THE GLORIOUS PRESENCE

"A handful of great sayings—the distillation of millenia of thought—"form the basis for this volume. Built around commentaries by the great Indian sage and philosopher Shri Shankarācharya on the Vedanta-Sutras of Badarayana, along with his commentaries on the Upanishads and the *Bhagavad Gitā* and some of his smaller popular works, the book sets forth a philosophy of living that is, in the words of the author, "simplicity itself." The ideas are presented carefully, sympathetically, and clearly, with many analogies and illustrations drawn from universal experience, thus showing the timeless relevance of these ideas to the life of "everyman."

Professor Ernest Wood made his home in India for almost forty years. He was a profound scholar and an unparalleled teacher. Deeply interested in education, he served as Headmaster of a high school preparing students for the University of Madras; was Managing Secretary of a group of 37 schools and colleges; Principal and President of the Sind National College and Manadapalle College; founder of two university colleges; and first Organizing Secretary of the independent Indian National University. Following World War II, he came to the United States and was for several years President and Dean of the American Academy of Asian Studies, a graduate school in San Francisco. Retiring from that post, he joined the staff of the University of Houston, Texas, and, with Mrs. Wood, organized and maintained the School of the Woods for pre-school children. Professor Wood is the author of many books, among which *Concentration: An Approach to Meditation*, *The Pinnacle of Indian Thought*, and *Seven Schools of Yoga* have been published as Quest Books.

Books by Ernest Wood

CONCENTRATION: AN APPROACH TO MEDITATION
MIND AND MEMORY TRAINING
THE PINNACLE OF INDIAN THOUGHT
SEVEN SCHOOLS OF YOGA
THE STUDY OF PLEASURE AND PAIN

The Glorious Presence

The Vedanta philosophy including
Shankara's Ode to the South-facing Form

by

Ernest Wood

A QUEST BOOK

Published under a grant from the Kern Foundation

THE THEOSOPHICAL PUBLISHING HOUSE
Wheaton, Ill., U.S.A.
Madras, India / London, England

First Quest Edition published by the
Theosophical Publishing House, Wheaton, Illinois,
a department of The Theosophical Society in America, 1974

Wood, Ernest, 1883-1965.
    The glorious presence.

    (A Quest book)
    Includes a translation of Shankara's Dakṣiṇāmūrtistotra (Ode to the south-facing
form): p.
    1. Vedanta. I. Śankārācarya. Dakṣiṇāmūrtistotra. English. 1974. II. Title.
B132.V3W6 1974   181'.48   74-1045
ISBN 0-8356-0446-2

PRINTED IN THE UNITED STATES OF AMERICA

CONTENTS

PART IV. COMPARISONS

AUTHOR'S INTRODUCTION

Three great questions arise now and again in the minds of most of us: what am I, what is the world, and what is living?—the last question again being resolved into another three: what is the world doing to me, what am I doing to it, and what are we doing together?

People who have tried to solve these questions throughout the ages have been called philosophers. The word means merely "fond of thinking," but it has always had a special reference to life, so we can enlarge the meaning to "fond of thinking about living."

Many people simply go on living without any question about it; they think about all the bits of business that come up during the day, but do not think seriously about life. On the other hand, the philosopher thinks about life, and, if really a philosopher, lives in this world just as much or more than the other man while doing it. It is an error to think that a philosopher is not active in life, is merely an armchair man, or a yogī sitting in a forest.

Many of the great philosophers have been athletes, as in the case of Plato and Socrates. There is a story about a young man named Alcibiades, who was handsome, proud, rich and fond of dog-fighting and roystering. One day he came to one of Socrates' gatherings with a view to heckling the speaker and breaking up the meeting. Socrates, however, was not upset, but soon showed the assembly that Alcibiades was a fool. The young man then admitted that Socrates could beat him in argument, but said that if he would wrestle with him he would soon show who was the better man. To his surprise, Socrates agreed, and gave Alcibiades such forcible treatment that he was out of action for a month, after which he became a

7

firm friend of the philosopher's and established himself as his "chucker-out."

That there *are* armchair philosophers is, however, well known. But they do not usually withdraw themselves from life. On the contrary they are much interested in it, and very busy indeed reading about what people all over the world are doing and thinking. Such philosophers have nearly always been very up-to-date on the news, and for the last few centuries very well-informed in both natural science and religious tradition and opinion. In India, many of the ancient philosophic recluses traditionally attended immense gatherings convened by the rulers of their days for discussing all these matters, and they were so human and sometimes became so heated in the course of argument that their language was occasionally by no means parliamentary—but my special point is that they were nearly all well versed in the sciences of their day, and were often called upon by kings for advice in practical affairs.

It would not be very sensible for any man to try to discover the truths of philosophy all by himself. Indeed, one cannot have a clear field for this, because we have heard so much of it one way and another during our childhood. It is indeed the path of wisdom to know what others think, to listen to speakers who voice opinions different from our own, and also to read their writings.

The philosophers who wrote were teachers. A teacher is one who selects the treasures of knowledge acquired by mankind in the past, correlates them to present gains, and passes them on to the future. The information which great minds toiled for centuries to obtain can thus be imparted to us in a very short time. Most of the world's noted philosophers were also speaking-teachers, but some few were armchair teachers, who merely wrote. The exceptions to this which I have known have been certain Hindu recluses, who were ready enough to reply to the questions of those who sought them out, but would only speak on those terms—because they held the view that it is foolish to proffer knowledge to those who are not awake enough and interested enough to ask definite questions. Even then, sometimes the enquirer had positively to wring what he wanted to know out of them. Similarly, one American philosopher of comparatively recent times, when questioned why he wrote rather tersely and not in such an explanatory manner as some desired, replied, "Really, I must leave people *something* to think about."

The teacher of today has the whole world to choose from in his work of passing on the great treasures of human thought, and has the whole of human historical time, from the very invention of writing, and even before that, since the early writers passed on by memory what had come down to them by word of mouth, traditional stories sometimes sparkling with diamonds of thought. In our day we cull from the whole world—Jewish and Christian Scriptures, Egypt, Persia, India, Greece, Rome, mediaeval and modern Europe, and, more recently, America. Everywhere these mines yield treasures.

One of the most striking features of all this philosophy is that it shows life and thought to have been basically the same in all climes and times. This is so because man is man everywhere; as Robert Burns put it, "The rank is but the guinea's stamp, the man's the gold for all that." The basic facts about man and his world and what is going on in their interplay are just the same now in New York and San Francisco as they were in Ancient Greece, or in Egypt or India. Children are children still, and lovers lovers, eld eld, and, when all is over, the same old truth awaits each of us: "Home art gone, and ta'en thy wages." Wages? Yes; the more we look into what is happening to these people in their skyscrapers or their huts, in their city streets or country fields, in their business suits or overalls, in their trousers or skirts, in their regalia or loincloths, the more we discover what it is in a man that is the man, and that it is in knowing that and being that, with the minimum of obscuration in life, that our enjoyment and benefit are found. Is it not richly good that steel be steel, an apple an apple, and a man a man! How glad we are to see one that is one! How bright the day in which we have walked with a man, and heard three sentences of his! And all because what he boldly proclaims, we lisp. All because we are like statues coming hesitantly to life.

Where thoughtful people foregather, we are accustomed in these days to hear them speak of Greek thought, Hindu thought, Chinese thought, European thought. It is a happy augury that they do this with a feeling of expansion and gain. "Listen to this," says one, "from Kalidasa. . . ." Then another speaks of Lao-Tsu or Confucius, another of Shakespeare or Kant or Hume, another of Plato or Pythagoras, another of Plotinus or Philo, another of Burns or Whitman. To converse with men whose minds are not in bonds is the height of companionship, where no offense is intentionally given or, what is even more important, stupidity taken.

I am not quite sure of my last sentence. It does not seem quite right. Perhaps it is better that offense be given and taken sometimes, that flint and steel should strike sharply and produce fire, among those who have not learnt the secret of phosphorus. Someone jostles me in the street, begs pardon, receives my smile, and is soon forgotten. This will not do in philosophy. Let my companion's thought pierce my heart, rather than that he should glance at me aslant and keep silent, for the barb of truth is tipped not with venom, but with nectar.

Another correction is now needed. I have written too much about well-known names and of the value of conversation, when after all it is only in living that truth resides. A fine crew we should be, were our chief interest in gathering together to talk. And a poor philosopher is he who gathers his "gems of thought," or cudgels his brain to evolve some of his own, only with the purpose to talk. Sometimes, after a lecture or conference someone will approach the speaker and say, "Thank you, very much. Your talk has been most helpful to me. I would not have missed it for anything. It is just what I have been thinking for a long time." Good, indeed. Shakespeare spoke to Shakespeares. All of them learn in their offices and shops, and in town and field. Occasional conversation clarifies the thought and empowers the arm, but the fullness of life is in living, and understanding should flow in us like food and drink, not be imbibed as a stimulant.

The values of life are found in all necessary circumstances, if they are received with some measure of thoughtfulness. Chafing is prejudice, closing the mind, throttling the life. Silks are good, cotton too; gold is good, clay also. I have sometimes been tempted, when in villages in India, to say to myself that this is home. The mud walls are gentler to the touch than plaster or paint, and one can step just over the threshold into a world of earth and trees and clouds where one is not caged, but every sense can breathe. What if a man does drive a wooden plough, if it gives "enough"? But I know it is not enough if it leaves us sleepy-minded. People need the goads of natural reward and punishment to wake them up, and so they have had the unconscious wisdom to create all this "modern civilization" in which we plunge ourselves with terrific energy into endless labors in order to have flush toilets and electric light. Perhaps our brains need rattling, and when we have had enough of it we shall begin to ask what it is all about. With all this, we feel "in our bones" that we are destined to reach power along with peace materially as well as in the mind.

Still, we recognize that to those who were "awake" the simpler life of older times gave great opportunity for thought. It may well be that while living the simpler life of earlier times and easier climes than ours, the old philosophers were in an excellent position to think about the essentials of life. It is no wonder, then, that some of our ancestors in ancient India

reached the very pinnacle of Aryan thought, with that combinativeness or inclusiveness of mind which is characteristic
of our race.

What I have called the pinnacle of Aryan thought consists
of a handful of great sayings expressed in not more than half
a dozen words apiece. These were the distillate, so to speak,
of millennia of thought. The ancient Hindus, being a me-
thodical people, collected all their lore of living into four
books, which were at first passed on in memory from teacher
to pupil, and afterwards inscribed on palm leaves. These were
called the Vedas, the wisdom. Certain sections or chapters in
these books were specially devoted to the philosophy of life.
These were called the Upanishads. They also contained various disquisitions, and accounts of incidents in the lives of
ancient philosophers, who are regarded as having been not
only wise men, full of well-digested experience of human
life, but also as the recipients of much intuitional knowledge,
on account of which they were called Rishis, that is, Seers.

In the next period the important philosophical teachings
and sayings were gathered into strings of aphorisms, containing brief explanations of these sayings and their implications.
These books in turn gave rise to commentaries written by
many later teachers.

Sometimes the Upanishads are called the Vedanta, a word
meaning "the end of the Vedas"; sometimes the word refers
especially to the Great Sayings; sometimes it is used for the
aphorisms, and sometimes for a system of philosophy based
upon these. In the present volume I have taken as my chief
guide the *Vedanta-Sūtras* of Badarayana, with the commentary of the famous philosopher Shri Shankarācharya, eluci-
dated by the *Panchapādika* of his pupil Padmapāda, with
its *Vivarana*, and again the *Vivarana-prameya-sangraha* of
Vidyāranya. Along with these I have taken Shankarāchārya's
Commentaries on the Upanishads and the *Bhagavad Gītā*, as
well as a number of his smaller popular works, such as the

Crest Jewel of Discrimination and *Direct Experience*. For the feeling-thought expression—since Shankara was by no means a dry-as-dust philosopher—I have been most charmed by his *Ode to the South-Facing Form*, which presents a series of meditations, which I have translated and explained in Part III of the present book. To all this I have added the results of much experience in India—which was my home for thirty-eight years—and much of the fruit of innumerable conversations with people whose lives have been devoted to this kind of thought, as well as some of my own thinking, including what seems to me the clear bearing of it all upon our modern natural science and psychology.

Written down like this it sounds a formidable business—and yet it is simplicity itself. There are just about half-a-dozen straightforward, simple ideas, stated or implied in the Great Sayings—that is all. I am not going to state them in this Introduction, because I want to bring them out carefully, delicately, almost reverently, like jewels from a casket. I want the reader to linger with them a while, so as to know them well. Therefore chapter by chapter I have followed a teaching method, unfolding one thought after another upon which it rests, and at each step showing its bearing on "ordinary" life. Well has it been said: "No man can be the same after knowing this."

PART I

THE MEANING OF LIFE

CHAPTER 1

THE GENERAL ARGUMENT

The Vedanta Philosophy has as its basis the belief that the universe of our experience is only one reality and it can be known. I use the word belief, advisedly, because its chief exponents say they first derived this piece of knowledge from the ancient scriptures, written not by ordinary, but by illuminated men. Among those exponents none is more highly regarded than Shri Shankara Acharya, who lived, some scholars say, about the seventh century A.D.—though some traditions maintain a much earlier date than that, even to the third or fourth century B.C. These dates do not matter, however, in a book of practical philosophy, such as this is intended to be. Our object as thinking people is to observe man and his world as accurately as possible, and thus obtain knowledge which leads to enlightenment and power.

We know enough about ourselves and the world to be well aware that there is very much more that we do not know. We are quite sure also that there is something wrong with our commonly accepted ideas about such basic things as time, space, matter, form and consciousness. The old philosophers put before themselves the questions that we set ourselves today, but they did not sink back, as many of us are apt to do, and say "The real truth is unknowable." They put forward the questions: "Who am I really? How was this world pro-

duced? Who is its maker? What is its ultimate substance?"
Guided first by the testimony of their predecessors, supported
secondly by the use of reason, thirdly and finally they claimed
they answered those questions by direct experience.

Their first postulate was that the truth is ever-present—as
all must admit. Their second was that if we do not see it the
defect is ours—we are making some sort of mistake which
stands as an obstacle to clear seeing. Their third was that the
ultimate truth was known by some men in the past, by direct
experience, and can be known now by any intelligent man
who will take the trouble to do so.

"If truth is truth, how can it be unknowable? Wake up, O
man, and look straight, without prejudice, at the facts of
being!"

Shankara did not leave the Vedanta teaching as a matter of
religious belief, however, but said we must verify it by thinking, and then realize it by experience, as did the illumined men
of old. This may seem a startling claim, until we remember
how busy we are in these modern days, how preoccupied with
"a number of things," how little we really want "to know"
and how much "to have," and remember also that this condition of ours *may be* a grub-state in which we are preparing
to be butterflies, as religious teachers have asserted again and
again.

Let us then proceed to reason on the materials of our own
experience with regard to the Vedantic statement that all
things are really one thing.

Every object we know is dependent on something else. Not
a particle of dust can escape from this world and go away to
live somewhere else all by itself. Burn a candle, our scientists
tell us, and take the proper means to collect the gases that
come off it, and you will find that you have just as much matter as you had at the beginning—the weight of the candle and
the oxygen absorbed from the air are equal to the weight of
the carbonic acid gas and water vapor produced. The high

temperature has caused burning, which has altered the shape or form of things but has not removed anything out of the world. This belief that our world is one indivisible thing is held by modern scientists today, and they come very near to proving it also—at least nothing ever happens to create a doubt of its truth. Our first established axiom, then, is, that the world of our experience is "in some way one."

Our next enquiry is: Have we any way of finding out in what way it is one? Can we say what sort of a oneness it is?

People have tried to do this in at least two different ways. Some have said: "There must be an ultimate material substance." Atomistic theories have been put forward and held for a time. Among these the latest was the belief that the chemical atoms—the ninety odd kinds of atoms known to our chemists—are the ultimate bricks of which all forms are built. A century ago it was thought that they could never be split —that they constituted the ultimate reality of the world. The very word atom refers to this idea, and means something that cannot be cut or divided. These atoms were held to have their particular properties and to play upon one another—or interact—with exhibitions of force. As to mind—thought, feeling and the will—it, too, was but the play of atoms in a brain. So the basis or one permanent reality was said to be matter. This was the theory of substance.

But the chemical atom *has* been cut and found to have finer constituents, and the scientific mind has been driven by experience to the belief that there must be an infinitude of cuttableness, or else that force is the ultimate reality and matter is only a form of force, that the world is a huge river of forces, and where eddies form matter appears.

Another view, the idealistic, suggests that mind is the world-stuff, and all the forms that we know, including the atoms and the forces, are basically only thoughts. This too, will not stand criticism. Clearly, the clouds drifting in the air form various shapes which have not been thought by any mind. Each one of us also knows full well that we go to sleep each night, not because we have thought "sleep"—quite the reverse—but because "circumstances" have made it impossible for us to carry on without a rest. And we know that the world goes on its way while we are asleep.

One thing is sure, however—all is one; the world, mind and all.

Our second axiom arises from the fact that the basic reality is not any one of the things that we know in ourselves or in our world, that is, not one of the "many," but is a principle of unity inherent in all things, not absent from any.

The emphasis here is upon the word "inherent." If there were a Power which united all things—if they were all held together as if in the grasp of a giant hand—there would not be unity, but duality, the hand and the things held together. So "inherent in all" is the statement; and this must not be thought of as a property or quality belonging to each thing, but as its essential being, lest we fall into duality again. So:

Being *is* unity.

I must now, I think, give some examples to show how everything depends upon everything else, and, in fact, *is* everything else as well as itself. I take first the table on which my writing pad is resting. The table stands on the floor boards, these rest on beams, those on walls, those on concrete foundations, those on the earth, and the earth has its position on account of the gravitational effect upon it of other planets, the sun and the stars. So the table is where it is because everything else in the universe is where it is. If I take the table and move it to the other end of the room I have shaken the whole solar system—though not very much, of course!

Does this seem to make the table an entirely dependent thing? Not really. Any such total "determinism" would be quite illogical. I will show this by reference to a planet pursuing its orbit round the sun. This planet is pulled by all the other stellar bodies, but it is also a puller of all those others, since every other is pulled by all the rest, including this one. So the planet has some inherent power of its own. And you, my reader, and I, when we walk along the ground, are similarly not simply the total victims of a so-called law of gravity; we are also pulling the earth up to us; we have our own inherent "floating power." We feel it and it is true, but I mention it here only in order to illustrate the undeniable fact that the ultimate reality is in us and in everything, and is what we all essentially are. Without the acceptance of the idea that we have some essential power of our own we could not move, the mind would inhibit us, instead of aid.

Now to another example, applying the same principle in the sphere of knowledge about things. Here I must ask for considerable patience in what may at first look like a digression, but will be shown to be essentially relevant before I have finished.

Suppose you take a large sheet of paper, draw a circle in the centre with the word "cat" written in it, and then a large number of radiating arrows, somewhat thus:—

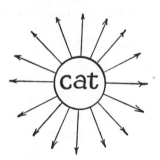

The next procedure is to lay your sheet of paper on the table, gaze gently at the word cat (do not strain your eyes), thinking of it, and see what comes into your mind. Perhaps "mouse" or "milk" will arise. Whatever it is, write it (without thinking *about* it) at the end of one of your arrows. Suppose you have written "mouse"; do not go into a daydream about mice, but come straight back to cat, and ask yourself, "What next?" If it is milk, write it down. You can write down a great many things in this way. You will probably think of the parts of the cat (claws, tail, eyes, heart, spleen and liver, etc.), the qualities of the cat (softness, looseness, alertness, fastidious-ness, etc.), the status of the cat (animal, mammal, quadruped, carnivore, feline, etc.) and many incidents in connection with cats you have known, or have read or heard about.

Your chart being prepared, with a quantity of arrow-words filled in, you can begin to think. Take "mouse" first, and pic-ture the cat with the mouse—how the cat waits for it at the mouse-hole, how it plays with it, how it pats it with its paw, how it finally finishes off the mouse. Try to imagine all the details as fully as possible. Then observe that in so doing you are knowing the cat—and that is what the cat is. Without mice cats would not have become exactly what they are. So you do not know all that a cat is unless you know it as an animal which has been partly formed by mice, and bears their imprint at the present time.

You may go on to milk, and all the other fifty or sixty arrow-words which you have written, and treat them all in the same way. (Incidentally, this is not waste of time, but a good mental exercise.)

You will surely soon come to realize that things are not such independent, clear-cut, definite-boundaried objects as most people assume that they are. Each one is what it is be-cause there is a principle of oneness which is the essential cause and basis of all. Each is in some way all. That is the nature of being. Nothing *is* that is not essentially all.

Look again at the cat diagram, and consider the mouse. You could make another diagram for the mouse, and in the same way come to know better what the mouse is. Then remember that the better-known mouse would in the first diagram give you a better knowledge of the cat than you got with the less-known mouse. And all the fifty or sixty mouse arrow-words could have the same retroactive effect. Thus the whole reflects into every part.

Now I will take causality. Suppose I go out in my car, and there is an accident. Someone runs his car into mine. We jump out and begin to collect information. It appears that Mr. Bumbler, my unwitting assailant, has been drinking too much. So we say that drink was the cause of the accident. Sometimes this is pleaded before the magistrate, "I am not really responsible for my action; I was a little drunk," and if the matter is pressed further, "No, I am not really morally responsible. I did not want the drink, but my sister was having an engagement party, and I just could not refuse another, and then another." Well, it does appear that a great many causes are here, including the men who invented and designed the cars, the road-builders, and—I am afraid—even those apparently innocent persons, the Pilgrim Fathers who came to this country several centuries ago.

Or perhaps Mr. Bumbler was not tipsy, but was hurrying to the railway station to catch a train. Now we are in for it—a train which was timed to depart half-an-hour later was one of the principal causes of this accident, and what shall we say about the man or men or woman or women who worked out the railroad time-table? If only he, she or they had timed that train even half-an-hour later still, this accident would not have occurred.

I am leading up to the over-all character of causality. You cannot say that mere succession is the essential mark of causality. In the day and night sequence, for example, which is very reliable, day does not cause night, nor does night cause day, but the rotation of the earth in relation to the sun is the cause of both night and day, and of their sequence. It is the enveloping cause. We cannot get away from one ultimate enveloping cause, present in all causes and constituting their essential nature, even though we do pick out particular causes for particular practical purposes—for example, to write I first obtain a pencil or a pen—ignoring the more enveloping causes. To this class of relative actions belongs the idea that we move westward from New York to San Francisco, when in fact we are moving eastward all the time, with the rotation of the earth, and that in turn is only relative to something else.

As I said before, if I move the table I shake the stars. It follows, further, that if I could totally blot out one thing (not merely move it or transform it) I would in that act blot out the whole universe.

At the risk of being tedious I must go further, and apply these principles to the mind, not merely to forms. Now, the mind is a peculiar sort of a thing, in that it plays a strange role in the time-sequence of things. Let it be Tuesday now, and a man says to himself that he will take the 10:20 A.M. bus to San Francisco next Saturday morning. He does this as the result of thinking about the future. Saturday morning comes and there he is at the bus, and in the bus, and the bus goes off. It is then a present occurrence. He has brought the future into the present, has he not? He has reversed the order of causation, looked into a future, and converted that future into a present.

So, in a world where mind is part of the causality, there is even more enveloping, more over-all effect than ever, because the future as well as the past makes the present.

Someone will say I am building this up a bit too much, that the bus was to go anyhow. But the other forty passengers also planned in the same manner, and suppose they had not done so and no passengers had turned up, and the bus-conditioners and the driver also for some reasons of their own did not turn up, that Saturday 10:20 A.M. bus would not have been a present occurrence on that Saturday morning at 10:20 A.M.

We can see something of this operating in Nature, apart from humanity. There is a small oak tree in the garden, which sprang from an acorn. It will grow up into a large tree and will stop at a certain point. It will not grow a thousand feet high, and it will not turn into a pine tree. Someone may say that this growth is due to "something in the seed," yes, "something unfolding and developing." But let them imagine that seed in its smallest beginnings. Does it have a beginning? In all the millions of acorns on one tree, the same potentiality is wrapped up, and what a potentiality there is in each one acorn —not merely to produce a tree, but one that can produce millions of acorns, each one of which can produce etc., etc.

Is it more preposterous to think that perhaps there is a mind which is calling the seed out—the perfect tree-to-be is calling the seedling to its fulfillment? That in the evolution of all living forms there is mind exerting some degree of desire, and thereby determining their future, just as when a man determined to go on that Saturday morning bus?

It is not preposterous, once we admit that there is mind in man, and something of mind in the animal and the plant also. Reactions in plants indicating some degree of mind were shown by the late Prof. J. C. Bose of Calcutta, and somewhat the same has later been done by others also.

People say: "We are commonly aware of the influence of the past in the present." Influence—flowing in—is indeed the proper word, because the past has not become totally non-existent in the moment of its passing, for if it had done so it would not be causative in the present. They go on: "But we are not commonly aware of the influence of the future in the present." In-fluence again.

We may reply: "Your second statement is wrong." It is exactly like the statement thrown at Galileo and Copernicus when they declared the sphericity of the earth: "But we are commonly aware that the earth is flat." That second statement is due to an ignorant habit of thought, to a habit of keeping the eye on the material element in the changing world and ignoring the mind element.

Such thought-habits can stand in the way of our knowing the truth about ourselves and the world—a truth which is present, and must be knowable.

Frequently, thought and talk about the present is unfruitful because a common assumption is allowed to block the way of knowledge. To clarify the position let us distinguish between the *point-present* and the *practical-present*. The point-present is the moment in which there is no change. It is as paradoxical as the mathematical point—which is often considered to have no size, but nevertheless to be capable of accumulation to form a line! The practical-present is quite different; it contains some past and some future. This is the actual present time that we experience in our lives, and it can be larger and smaller in different persons. It involves *grasp* or scope of time, not merely grip. Our mental trouble arises when we begin to analyze and try to find constituent elements—instead of accepting experience and seeing what it brings forth. There is a very real sense in which it can be said that the mind *is* the future affecting or modifying the present.

Let us go into this carefully in another chapter. We shall find, I think, that the future is trying just as hard to be born as the past is trying to die into the present, and so learn that the time as well as the space factors are bearing upon the present.

CHAPTER 2

THE MIND IN EVOLUTION

Let us start with another axiom:

The mind is the servant of unity.

The mind is like an artist, a painter who tries to see beauty—and does in fact see it—and then tries to picture it. There is a vast difference between a picture on the artist's canvas and the splashes of mud on our clothes made by a passing car on a dirty road on a rainy day. Although the painter only makes marks on his canvas, those marks are dominated by a unity. If in the picture he paints he cannot see the unity he cries out with disgust that it is no picture but only a daub, crumples it up, throws it in the bin, and tries again.

The mind is like a scientist. A man who wants to know, for example, what lightning is, and not simply to believe that it is the terrible glance of an angry god, as perhaps his father and mother believed. He sends up kites, as Benjamin Franklin did. He devises many experiments. And he discovers something which unifies his thought-picture, and shows him the unity of electricity in the eel, in the cloud, and in the power-house that he himself can now construct. It is realization of unity that he calls knowledge. Knowledge depends principally on a mental act of unity. The advance of knowledge is the discovery of unity. Power in human life flowing through tools and machines into new structures is due to applied knowledge of unity. This principle was shown in the cat exercise in our last chapter.

The mind is also like a philanthropist or a devotee, who looks to the feelings of goodwill and affection—or, in brief, love—to produce social unity and the salvation of mankind.

"We are brothers; sons of one sweet mother." "We are devoted to the Father without whom even a sparrow does not fall to the ground." All these disciples of the two forms of love—brotherhood and devotion—are seekers for unity, and, in so far as they are able, workers for unity among human beings, conceiving the desire for unity as something inherent and natural, not as secondary or imposed. Though they recognize the wonderful benefits of economic co-operation, they assert that such material considerations do not contain either the safety or the pleasure of companionship, which is fundamentally a feeling of unity, and the basis of that "divine arithmetic" of life in which two plus two do not make four, but forty or even four hundred. In fact, perfect love, they say, could manifest through its perfect unity such a perfect power in human life that every man would soon be almost a god—if only all men would love one another.

In such ways does the mind seek and practice unity. Knowledge, goodwill and power are thus seen to be expressions of unity itself, operating in the mind through thought, feeling and the will.

The second fundamental statement is that:

The mind is the basis of evolution.

We may go back to Herbert Spencer for the clearest definition of evolution. He said that the evolution of any form is a progressive change from a state of incoherent homogeneity to one of coherent heterogeneity of structure and function. Some of these words may sound formidable, but the ideas are really as simple as A,B,C. On the table there is a small tray full of pins. The pins are apparently all alike, that is, "homogeneous," or of the same nature. This idea of homogeneity is simple nowadays, when every housewife knows what homogenized milk is—milk which has been so treated that samples taken (it can be done through a straw, in the kitchen, or a pipette in the laboratory) from near the top, from near the middle and from near the bottom of the bottle, all have the same consistency; the lighter fats no longer float to the top, as in a bottle of nonhomogenized milk.

Furthermore, the pins are not operating jointly, are not working together, are not cohering, so are "incoherent." The pins offer a good example of incoherent homogeneity.

But in any form in which evolution has taken place there are many heterogeneous or varied things which are coherent. We may call such a form an "evolute," as distinguished from a casual form, such as a drifting cloud, which is not an evolute.

Mind goes to work—especially the human mind—and produces artificial evolutes. An automobile, for example, or a printing machine. In these articles there is coherent heterogeneity but there is not perfect coherence, since the driver who is not part of the car must direct the steering wheel, and someone must pull the levers or press the buttons at the correct time. In the natural evolute, such as a man, the mind is inherent, not separate, as is the driver in the car.

In the perfect or natural evolute every part works for every other part. The human body is the best example. Eyes work for feet and feet for eyes. If you wish to see what is in another room, you do not tell your eyes to look until after you have told your feet to walk through the door and round the corner, carrying the eyes into that room. Similarly, you do not tell your feet and legs to walk until you have instructed the eyes to look where the feet are going and see that you do not sprain your ankle or run your nose into a post. Some say that all the parts of the body work for the stomach, but it is equally true that the stomach also works for all the parts and sends something to the remotest cell.

The natural evolutes are called living forms. They are characterized by the instinct of self-preservation. I believe that we are justified in saying that there is something of mind wherever there is evolution going on. The very terms self-preservation, self-expansion and self-enhancement demand it.

With our conception of mind as an element in Nature, we

have no difficulty in thinking of mind not as something that springs full-blown onto the pages of natural history at some particular point in that history, but as something which may be traced backwards from the height which it has achieved in man to a fainter and feebler past condition, so faint and feeble as to be almost unrecognizable.

To grasp the full import of this we shall do well to review some of the main steps on the evolutionary road. Let us assume for a while that even the chemical element or atom is an evolute, and exhibits an adumbration of mind, suspending judgment on this until we have completed the picture. The proposal is that even solidification is a manifestation of mind-entification. Why should life be thought of as only in visible movement? The plant moves less than the animal. The mineral less than the plant. Let me exaggerate—in order to emphasize this idea—and with the same kind of imaginative sympathy that we apply to other people, to animals and even to plants think that the mineral positively enjoys the feeling of solidity and stability, and in some way works for an increase of this enjoyment as it proceeds from hydrogen onwards to uranium and its peers and compounds. Nay, is it not the very attainment and enjoyment of solidity and stability that lies at the root of the instinct of self-preservation in the plant and the animal and even in man? In this light it is an action of self-preservation in terms of material form. There is a small poem, whose author I do not know, which can help us to imagine this condition:

> I wish I was a little rock,
>   A sittin' on a hill,
> A doing nothin' all day long
>   But just a sittin' still.
>
> I wouldn't eat, I wouldn't drink,
>   I wouldn't even wash,

But I'd just set and set and set,
An' rest myself, by gosh.

We can almost see the progress of an inner conflict between self-preservation and self-enhancement in the primitive mind, when the mind emerges into more and more moving forms. The adventurousness of the self-enhancing mind becomes more evident step by step, but the mind never entirely burns its boats, never completely lets go of its anchorage in stability and solidity.

This conception of the presence of mind throughout Nature solves the problem of materialism versus idealism. It agrees with the materialist assertion that man and the mineral are kin but adds the rider that if in a world of evolution or growth man is a developed mineral, the mineral must for the same reason be an undeveloped man. We must then attribute to the mineral something of the mentality of man, since we cannot deny the experience of mentality in ourselves; although we must be careful to remember that while using the term self-preservation in connection with such primitive mentality we are not in the least implying that it, although conscious, has any *thought* or *idea* of "self." Even in the human babe there is no idea of self as an entity, though there is a very decided mind-urge in it, with strong consciousness and feelings and the will to live.

We can trace the development of the *idea* of self as the child grows. Putting this matter briefly, we are justified in saying that as the child gradually obtains definite ideas about outside things, that is, as the vague cloudy presence that is the mother gradually assumes clear outlines and becomes a recognizable entity to the child, so does the child gradually become a recognizable entity to itself. The recognition of things as entities, or entification of objects in the mind, by sense-perception and mental analysis acting together, is soon followed by "self-entification"—the formation of a *mental* picture of an object of experience called "self," which we remember in memory, and can recognize every time we see or remember it.

The mental process which I have called entification, by which the mind acquires a definite idea of a given object as a separate entity, depends very much on the point of view. To take an example: when we look at a map of the world we see at a glance the continent-forms of America, Africa, etc. This is so because we are land-animals, and when travellers, are interested in land-forms. But suppose we were creatures living on the surface of the ocean, we should then, on looking at the maps, see the ocean-forms. As it is we do not see or think of the ocean-shapes, unless perhaps there are some ships' navigators who do. The map is the same for both land-forms and ocean-forms, but each mind looking at the map follows its own selectiveness. Similarly, looking at the hexagonal tiles on a bathroom floor, we see them fall into different patterns as the mind changes.

Observation of the psychological process of entification of external objects and also of self is of great value in the understanding of mind and life. In the case of self the process goes on over the years, until a definite personality is formed by reaction between the mind and the resistances or experiences it meets in the world. The personality, being the product of this mutual action, is thus partly mind-produced. It is not the case, therefore, that the personality is something that grows in the field of Nature, and afterwards comes to be known and recognized. Even the body is to some extent modified in its growth by the mind's thought about it, and when it comes to expression, mannerisms, habits, etc., the mind-influence is very great. In a limited sense, the body is the artist's material (with a limited form-scope), the artist being the mind, and in this sense the word personality is very apposite.

The word personality means, etymologically, a mask, something that is spoken through. In the old Greek drama the masks which were used by the characters on the stage were so named. Personality is thus a presentation or appearance. This personality appears always somewhat different to its various observers —to the man himself, his wife, his parents, his children, his business associates, his friends at the club or the Lodge, and all the rest.

This self-entity, which is an idea imposed upon the essential self, is what we usually call our personal self. How much of confusion and error there may be in this idea of self becomes later a matter of study for the philosophic man—which we need not enter upon here, as it will be more relevant to a later chapter. I have mentioned it in order to show that we can posit something of mind-urge and feelings and the vaguest rudiments of ideas, even in the mineral, without the least supposition of the self-entification or personalization complex that is so prominent a feature of the mental scenery of each one of us human beings.

Let us return to the main line of our present review of steps in evolution. That the mineral is quite a high evolute would have been a conception very acceptable to the ancient philosophers, as they held quite definitely, in their department of thinking about natural things—the ancient scientific opinion —that in the distant past the conditions of matter descended progressively from the skylike to the atmospheric or gaseous, then to the fiery, next to the watery or liquid, and finally to the solid or earthy.[1]

The Sanskrit words in our footnote do not matter—I have mentioned them only in order that scholars may check my statement for themselves. This means that far in the past of our globe and even of our solar system, it was believed, the whole thing was a mass of ether or skylike substance. In course of time some of this densified or dropped, as it were, into a state of gas—our globe then being a mass of vapors. Next, some of it dropped into the fiery state, then into the watery,

[1] *Ākāsha, vayu, tejas, jala and prithivi.*

and finally, in the fifth act, some of it climbed down into the solid condition. So at last we have a world containing all the five "elements" named by the ancient world, which used the word elements[2] not at all in the more limited sense in which we speak of chemical elements today.

The term "elements" is probably more exactly or correctly applicable to these anciently—and currently—known states of matter than to the chemical elements isolated in our laboratories and classified in our chemistry textbooks of today. Without going into detail about these things—a side study which would delay our argument—let us briefly notice that our knowledge of chemical elements as capable of change of state at different temperatures and under different pressures does not at all conflict with the old classification.

When speaking today of the state of an element as solid, liquid, or gaseous, we always bring in the formula NTP, meaning "at normal temperature and pressure." When we say that mercury, though a metal and heavy, is a liquid, we mean mercury at NTP. Why this should be so is not the question here; we may expect our scientific researchers to find that out some day. We know that we can solidify mercury, and also transform it into the gaseous state. Similarly, the chemical compound carbon dioxide is a gas at NTP though we can convert it into a liquid or a solid by changing the temperature and pressure. The ancients did not imagine all gaseous substances to be homogeneous. They knew something about varieties of gases in the atmosphere, some of the properties of which they mentioned with sufficient precision to enable us to identify them with considerable probability as our modern hydrogen, oxygen, carbon dioxide etc. I have before me a paper on this subject read before the American Chemical Society at Detroit in September, 1927, by my scholarly friend Dr. V. R. Kokatnur.

In the old Hindu books of analytic philosophy (*vaisheshika*)

[2] *Bhūtas.*

the five kinds of elements I have mentioned were regarded as states and forms of matter, not, however, as being purely and totally different, but as having proportions of one another in their composition. Thus, if we represent skyey (or etheric), aery, fiery, watery and earthy matter by the letters S,A,F,W, and E, it would be said that the manifest *earthy* material that we see and feel is compounded of $\frac{1}{2}$E, $\frac{1}{8}$W, $\frac{1}{8}$F, $\frac{1}{8}$A and $\frac{1}{8}$S. Or again, the skyey or etheric is compounded of $\frac{1}{2}$S, $\frac{1}{8}$A, $\frac{1}{8}$F, $\frac{1}{8}$W, and $\frac{1}{8}$E. This idea may or may not have exact knowledge behind it; its special interest for us in the present context is that it maintains the principle which I have earlier enunciated, that nothing is entirely itself, but the whole universe is in a flow of universal in-fluence in which everything is in some degree potent in everything else, or, in other words, in which there are really no absolute entities.

The bearing of these statements on our theory of early evolution is quite important, for we see evolution coming down, as it were, from the skyey or etheric by degrees to the earthy or solid form, in which matter most asserts its self-preservativeness by resisting the intrusion of other matter. We used to speak of material objects as things which occupy space and resist the intrusion of other similar objects into their space. I do not want to bring up a discussion about the nature of space at this point, so I will modify the foregoing statement a little, and say that a material object is that which has boundaries or surfaces. In this view even the skyey matter is still matter, and if it is to be equated to our modern ether (as is wished by some) our ether must also not be entirely simple, but must have a modicum of solidity in its constitution.

Having made it clear that all the S,A,F,W,E is to be regarded as material, we must now introduce another subdivision in Nature. When writing of the five kinds of material things as above described, the ancients did not omit another important scientific observation of the world, or the totality of Nature. They said that matter had three essential qualities.

Nature is more than matter. Nature is, in our experience, composed of (1) matter, (2) energy or force, and (3) constancy or law. This is the subdivision of the real world that all our science teachers put before us in our school days, as soon as we began to study Chemistry or Physics. Our teachers then said: "Now you are going to study material objects, also forces, also natural laws. Material objects are composed of the chemical elements; forces are such as heat, light, sound, electricity and magnetism; natural laws are seen in the constancy of material operations, since Nature is not fantastic but is steady and reliable. Without such constancy and reliability this could not be an intelligible world; no knowledge would be the same tomorrow as today and no machinery would work."

In our later studies we learn that the division of the objects of experience into matter, energy and laws is not absolute, for here again the general principle of in-fluence applies, so that in matter there is always some energy and law, in energy there is always some matter and law, and natural law is not law in the sense of an order imposed upon matter and energy but is a constancy inherent in them. So these three are constituent qualities of Nature. They are more elemental than anything else we find in the world, and are thus the background of our modern scientific thinking. They are always together, but never equal, in anything we know. In our modern scientific manipulations we cannot resolve matter into nothing but force —we inevitably talk about quanta, the corpuscularity of light and electricity, and a granular ether. If we discover that matter is essentially force, and then we want to know what force is, we soon find that it is in some way matter. The ancients had definite names for these three[3] and applied them also adjectivally to describe the characters of all kinds of things. Thus, a person might be described as material, or forceful, or law-abiding.[4]

[3] *Tamas, rajas* and *sattwa.*
[4] *Tāmasa, rājasa,* or *sāttwika.*

The three primal constituents of Nature are not equally present in any thing. The five elements present a predominant matterness, while the mind and its ten adjuncts present a predominance of law. The ten adjuncts are: five organs of sensation (the ear for sound, the skin for touch, the eye for sight, the tongue for taste, and the nose for smell), and five organs of action (the mouth for speech, the hands for holding, the feet for walking, and the organs of generation and excretion). Behind these organs is the mind, which receives, interprets and correlates the sensations, thereby forming ideas or items of knowledge, then works upon these with thought and feelings, and finally arrives at decisions which it transmits through the five organs of action into action upon the world.

The mind in anyone is to be thought of not as a *thing* that possesses mental functions, but as a representative in him of natural law—it is the presence of law in that place. Law not only makes mind possible. It *is* mind operating in Nature. It introduces time, or change, and includes the past and the future. If there was a yesterday and there is a today, and there is in today anything that was the same yesterday, it means that what was gone has come the same again, not that yesterday has somehow become today. Can the past *alone* make the new present? Can there be purely material causation? If the material past *alone* produces the present will not today be the same as yesterday, with no change?—and therefore no time? In the changes in Nature we are seeing the operations of minds. The present is the past modified by mind. Nature in all her moods proves to be the same kind of mind—what lies in that unseen region of our being which is between the working of incoming or afferent or receptive or sense organs, and the outgoing, or efferent, or action organs. From that unseen chamber it exerts its influence upon the world.

Law in Nature, which is constancy and reliability, is laid down to the presence of mind everywhere—even, as I have been saying, in the mineral forms. Relatively speaking, the matter and the mind are respectively the great passive and active principles in the world, and the process of living is on the line of the interplay of these two, where forms are produced, and preserved and destroyed. Mind being the positive factor in this interplay, is the builder of forms and the source of evolution. Everywhere, among living things, where mind builds there is progress of forms from a state of incoherent homogeneity to a state of coherent heterogeneity of structure and function. And mind itself becomes more efficient as it produces these things, so that it undergoes a retroactional development. It, too, evolves in its own way. An example: the chief value of an artist's work is that it produces an equivalent effect in his own mind. A rough way of putting it is to say that the mind grows by the exercise of its powers. This is, of course, a growth of capacity, not a process of material accretion. This growth is seen in the stages of evolution in Nature. Materiality (stage 1) is so great in the minerals that we see in that stage the mind slowly learning to appreciate materiality, so that it may in due time know it and own it. In the second stage, in plant life, we find the quality of force or energy emerging and gradually becoming dominant in the form. This could be described as a new adventure on the part of mind, and an achievement of self-enhancement over mere self-preservation. We have only to observe the plants of the tropical jungles to realize the great force that is now expressed. The plant stands on its root, but from there it pushes out with prodigious effect, so that sometimes great rocks are split asunder and huge buildings overthrown. A tiny rootlet gets into a joint, and in time tons of masonry are lifted and pushed aside. But it is mainly an insensate force. The mind of the plant, we may say, is preoccupied with the learning and enjoyment of force. We often see a reproduction of this "plant-stage" in the recurring cycle of human life in the behavior of growing boys, who sometimes delight in the unintelligent experience of feeling force, by stamping, shouting and pushing about the place—an experience which will no doubt enrich their minds with a sense of the reality of force and will stand them in good stead later on when they reach years of discretion, although in the meantime the demonstration of unintelligent force is often very painful and distressing to their elders.

In the third stage—that of the animal—we find that the mind is ready for another adventure. The will of the mind now gets up from its root and goes about on legs. Let us consider a fox, when it gets up in the evening to go in search of hens—to take only one example from among the infinite variety of animal Nature. It smells them in the distance, and must then undertake a journey in order to reach its objective. It will find many and varied things confronting it in the course of that journey, in which it has to cross fields and gardens, see trees and houses, negotiate fences, walls and other obstacles and perhaps even encounter dogs and people. To fulfill its self-preservation in this new life of self-enhancement the fox must awaken and develop that specific function of the mind that includes the recognition and memory of objects and their specific qualities and actions. Without this it would run its head into a tree instead of walking round it, and would not be able to avoid the numerous other perils that beset its way. As it is, it somehow gets into the hencoop and seizes one of the birds by the neck. At the moment of seizure it stops its mental operations and enjoys the food, with all the feeling of force which accompanies that operation.

The fox is learning natural law, the constancy of things and operations of Nature. The tree is there today and tomorrow, not much changed. It is as sedate as it was, and has not suddenly started dancing a jig or turning itself into a dog. In this conservative, sane and sober world the mind of the fox can grow. Operating among orderly and reliable things, that mind itself becomes steadily more orderly and reliable. People too, are like this; they can lose their minds in hysteria and anxiety neuroses if their world becomes too varied or too uncertain for them. When we reach the age of reason we like our world to be conservative, orderly and reliable, favorable and conducive to quiet thought. Rather than the energetic philosophy of "Row, boys, row!" we would have that of "Let us put up a sail."

In what I am now calling the fourth evolutionary stage, we come to man himself, who has evidently embarked on another type of adventure. At the present point in this evolutionary process we find ourselves most vulnerable. What man has, however, but the animals have not to any extent, is the combinative mind, which has developed along with our increasing vulnerability. I first realized the far-reaching importance of this when I read, forty-five years ago, in one of the old Sanskrit books, a description of man as "The weak and strong, the ignorant and wise." Surely he is the weakest of all animals. He has not the teeth or claws to fight like a tiger, nor tusks, like an elephant, nor horns, like a bull, nor can he kick and stamp, like a horse or an ostrich, or swing a wicked tail, like an alligator, or inject a shot of poison, like a snake. He cannot retire into a shell, like a tortoise, nor escape at speed, like an antelope. He has not a covering of hair, wool, scales or feathers to protect him against adverse weather. He has not even the natural instincts of a fly.

Without natural weapons, clothing and instincts man is indeed ignorant and weak. Nevertheless, he is the powerful and the wise. With the aid of his combinative mind he has made for himself the weapons that have set him up as the safest and most masterly of all animals. He has made for himself clothing to fit all climes. He can live on into ripe old age. He has spread himself everywhere, and learned how to make use of things with his small, soft hands. With the development of this combinative mind his achievements know no end— tools, engines, machines, steam, oil, electric and atomic power all aid his arm, and telegraph, telephone, microphone, telescope, radar, phonograph, radio, television and a hundred other inventions and designs augment his senses. And with the aid of newspapers, books and magazines the wisdom of the ages and the techniques of the moment are available to each. Above all, man has learned co-operativeness, which multiplies his gains enormously—in my youth fifty years ago it was computed that each civilized man had "fifteen slaves," but by now it must be more than double that.

The point of all this is that for man necessity became the mother of invention, and invention the mother of new necessities—by which man became weaker in body but stronger in mind as the process went on.

This combinative mind is the same as what is called the abstract mind. It is curious how this word "abstract" has come to be used for a perception of unities, while etymologically it should mean quite the reverse. To abstract means to take away or single out something from a group or mass or composite. But when we look at a cat, a dog, a horse, a sheep, an elephant, or a cow, and say, "This is an animal," surely we are not intending the idea that "animalness" is a part of "cow." Such an idea is born only from an exclusively materialist or atomistic mental background, in which the world is believed without reason to be a collection of particular things.

Is it not correct to say: "We see an animal, and closer inspection shows it to be a cow?" Still closer inspection reveals it as a black cow or a red cow. It is because the human mind sees the general first and the particular afterwards that it can take a grasp of several or many things in one thought, see their unity, and then get a new idea, a new combination embodying a new unity, which in due course will come out through the action-organs as a new kind of a chair or of a flying-machine, or a new piece of understanding. The point is that "animal" is a reality, is a way of seeing facts as they are—not as particulars, but as subdivisions and modifications in the unity world of universal in-fluence.

That there are no ultimate differentia is a corollary of this idea. There is an ultimate unity, but there are no ultimate differences.

Another formulary of the ancient Aryan thinkers states the trinitarian character of objects. When we deal with an object, it says, we have before us (1) the object, (2) its qualities, properties or attributes, and (3) its motions and other actions.[5] Let us make this very clear with examples of different kinds taken at random; a block of glass (which I am using as a paperweight), a horse (there is a nice porcelain one on a bookcase in front of me), and a planet (I was looking at a picture of the night sky just now).

Exhibit 1

Object: piece of glass.
Qualities: cubical shape,
               hardness,
               translucency, etc.
Actions: presses on papers,
               reflects some light, etc.

Exhibit 2

Object: horse.
Qualities: hunter,
               white,
               good-tempered, etc.
Actions: runs,
               jumps,
               kicks,
               bites,
               eats, etc.

Exhibit 3

Object: planet.
Qualities: point of light, etc.
Actions: orbital motion,
               radiance,
               gravitational influence, etc.

[5] *Dravya, guna* and *karma*.

I have somewhat misrepresented our ancients in writing (1) an object, (2) its qualities and (3) its actions, as a temporary concession to the modern dualistic mind. Really they spoke of the presence in one place[6] or ground of thought, of three inseparables:

(1) object, (2) qualities, and (3) actions.

Inspect now our three exhibits. We are not in fact aware of a piece of glass, or a horse, or a planet, as an object which possesses those qualities and performs those actions. We are aware first of certain actions taking place, then of certain qualities present. It is this bundle that we call an object. It is the bundle that we know, and that is effectual in Nature. In the nondualistic philosophy of unity the essential thing about the planet is its orbital motion. When and where that motion is interrupted, or resisted, or disturbed, qualities (or forces) become evident. Forces are broken motion, or "potentials" (as Professor Clark-Maxwell would have put it)—neutralized or active potencies. Nextly, arrested forces are objects, neutralized potentials.

The explanation I gave of the way in which the human mind has supplanted natural clothing, weapons and instincts in the human evolute, and the description of the combinative quality of the human mind, as compared with the noncombinative mind of the animal, may have seemed somewhat of a digression. This was not really so, because the object of this chapter was to show how, in the course of evolution, the mind was mainly interested successively in materiality (in the mineral), force (in the plant), law (in the animal), and unity—the combinative mind—in man. We ought now to notice that the combinative power is a power of increased association with the mineral, plant, animal and fellow man. The power lies essentially in the coverage of this mental grasp of unity, and this consequent alliance with far-reaching forces. In his acts man does not violate or compel, but makes alliances—alli-

[6] *Bhūmi.*

ances with earth and water, fire and air, mud and the cosmic rays. What a bundle he is! What coherent heterogenousness is here, in this being who regards himself as the highest product of evolution on earth!

CHAPTER 3

THE PSYCHOLOGICAL LOOM

This morning at ten o'clock, after about four hours of steady writing, I finished the previous chapter of this book. My wife, seeing me at ease, posed the question: "Shall we go out?" To this I replied, "Yes, if you like," and the following conversation ensued:

"Shall we go to the beach, and watch the people bathing, and swimming, and eating their sandwiches on the sands, or shall we go shopping, or shall we visit Judge and Mrs. White for a game of chess and a conversation on Vedanta, or——"

I interrupted: "Enough said. Let us go to the beach, and afterwards, if there is time, to the grocery store. As to the chess, what do you say to leaving it for a rainy day?"

So, very soon we found ourselves on the beach, and there, as it happened, not exactly watching the swimmers, but engrossed in the doings of two tiny children—one in red pants, and the other in blue—who were being inducted by their mothers into the delights of sea-water immersion.

That describes what I was *doing*. But let us ask the question: "What was I *being* at that time?"

Without making a long story of this, I will say that this person was mentally very fully occupied with the doings of the two children, and at that time he had no thought of himself as writing, or eating breakfast, or going shopping, or of yesterday, or tomorrow, or even of the other people swimming and eating their sandwiches. He was concentrated upon the children.

Such things are a common occurrence, and they present a gold mine of information. It is vastly important, this phenom-

enon that a conscious being can without losing himself or herself come out of his or her infinite variety of mind into a
finite act by the miracle of concentration. At any time any
one of us can say to himself: "Thousands of things I could do,
but now, at this moment, I do only this one; many possibilities
I could be, but I am this one."

You will, perhaps, say that that watching of the children
was only for an hour. Yes, but at the end of it we went shopping, and we looked at eggs in cartons, and then we looked at
cans of peas, and so on. At no moment was I the whole of
myself. This is true of every one of us—that in a whole day
one is not the whole of oneself; nor in a whole year or in a
whole lifetime has one ever been or will ever be the whole
of oneself.

Of course, each one as defined by body and mind has his
limitations of personality, has his fixations, which, however,
even if very obdurate, can theoretically be unfixed by suitable
acts of concentration. He is to some extent like a swimmer
who has swum into the middle of a certain pool and must now
swim some more to come out of it again, or like a chess player
in the middle of a game, who has accepted the rules of the
game, involved himself in a position, and must by honorable
obligation with his opponent play the game through. Probably he is even more in the position of an actor on the
stage; Sir Laurence Olivier is playing Hamlet, and has entered into the part with such concentration that he practically is that Hamlet and has forgotten Olivier for the time
being; a simile that would consort well with the belief of the
Vedantists that our whole role in one lifetime, or rather body-
time, is only one phase of a longer life, described as a series of
body-times, in which different phases and aspects come into
operation. Be this belief true or not, the principle holds that
the life-urge has no material definition, but within its infinite
sphere goes on contracting and expanding alternately as its
interests change and fulfill themselves.

O miracle of concentration! This person is the infinite Being in one of his moods. For if one can concentrate oneself down to being the looker at the sea-bathing children, surely the infinite Being, without prejudice to his infinitude, can stoop to a mood-being of John Jones, of Emily Wilkinson, or any of the rest of those lookers and bathers and eaters of sandwiches! "What man has done man can do," says the proverb. Yes, and what man has done, surely the infinite Being also can do.

Let no materialistic metaphysics (of all paradoxes the worst) put its foot in here. Let it not be said that the infinite cannot be finite, that the unlimited cannot be limited. We see it happening, even in the mind, which has not dimensions and boundaries, like a box, but has a moving centre of power with no circumference or surface anywhere, except such as it adopts for a given time. Besides, if you say that the unlimited cannot limit itself you have denied its unlimitedness.

All this is not pure metaphysics. It is applied metaphysics operating in daily life, whenever the mind concentrates upon anything at all.

This operation is what the old Vedantists called *māyā*, translated often as "illusion." The derivation of the word *māyā* seems to be related to a verbal root *mā*, which means to measure off, to mete. From this comes the idea of the setting up of a definiteness within an indefiniteness, that is, a creation, the production of three-dimensioned forms in dimensionless space. Among the old Vedantists *māyā* is equivalent to creation in this sense. When they called it illusion they meant that the seen was not the whole truth, and therefore was false, because it could be known as it really is only along with the wholeness. The *māyā* is thus not true, but not entirely false, not real and not unreal, but indescribable. How can there be anything that is unreal and indescribable? There is not, and that is why it is called *māyā* and is expected to disappear, like a dream, when the sleeper awakes.

The idea of *māyā* thus contains more than mere illusion, though we can accept illusion as a secondary meaning, as an attribute or quality of this creation. If, however, it is said that this world of limited experiences is illusion, it must be replied that the word "illusion" and also the thought of its meaning are limited things of this world, and therefore the "illusion" is an illusion—and where are you then? But if one says: "Inasmuch as the children on the beach are parts of the created limited world they are not merely what we see, and our seeing of them as children only and our thinking of them as children only is illusory," we can all agree.

It is a delusion if we see something where there is nothing; an illusion if there is something there, but we see it not as it is. So what *māyā* really means is the truism contained in the old saw: "Things are not what they seem."

I have jumped, perhaps, rather far from the children to the world in the course of the foregoing argument; with good reason. Let us focus our thought more definitely by a quotation from one of the best of the old Vedantic books, the *Mānasollāsa* by Sureshwara Āchārya, it being a commentary on Shankara's *Dakshināmūrti Stotra*. Chapter II, verse 44, says: "By *māyā*, operating in the form of will, intelligence and activity, have they been displayed." The "they" means all the things in the world and the world itself, as is mentioned in earlier verses in the same philosophic poem.

Now let us look at *māyā* as operating in the human mind. I wish to use here for a short time three original Sanskrit words, translated as will, intelligence and activity. I want them because they bring out the significance of these three functions remarkably clearly.

The *Mānasollāsa*, by stating that all events are the products of will, intelligence and activity, and that these are the work of the infinite Being in a limiting or mayavic mood, gives universal significance to the process of concentration which we find in operation in our own minds all the time. Every time that we "pay attention" to anything we are voluntarily "measuring off" that thing, and there is at the same time an operation of ignoring, even forgetting, everything else. Sometimes we use the power of concentration in order to observe and learn, sometimes to plan and make. In bigger or smaller matters, according to the measure of the moment, we concentrate to create our little game of the moment, or the hour or the year, or the whole body-time, in this big room called the world, which is "the hall of all games."

The three words above referred to—*ichchhā* (will), *jnāna* (intelligence), *kriyā* (activity)—have technical significance in this philosophic system. Used here as attributes of mind, they are the equivalents of will, affection and thought.

That the action-aspect of the mind is thought becomes evident when we notice that ordinarily we, as mind-beings, have thought at the back of our bodily actions. We may say, "With my hand I lifted the pen and wrote," but really the action was only the outside end of a thought. One could quite truthfully say, "I lifted the pen with my thought," because thought lifted the hand that lifted the pen. The degree to which the thought-pictures in the mind govern the action of the body is surprising when one contemplates it for the first time. The standard example of "walking the plank" (described in Chapter 8) illustrates very well what is happening all the time. To sum up: the *activity* of mind is thought. It includes perception of things and also planning.

Jnāna, intelligence, is more than such bare thought. It implies understanding of life, not merely remembering, recognizing and planning. The word "wisdom," as distinguished from mere knowledge, is probably the best translation for *jnāna* in this context. To know *life* is wisdom. To know *things* is mere knowledge. When we get up in the morning we require knowledge to take our bath, shave, put on our clothes and go down the stairs to breakfast, but when we sit down at the table it requires wisdom to deal with father and mother and sister and brother, or wife and children, who are sitting there. This wisdom includes a sympathetic understanding of how all those minds work, and what is going on inside them —with all their pleasures and pains, joys and sorrows, frustrations and elations, hopes and fears. It involves a considerable amount of sympathy with them, for the unsympathetic person never really knows others—he shies away from them, and thrusts their pleasures and troubles away from his mind, being only intent upon his own, so that people who amuse and aid him are "good sorts" and the others are bores to be avoided or "put in their places" as the case may be. There is always some affection or love in wisdom, and this touches in some degree every occurrence in our lives which involves intercourse with another living being. And, in its turn, there is the reaction in us, producing an increase of wisdom corresponding to the amount of intelligent goodwill, friendliness, affection or love that we have put forth.

All this sounds like a three-minute sermon, but it is really only an effort to state that the mind has three powers; will, love or affection, and thought. Thought involves knowledge of things; love, knowledge of others; will, knowledge of self —the man who does not "know his own mind" is not likely to "make it up" for himself, and the lady, dear soul, goes "up and down, up and down, like a cork on a wave."

I have written at some length of the way in which we concentrate or "limit the attention to a particular ground" (as, for example, the sea-bathing children) in order to know. It should be mentioned that we perform a similar self-limitation whenever we intend to do something. The carpenter, going to his workshop in the morning, may say to himself, "Now, what shall I make today? Shall it be a table or a chair, or a bookcase, or a desk, or—?" He is capable of many things, but he will decide perhaps on a chair, and then concentrate his doing within that field until that work is done.

It is here that we are brought face to face with the shuttle action in the loom of life. The carpenter concentrates upon his work upon the chair. He uses all his will and affection and thought within that limited field. He keeps himself to the task —that is will. He has an idea that someone will sit in the chair, if it is an armchair, or on it, if it is a chair without arms, and, having some feeling for others, he wants it to be a useful and comfortable chair for them—that is sympathy, affection, goodwill, or—in the language of philosophy—love. Thirdly, he considers his materials and their qualities and his tools and how to use them, and studies the shaping of the parts of the chair and how to fit them together, and then the polishing and the varnishing—that is thought. And finally, he says, "It is done," with a sigh of satisfaction, a release of tense breath which at the same time marks the release of his mind, and the ending of that particular act of concentration.

Expansion comes in during the work. The mind expands or enhances its powers. The work has left a visible chair on the floor, and also an invisible growth inside the man. There has been an addition to the mind, a new perception here or there, an intuition, a realization of something not realized before, an awakening of something—an evolution of the mind. We can consider it as parallel to the evolution of the body and its outposts, as we may call the things which it makes, the artificial evolutes; remembering the difference, that heterogeneousness in the case of the mind appears in the coherent powers of mind.

There is real expansion in this, for step by step the mind becomes capable of greater grasp. Concentration gives grip. In that, our conscious powers are at their best. The work expands the grip, and so enlarges the grasp. The fulfillment of the work is power, greater grasp without loss of grip, so that afterwards we can deal with more difficult, complicated or subtle problems and jobs with the ease and certainty with which we handled simpler ones before.

This is precisely what the process of life is doing to us.

Two words are constantly mentioned in the old Vedantic literature, to describe what happens when *māyā* gets to work. The two powers of *māyā* are described as covering-up and throwing-out.[1]

We have to assume, then, that, at some point in the infinite, *māyā* takes charge, and operates its power of concealment, shutting out or shielding off everything else, or, as one text puts it, "causing conditioned existence." Then the other power comes into operation, and there is a great proliferation within the marked-off field. It is like the establishment of a conditioned entity or mind, and then the working of that mind into a quantity of creations. It is like the landing of the Pilgrim Fathers in a new land, and then up spring houses, farms, and all the adjuncts of civilization. It is as though a creator let forth an "abstract" thought, such as "feline animal," and out come cats, lions, tigers, leopards, pumas, ocelots and all the rest. Or as though the limiting thought or act of concentration were "a world," and then begins all the evolution in that sphere. Or as though you or I said, "I will now be an artist," and soon paintings of all kinds are littering the place.

Any talk of a beginning to all this is all speculative, of course. True, it is based on experience, reason and analogy, but it can be regarded only as a symbolical idea. All our thinking, like all our living, must begin from what is and where we are. We find ourselves as though upon a stairway, as Emerson put it, looking up and down, and seeing some steps below us up which we have come, and some above us which we will now tread, but seeing neither top nor bottom of this stairway. But from where we are we can see and learn the nature of the process that is actually going on, as we are doing now.

The process applies to both knowing and doing. A student wants to acquire, let us say, a French vocabulary. There are perhaps twenty words on one page of his textbook. He con-

[1] *Āvarana* and *vikshepa*.

centrates on one of them; gets its sound right and considers its meaning; learns the modifications it undergoes—until he has observed and learnt all its proliferational ideas. Then his concentration on that word ends, and he forgets it while he goes on to another word. Forgotten, it is not lost, however; the word has gone into his memory, from which it will come out at the proper time if he has concentrated well upon it. Having set it aside, he now turns to the next word, treats it the same way, and so on. So valuable is this principle of concentration or self-limitation that in teaching Sanskrit I have found it beneficial to get students to concentrate on the sound of a word until it becomes familiar to them, before giving them the meaning; thus they had more perfect concentration than if they tried to think of the sound and the meaning both at the same time. The importance of this process of simultaneous concentrating and forgetting is seen in a general way in a school, where every student knows that he must not think of geography while the arithmetic lesson is going on. Later, when his grasp has grown, he will be able to use any of his French words in the bigger concentrative field of a conversation or a letter. In the meantime this process of concentration is a voluntary ignorance, which is nevertheless the road to knowledge.

Another point of great importance in our evolution—which is to a large extent self-directed evolution—now comes into view. While the evolution of our bodies is complete—we are evidently not intended to grow ten feet high or sprout four arms—that of our minds is not. For the intelligent person, however, the practical completion of mind-evolution is not remote. Let him train his mind in habits of concentration and well-directed thought, so that in its own sphere it will be as orderly and obedient and useful as the body is in its, and he will then be ready for another step. The body being mature, we proceed to develop the mind. The mind being mature, what next? It is evidently a stairway that we are on, not an inclined plane. The ancients say that when the mind is mature we shall be ready to think upon the "infinite self" which is the heart of our own being, until we complete and go beyond mere thought and live in the light of that Being. This is to say that we do not need mental genius any more than the bodily "genius" of extreme muscular cultivation, but we do need a mind released from slavery to bodily appetites and able to think. Such is held to be the destiny of our present "concentration" and unfoldment in the human form. Some day this child will have finished this schooling and will slip into a higher life. Having come into it a grub we shall go out a butterfly, all grubness given up.

In the third part of this book I will make a translation of the famous *Dakshināmūrti Stotra*, or *Ode to the South-facing Form*, which shows how our ancient Aryan seers taught men to fulfill this destiny, combining devotion with the profoundest thought. This combination could be so because their conception of the infinite Being was not materialistic. They did not make the mistake of abolishing the old gentleman with a long beard and a good temper beyond the clouds, only to replace him with a blank sheet of paper or a material void. In the meantime, let us go on to Part II of this work, dealing with the means to maturity of mind.

CHAPTER 4

COMBINATIVE CHANGE

Every man is to a large extent the supporter of his own ignorance. He often fears to know the truth, and clings to fancies. He bathes in drifting tides of thought on the edge of sleep. He clutches at slipping memories. He trembles in his castle of illusion when he hears the call of his future: "Awake! Arise! Seek the teachers and understand!"

The teachers? Yes. It is the belief of the Aryans that every man can find someone who knows better than himself. Not "knows more things," be it observed, but "knows better."

Probably the best piece of information about himself that can be given to any man is contained in the words: "Your mind is only half-grown." And the best advice: "Compare it with your body, which is full-grown, and then undertake some study of the matter, in order to know what is needed and desirable, and some suitable mental exercise to complete its growth." We know, of course, that experience will gradually mature our minds, but the process can be greatly accelerated by a little self-education.

In every man there is a process of evolution, in the sense of unfoldment and fulfillment of both body and mind. When we study Nature, including man, we find two departments of enquiry before us; things and changes. Nature is composed of things which are changing. That is the way in which we

53

usually think of the world. But it would be equally logical to regard Nature as composed of change which is "thinging." Change is much more permanent than things. It is going on all the time and everywhere—more quickly in some things and more slowly in others. The slower a thing changes the more we are aware of its "thingness." A cloud seems less a thing than a mountain does. So we can, if we like, regard Nature or the world as a stream of change in which the things most definite to us are the portions where the movement is least.

When we consider the evolution of bodies and minds, then, we are studying the nature of change with reference to these two facts. Thus we have to study the "thinging" in change in order to understand growth or evolution. The background thought is: a change is going on; how does it alter this mind? What is mind-maturity, and how does it proceed? To answer this question there must be observation, thought, and then meditation, which is the play and then the poise of the mind on a subject of enquiry for a considerable time.

As already mentioned in Chapter 3 everything is triple: (1) the object, (2) its qualities and (3) its actions. An example: an iron girder, which has the qualities (among others) of solidity, hardness, heaviness, tensile strength, malleability, and metallic lustre or sheen, and has the actions (among others) of rusting in damp air, and of supporting a weight. Another example: a dog, which has the qualities (among others) of middle-sizedness (among animals), hairiness, and flexibility, and has the actions (among others) of running, barking and biting.

In the field of Science, men study these three features of the things in Nature with meticulous and unremitting care; but they do so not purely from a desire to know about them. There is another purpose in view, namely, to change them. The spirit of change is in man. He wants to alter things. In this he has great power, when he knows the things with accuracy, because he has not only the observing mind, but also the combinative mind. Combinativeness is man's special capacity in the field of change, his phase or stage of evolution. He can alter things, and also put them together, first in imagination and then in fact, and use them for his own purposes—making more complicated objects by his power of combinative thought. His study of things—all three features, I want to emphasize—has fed more and more materials to his combinative power, so that he has been materially rewarded beyond all expectation with the fruits of applied science, which will no doubt go on to make human life so rich that our descendants of a few generations hence will look back upon us as quite primitive men. Solids, liquids, fire and gases have come into his net, with all their forms and qualities and actions, and in his latest achievements he has taken in the ether or "skyey matter" as well.

Even outside the operations of man, every object changes quickly or slowly. The milk goes sour, the cake of soap diminishes, the bar of iron rusts away, the dog grows from puppiness to maturity, and passes on to elderliness, old age and death. Men have cherished a hope of finding "the substance of objects," something unchanging—the chemical atom, the electron—but all are changing, and "substance" remains a pipe dream, a fantasy. The search for it is really an obstacle to knowledge, if there is no being without change, and that is surely the case. Our best knowledge on this point is that substance does not exist in Nature, but is a superstition of the scientific mind, an unjustifiable assumption and belief. To understand Nature or the world, and ourselves, we must leave it out of account. We know forms and even matter, but not substance.

Change is of two kinds: (1) mere change of form, as when drifting clouds take different shapes from moment to moment, or when the forms of mountains and rivers are brought about by the interactions of earth, water, fire and air, or when the housewife throws her garbage in the bin: and (2) combinative change, which is evolution, as when a plant grows or, in a secondary way, when a man produces a machine or builds a house. Combinative change produced by man has the same character as evolution in Nature, in that it makes objects in which the parts inherently cohere to produce a new object, with new qualities and new actions.

The reader may very reasonably ask why this emphasis on forms and form-making, when Vedanta is concerned especially with the path of knowledge, not the path of action. The answer to this is that really we make forms only to assist us in knowing. A composer of music cannot be quite satisfied with the melody that forms itself in his mind. It is not real enough, until he has played it out on the piano.

Our power of concentration of attention, or of mind, is at its best in dealing with actual forms. This outward process of making and using things is therefore necessary, in order to produce the maturity and strength of mind needed for the next step. We must have "coherent heterogeneity" of mind, or, in other words, the mind must become "as good as the body." Applying it to things in the combinative way helps to bring that about.

The Vedantic books ask: "For whom is the Vedanta?" They also give the answer: "For the qualified person." [1] The qualified person is he who has attained maturity of mind. He will have a usableness of mind that compares with the usableness of his body in ordinary life. This means a mature mind. This maturity is the completion of the mind's evolution. At the beginning of this task let us compare it with the body. As explained in Chapter 2, the very height and crown of evolution, that is, of coherent heterogeneity, is seen in the human body, with its great variety of limbs, organs and functions all working together for its self-preservation. "With legs and feet we see" is true, inasmuch as when I want to see something in another room, I first tell my legs to walk and

[1] *Adhikārī.*

take my eyes into that room, and "With eyes we walk" is also true, inasmuch as when I want to walk anywhere I first tell my eyes to look for obstacles, lest those blind legs of mine run my nose into a post, or themselves take a tumble on the steps.

On this account we say that the human body is a high product of evolution, meaning not that there is an invisible mystery person or power named Evolution who is doing all this, but simply that there has been a progressive change with this result.

Now I will give you "the doctor's bulletin" on the evolutionary state of the average mind: "We are happy to say that we find a sufficient quantity of heterogeneous ideas in the patient, but must report the presence also of a considerable degree of noncoherence in the shape of drift, dullness and disorder." So while we are studying Nature and increasing the heterogeneous ideas in the mind, we had better attend also to our instrument of knowledge of Nature, the mind, especially in the matter of coherence. We can hardly expect coherent understanding in an incoherent mind.

CHAPTER 5

WHAT DO WE WANT?

The ancient Aryan thinkers who collected, collated, classified and commented upon the thought-traditions accumulated
by their distant progenitors performed a rational and ethical
service of the greatest value to posterity, when they put together a set of brief sayings, which they called the Vedanta
(the end, or highest point, of knowledge; the "last word"), and
presented them for study along with the further statement:
"You will not be able to understand or realize the full import
of these Great Sayings unless you first put your mind in order
by certain practices or disciplines, which we will describe."

They said in plain language: "Be thankful that you have
been born a man, and, further, a thinking man, which is a state
which can lead on to the fulfillment of life in happiness and
freedom, and do not be such a fool as to throw away your opportunity by a life of idleness, frivolity or dissipation."

In this book I will describe the Disciplines first, and give
the Great Sayings afterwards. But I must at the very beginning put in a word about *the question* put to every aspirant
or candidate for knowledge, which was and still is: "What
do you want?" It is a question every man should ask himself,
and he should probe his own motivation until he gets beyond
the shallows of thoughtless motive in his life, and discovers his
own depths.

There is a purely apocryphal story of a young man who
applied for a job, and was asked a series of questions:

Question: "Why do you want this job?"
Answer: "To get some money."
Question: "Why do you want money?"
Answer: "To buy food, and eat."
Question: "Why do you want to eat?"
Answer: "To stay alive."
Question: "Why do you want to stay alive?"
Answer: "To look after my wife and children."
Question: "Why do you want to look after your wife and children?"
Answer: "Because I love them—I guess."

So he found his deeper motive, beyond reason.

In the field of Vedanta, Shankara posed the essential question thus to his applicants for knowledge: "Which do you desire to know, (1) how things are made, or (2) how they grow?" Most students of Vedanta will not recognize the two questions in this form until I explain them, for the original statement was that there are two ways for men, based respectively upon the desire to know Rules of Action,[1] and the desire to know the One Reality.[2]

Karmas are action-with-intent. Knowledge of *karmas* tells you how to get the things you want, not only in this world, they say, but also in heaven after death. There are whole books of practical and ceremonial actions prescribed for obtaining just what you want. These are called *Dharmas* or Rules of Action, by carrying out which, it is said, you inevitably succeed. In brief modern terms, there were techniques, which men could learn from their predecessors in every department of human activity. Teachers taught them, and books recorded them. In these modern days we have such things as moving pictures to teach some of the techniques of surgery. In religious circles people have prescribed techniques for

---

[1] *Karmas.*
[2] *Brahman.*

going to heaven after you die. The old books of Rules of Action were very precise: they told us that if you want to clean a cloth you must wash it, if you want to clean a plank you must plane it, and if you want to clean a piece of iron you must file it. Simply, we might call a cookery book the Rules[3] of Cookery; you take so much flour and water and sugar and butter, mix them with a fork in such-and-such a manner, shape the paste and keep it in the oven at a certain temperature for so long—and you will get cookies. If I say that the way to get the best out of life is to take care to use on all occasions all the intelligence, affection and will that we have, I shall be prescribing a general Rule.

I have thus dwelt upon the idea of Rules because it often comes up in oriental literature, which is very widely read in intellectual circles today, and I want to explain its very precise meaning. Our ancients were very firm and realistic in this matter. Let a man decide what he wants, they said, and then go after it with the proper methods of action, whether it is a little cake or a high seat in heaven. Probe your own motives and find out what you really want; then learn the techniques and act upon them.

The second way follows upon the desire to know the One Reality. Our motive in this case is the desire to understand life, not mere forms or objects.

We have already explained that in a universe from which no part can be cut off, from which not one atom can escape and go away to live somewhere else, all by itself, there must be one over-all and underlying principle or first truth. This fundament cannot be a lot of things; it cannot be ten thousand million things existing side by side; it cannot be even two things. Two things would not be complete; their not-getting-awayness would have to be present as a deeper or more enveloping truth.

[3] *Dharma.*

It being accepted that the universe must be one, we have next to enquire what is the nature of that unity. The universe is not one like our number one. In this connection I wish to point out an important fact in our numbering operations: five eggs in a nest are "a five"; four corners of a square are "a four"; three bottles on a shelf are "a three"; two eyes in the head are "a two"; and similarly, one of anything is "a one." So one is one, two is one, three is one, four is one and five is one. We can count one, two, three, four, and five, and know there are five things, because to us five is a kind of one. Otherwise we could only tick off the things, saying, "One, one, one, one, one," as a mother dog can do with her puppies. If when that mother is away for a while you remove one of the puppies she will not know that there are now only four instead of five, and that one is missing, because she cannot count and has no idea of "a five." With us, one is only a number like two or three; it is not a sacrosanct number, different in character or nature from the others. If it were, we could not count a half, a quarter, a fifth, and so on. From the standpoint of a half, one is a two, just as from the standpoint of a three six is a two.

We cannot say that the universe is one thing in our numerical sense, but only in the sense described in my last paragraph. We can, however, say that it is not two or more, because no part is separable. It is indivisible. So Shankara did not call his philosophy monistic or unitary, but "nondualistic." [4]

This is declared to be *the* eminently practical basis of philosophy for those who want "to know the One Reality." [5] The word which I have here translated as the One Reality is often translated "God," when God is defined as the over-all and underlying reality of the universe, not as a glorified ruler or king. Patanjali aptly put it that God is that Being who (un-

[4] *A-dwaita.*
[5] *Brahman.*

like men) is not pushed about by anything other than himself. Patanjali introduced the idea of God into his yoga system not for metaphysical theorizing, but as an object of meditation, because we become like that which we meditate upon, and all men in their hearts want to enjoy the unobstructed life of which God is considered to be the supreme example. Patanjali was not prescribing a heaven for men, with a God as the central object of enjoyment therein. He definitely states that the practice of poise-of-mind which he expounds is intended to be used for the attainment of perfect independence.[6]

What people are really trying to get is this independence; all the time they are trying to overcome obstructions to life. This world would be good enough, they say, if we could have it without obstructions to our enjoyment and its increase. An unobstructive thing or world of things is, however, unthinkable, being a contradiction in terms; since a material object is defined as that which obstructs the senses in some way. But unobstructed life *is* thinkable. Meditation on unobstructed life until we grasp its meaning leads to that goal.

The etymology of the word *Brahman*, which I have translated "the One Reality" is important. Why did the Vedantic sages of old choose this word to express their idea of God? It is related to the verbal root *brih*, which means "to grow." The principle of growth is that of evolution—coherent heterogeneity or integration. Integration means making an *inherent* unity. That process is the principle of life, which defies and defeats all arithmetic, because it is not mere addition, is not merely sticking things together.

In material things, and in the mind, when there is integration or inherent unity or coherence something new is born. The new object manifests qualities and actions not found in the old parts. Unite oxygen and hydrogen and there is water.

[6] *Kaivalya.*

Merely mix them and there is not. This sort of integration is an outward expression of an indefinable unity.

When there is an evolution, it is a principle of unity that is increasingly asserting itself in the sphere of an object. Man, in whom this principle most appears, not only manifests it as a power in his own person. His action in Nature also imposes it on other things. It is the source of the combinativeness which fills his world with so many new things—from a child's toy monkey-on-a-stick to automobiles and aeroplanes, houses and hospitals, printing machines and cyclotrons, microscopes and telescopes, telephones and radio, and a great variety of clothing and housing. When the combinative mind of man makes these things, it imparts to them something of that nature of unity which is at the core of its own being. When it is withdrawn they fall again into incoherence, back towards "chaos and the dark." The mind builds, but when mind is withdrawn, Nature's process spells decay. I have emphasized this matter, at the risk of being repetitive and even tedious—it is so important in the understanding of life.

The desire to realize this principle of unity, that is, to become conscious of it, not merely to think about it in words, is what is meant by the "desire to know the One Reality." If, in answer to that question which we are advised to put to ourselves: "What do I really want? What is my essential motive in living? Do I want to occupy my time with the pursuit of pleasurable actions or do I want to know the One Reality?" we can say, "At least sometimes I want to experience the One Reality," this pursuit is for us in our moments of strength, and the moments will increase. No real success, however, can be expected, says Shankara, while the mind is still half-grown— is still full of drift, dullness and disorder. While that is so, we are not qualified for the task. Fortunately, however, he prescribed the Four Disciplines,[7] by practicing which we can

[7] *Sādhanachatushtayam.*

quickly achieve the maturity of mind that will clear the way for knowledge of the One Reality.

The Four Disciplines
1. Discrimination.
2. Uncoloredness.
3. Six things to do.
4. Reaching to Freedom.

CHAPTER 6

MENTAL BALANCE

The four Disciplines[1] required to prepare the way for the knowledge of the One Reality begin with "Discrimination[2] between the permanent and the fleeting." This has to be examined from several points of view and with regard to different aspects of experience.

We shall understand the value for consciousness of "the permanent" if we first examine the value of the fleeting thing. When a man uses his combinative or constructive mind he enjoys himself. We all enjoy a puzzle if it is not too difficult for us. It is not that we want the pride of achievement so much as that we enjoy the feeling of living which accompanies the use of our faculties. I noticed in India, when a large number of carpenters were engaged on a building job, that when some portion of the work which allowed for a little personal initiative, whether intricate or ornamental—such as morticing, or the ornamental carving of beam ends or door battens—was given to them they were highly delighted. Thought, not force, is our delight. If we are playing a game of tennis or of chess, there is no pleasure in being knocked about by an expert, nor in overcoming a weak opponent, but there is great enjoyment in pitting our skill and wits against someone just about our equal, or just a little stronger than we are, because then we are in a position to use our own powers. Incidentally, this informs us that in any brotherhood movement it is the companionship of equals or near-equals that is of the greatest benefit.

[1] *Sādhanā.*
[2] *Viveka.*

Every man is ordinarily engaged in trying to adapt his environment to himself, that is, to alter his little bit of the world to suit what he wants. When he has got so far as to establish himself in comfort with some money in the bank, he begins to cast round for a hobby—he must find some new but not too difficult difficulties to play with. This is another indication that the need for change—not purposeless or thoughtless change—is essential in our lives.

It is in practical things that we must first discriminate between the permanent and the fleeting. The picture that is successfully painted, the work that has been completely done, the game that has been played, ceases to be interesting to us; but the use of faculty in the work or the game was not only a delight at the time but remains as a joy for ever. There is then an enrichment of consciousness that goes forward with us into new works and games.

This thought engenders a wise attitude towards the world. It teaches us that our real life is on the wing, but that we carry with us in the winging a constantly richer power of consciousness. We can take Blake's well-known verse:

> He who takes to himself a joy
>   Doth the winged life destroy,
> But he who kisses the joy as it flies
>   Lives in eternity's sunrise,

and add to it the thought that the kissing becomes more and more efficient as he goes along. And, above all, it is the kisser that matters, for *there* is the consciousness, and the joy of consciousness. Indeed, we may go so far as to say that there is no life but living.

The first Discipline, then, is to learn to value things for the promotion of life, not as though they had some value in themselves. One cannot rightly speak of a good chair without saying for whom it is good. Or, a good person—to whom is he or she good, and is the benefit permanent, for if not it is not good? The practice of valuation of all things and experiences from the standpoint of the permanent (the consciousness) and not from that of the fleeting (the world) is the first step in Vedantic Discipline.

We come next to the matter of being well-balanced in our discrimination. Such balance is indeed mental health or sanity. Sanity is the correct valuation of the ideas in our own minds. The following teaching should be treated in textbook fashion —that is, accepted as the findings of the teachers, and studied critically, as subject to amendment: "There are five kinds of ideas in the mind. They are Right Knowledge, Wrong Knowledge, Fancies, Sleep-conditions, and Memories." This statement was made by Patanjali, the yoga teacher, not in the Vedanta literature, but in his yoga aphorisms, but I bring it in here as a great help to our first Discipline. The mind is full of pieces of knowledge which we have acquired in various ways at various times. Perfect sanity is our unfailing awareness, whenever there comes up in the mind a particular piece of knowledge, that is, an idea, as to which of these five categories it belongs to.

Let me take Fancy first. To indulge in fancies is both pleasurable and useful. The world has always enjoyed a story, and little girls have always played with dolls. It might be very amusing to sit back in your chair and imagine for a while that you are the Emperor of China—instructive also. But woe unto you if you forget that this is a fancy, and mistake it for reality, for that would be insanity. The greatest calamity in human life is to go insane. We are, however, sane if we can indulge in fancies knowing that they are fancies.

Next let us look at Right Knowledge, that is, ideas corresponding to facts. We all know, of course, that our ideas about things are obtained from a very definitely limited point of view, that their truth is personal and relative. In practical life we do not ask for anything more than that. Regardless of any metaphysical theories, and regardless of all "the new

physics," I will go to the table half an hour from now and
"eat my breakfast," as the idiom goes. Within the sphere of
practical facts I must have the mental sanity to know, with
regard to any idea in my mind, whether it is a piece of true
knowledge or not. "There are three ways of getting Right
Knowledge: by Seeing, Reasoning or Being Told." [3] The term
"seeing" must include the use of all the sense-organs, and Being Told must have the addition, "by a witness whom we
know to be reliable in the matter concerned."

Vedantic philosophers mention three more means to correct knowledge, namely, comparison, presumption and absence.[4] I wish to limit myself to the first three for the sake
of simplicity. It is arguable, anyhow, that this extra three can
be placed within the first three, but for the sake of complete-
ness I must describe them in passing. Examples: I have seen a
cow in town, and afterwards when in the country I may see
a gnu, and conclude: "That animal is like the cow." In this
there is some gain of knowledge through similarity, seen by
comparison. Next, if a fat man does not eat by day, it is presumed that he eats by night. Thirdly, if we see an unoccupied
chair, we do not merely think "There is an empty chair," but
"There is an absence of person on the chair,"—we are conscious of the absence of some specific thing in relation to which
the thing seen has its proper existence. This is something like
the case in which an Irishman is reputed to have taken a picture
down from the wall and put it away in a closet, remarking
that it would look better out of sight!

Perfect sanity with regard to Right Knowledge is the
awareness of an idea as a piece of well-substantiated knowledge. A man and his wife are going, let us say, to the theater,
and the following conversation takes place.

"Is the house door locked?"

[3] *Pratyaksha, anumāna* and *āgama.*
[4] *Upamāna, arthapatti* and *abhāva.*

"Yes, I locked it myself; I remember turning the key in the lock."

The wife says: "But I am not sure that you are a Reliable Witness. I am going back to see."

When she returns, he asks: "Did I lock the door?"

"Yes."

"How do you know?"

"I tried the door and it would not open, therefore I Reason that it was locked, and I Reason also that since it has not a spring lock you must have locked it."

"Perhaps, then, in future you will regard me as a Reliable Witness with regard to the locking of the door."

"I might, but I am not sure."

This little fanciful story will not harm us if we remember that it is only a fancy. The point is that we ought not to regard any idea in the mind as a true idea unless we are well aware that it is supported by our own experience, or reasons or reliable testimony. This discrimination or awareness is important, and indeed necessary, to perfect sanity. "True" means "having practicable truth," not, of course, absolute truth. Belief without the support of experience, reason, or reliable witness really contains a degree of insanity. There is plenty of this kind of insanity about, attained through wishful thinking, self-hypnosis, affirmations, etc. This is part of the first Discipline called Discrimination.

All this is equally true with regard to Wrong Knowledge and Disbelief. When there is a statement, we have no right to say that it is wrong, is not corresponding to fact, unless we know it to be wrong by the same means of Experience, or Reason or Reliable Witness. An example of this occurred recently in a house which was let to certain tenants. For two or three months all went well, but then several times at night the most unearthly moans and howls issued from the basement. The tenants telephoned long distance to the owners. Those sounds had been heard before, they said, and a neighbor, when asked, told them there was a ghost. The owner pooh-poohed the idea. The story went abroad among the neighbors, and soon there was a story of a suicide there, which grew into a murder, then into a crime committed by a jealous mad woman. The tenants moved out, and a new resident moved in. The sounds occurred again, and the new tenant had the courage to go down to the basement to investigate. He caught the offender in the act—a cat which belonged to one of the gossiping neighbors! This justified the house owner's disbelief, based upon the unreasonableness of the story.

Disbelief and belief are equally unjustified, unless properly supported. The pathway of science has been blocked again and again by these two, not properly supported.

Again, when we look into our own minds and find an idea there, we ought to be able to say, "That is a memory," if it is a memory. If I do not distinguish between my memories and my present experiences, I am partially insane. Or, if there is only a drifting thought in the succession of associations of ideas—there, too, I must know it for what it is, as a piece of mental sleepiness.

The First Discipline is therefore based essentially on the Practice of Sanity. I must make myself aware of the nature of the thoughts in my mind, just as I must be aware in my body that I am walking, or talking, or eating, or whatever it may be, and must not mistake one action for another.

It is not Discrimination to sit down and try to picture an eternal thing as opposed to the fleeting things, as is sometimes thought. The nonfleeting is, of course, the One Reality, but you cannot make it an object of comparison with the fleeting things. Discrimination can take us only to the threshold of the throne-room of the One Reality, which will then come to the door and welcome us in—if I may be permitted a figure of speech. The One Reality is not an object of comparative thought, for as such it would be one among many. All that a man can get by such mental effort to formulate it is a Fancy, and if he repeats it until it becomes so real to him that he does not recognize it as a fancy he will merely become partially insane. It is to be remembered that Discrimination is only a discipline of the mind, to help to bring it to maturity; not the means of knowing, but only the key to the door of knowing.

Discrimination of the classes of ideas or pieces of knowledge in the mind is the basis of all rational living. The essence of it is that we stand on our own feet mentally, in health and strength of mind, and we view and review the world without being swept along a thoughtless path in life. It can also be described as "being true to ourselves," because even when we accept the testimony of others we cannot escape the responsibility of judging their reliability.

As all thinking is value-ing, and all value-ing is relative to and for a purpose, and as purpose is to produce an experience, and experience—if with discrimination—leads to re-valuation, discrimination is the enemy of old valuations and old purposes, and at the same time the nursemaid of the new. It hovers with anxious love, as it were, over the prospective birthings of knowledge, and has such faith in the rightness of truth that it will never whisper, "I hope it is a boy."

When the student has enough discrimination to feel that he can trust himself to look without prejudice at an evoluted form, or an evolute—as we may conveniently call those things which exhibit inherent coherence—whether a primary evolute which grows, or a secondary evolute which is made, to distinguish in that evolute the relatively fleeting and the relatively permanent, he will begin to "know the mind." Then he will, quite instinctively, not intentionally, begin to put values on things "for the mind" instead of "for the body," as was the case before. He will not commit the error of trying to make the mind, build the mind, shape the mind, sculpt the mind, paint the mind, prop the mind, elevate the mind. He will let it grow.

Then in the mind itself he will more and more distinguish the inherent coherency of it from all its works or functions. Yesterday he saw darkly, cloudily, weakly; tomorrow his vision will be clear and strong. This explorer goes on chasing his receding horizon until he suddenly finds that he has rounded the world of the mind—the mind is now mature, is one piece. The inherent coherency has done its work of growth. The Discipline called Discrimination is finished. The man is ready[5] for what is next.

[5] *Adhikārī.*

CHAPTER 7

EMOTIONAL BALANCE

One of the most important things to which my attention was directed in the course of my Oriental studies was the fact that every idea is accompanied by feeling. I was taught that there are five kinds of ideas in the mind, as already mentioned, and all of them are either pleasing or painful.

You cannot look at anything or anybody—even the least thing—or have the most fleeting thought before the mind's eye, without being either pleased or hurt in some degree. There is no harm in this fact, but there is harm if we go through life, as many do, without being aware of it. This is a matter well worth knowing, because to see what is actually going on within itself is quite a release for the mind. I would strongly advise the reader of these lines to spare a few minutes every now and then for the inspection of these things which are going on in their own minds.

These feelings are subject to the same classification as our thoughts. There are right feelings about a thing, also wrong feelings, and feelings that are purely fanciful. There are also the pleasures and pains of drifts and dreams—pleasant and painful sleep conditions of the mind—and pleasurable and painful memories.

The pleasures and pains of the mind are feelings of liking and disliking. You cannot dislike a thing or idea or person without some mental pain, and you cannot like them without some pleasure in the thought of them. Victor Hugo said that the supreme happiness of life is the conviction that we are loved; perhaps the words "supreme happiness" were excessive, but

we do like those who love us—that is, unselfishly love us without any appropriation; or any claims upon our liberty.

The word which is used to describe this second Discipline[1]
has been translated sometimes as Indifference, sometimes as
Desirelessness. Each of these is in some way misleading. There
seems to be no word in our language which exactly conveys
the meaning, so I have coined a new one which is a literal
translation of the original. The word is Uncoloredness. The
mind of a man who wants to follow this Discipline or, indeed,
who wants to have true sanity of feelings, or emotional balance, should not take its color from outside things. His emotional reactions to the world, and his emotional purpose or
motive, should arise from his own judgment, based upon the
mental balance we have studied in our previous chapter.

Ordinarily, when people see or think of a thing, the emotions of liking and disliking which come up are the result of
memories of pleasure and pain previously associated with the
thing. Liking follows pleasure and disliking follows pain, and
the next step is desire or aversion. There is next a tendency for
thinking and action to follow desire and aversion, and so the
man's life becomes directed by outside things. He is then said
to be colored from outside, like a crystal placed upon red or
green paper, or he is called, more emphatically, "a slave of
Nature." In this way there is something automatic about his
life.

The first step towards Uncoloredness is to watch what is
occurring in the feelings and emotions in the mind, so as to
know what is going on. The Uncoloredness that arises naturally when we see what is going on is in some degree absence
of desire for external objects, but also absence of aversion to
them. They will be emotionally appraised for their value to
the permanent man, instead of to the fleeting man of the body
or the puppet-man of the mind.

After we have achieved more mental balance by knowing

[1] *Vairāgya.*

to what classes the various ideas which arise in our minds belong, our second step in the fourfold Discipline will be thus to
become aware of the feeling-stream, and know its contents for
what they are. Many things and ideas which give us pleasure
really ought to give us pain, and very many more that give us
pain ought to give us pleasure. And in the result, in the active
pursuit of things that we think will give us pleasure, we often
bring upon ourselves great quantities of pain.

Some say: "Kill out desire altogether." No, no, be rational
about desire. We have no reason to kill out desire any more
than to kill out thought. To have no emotional purpose would
resemble having no mental purpose, having as mental life only
the drift, but emotional drift would be worse than mental
drift.

In life without a "want" there would be not only no action,
but also no thought. If a starving man does not want food, and
therefore does not go towards it, and does not even lift it to
his mouth when it is placed before him, he is either an idiot or
a would-be suicide.

We do not need, however, to chide ourselves for our mental
follies. All we have to do is to recognize them for what they
are. When we allow ourselves to look at things with full
rationality or mental balance, as proposed in our last chapter,
the feelings about things and the flow of desire will begin
to run along correct lines.

In the course of Nature, our universal and much-to-be-
respected Mother, our bodies were somehow started off with a
proper equipment of pleasures and pains. Hunger was pain,
and eating was pleasure, and these things were geared to the
requirements of the body for its preservation and progress. To
walk into a tree was painful, to walk round it was a pleasure.
Someone may say he would rather have the tree removed from
his path, and walk straight on! But the fact remains that walking is in itself a pleasure, especially among trees. All the operations of the limbs are a pleasure—within proper measure. I

should have said, too, that eating is a pleasure, within proper measure. Mother Nature arranged that appetite would cease when proper measure was achieved, and that excess would lead to pain. The human mind, however, makes mistakes in its immaturity, and its power of imagination leads to the seeking of more and greater pleasures beyond the limits set by natural life.

No one is so irrational as to wish pain to be entirely removed from life; we all know full well that we would do the most foolish and self-destructive things were it not for the coming-in of pain. And as to pleasure—who objects to that? In proper measure; in natural degree.

Nature went on with her teaching by pleasure and pain for long ages, and at length man appeared upon the scene. Man is the creature which lives in its mind. The development of the mind has reached such a point in man that he has come to be occupied as much with the operations going on in the mind as with those of the body—and even more. At this point of evolution we have a new species in Nature—a creature which does not use its cunning to adapt itself to its environment, as the animals do, but sets to work to plot and to plan in a reverse manner, adapting the environment to itself. Up rises that combinative and constructive phenomenon, the human mind—please excuse the repetition, in this important matter—that can drain swamps and move mountains and alter the courses of rivers, that can express ideas—not merely feelings—in language, that can make machines to run swiftly over the ground, to fly in the air, to go on the water and under the water, that, instead of hiding in a cave, can produce houses, schools, factories, hospitals, that can make clothing suitable to all climates, and weapons suited to all fights, and even—wonder of wonders—instruments for the education and development of the mind itself—newspapers, books, radio, music, the cinema and television.

The point which I wish to make in this chapter is that, in

doing all this, man transferred his pleasures and pains very largely from his body to his mind. Hence every thought is to him a pleasure or a pain. As I have already written, we do not always notice this. Now is the time to begin—this is our second, the emotional, Discipline on the path of mind-maturity. We must know what is going on here, so as not to be carried along on a stream of unintelligence which is bound to lead to pain.

When man tore himself away from the apron strings of Mother Nature, he began to be responsible for himself. And see what he did to himself. Imagination went to work and produced a dummy, a puppet man! He went to work among his collection of bits of knowledge, and constructed a composite idea of himself; then transferred his instinct of self-preservation into this mental and emotional creation! Each one of us has (not is) such a puppet man. Just look at it. "I am Mr. Wilkins, business man, family man, good fellow at the club, knowledgeable about music and cigars, standing here in my business suit, in my goodness, in my sensible ideas, in my harmless foibles, in my pleasingness to my friends and my God."

If someone impugns our mental sanity or moral goodness, we are hurt and we hit back or retreat into icy pride. We can stand some criticism of our business suit, perhaps, and it may be even of our knowledgeableness about music and cigars, but no one must touch that mind-personality and say that it is silly, or that its beliefs have no rational foundation.

The pleasures and pains of the ideas that furnish this mind lack the patient wisdom of Mother Nature, and are not geared to the welfare of the man. Mr. Johnkins said I was an ass, so I think of Mr. Johnkins with dislike (which is mind-pain), and I try not to think of Mr. Johnkins and not to meet him, or, if I do meet him, I let my dislike get between me and the enjoyment and benefit of his company. Other people say that Mr. Johnkins is a splendid fellow; it happens that he has not yet called them asses.

It is interesting to see how small likes and dislikes can destroy the rationality of our desires and actions. Just now I have been typing this on a suitcase balanced on a radiator (cold) in a room in which I am staying for two days, on tour. A minute ago my eye caught sight of a red tie-on label attached to the handle of this little suitcase and at once my mind was poisoned with the pain of dislike; I quickly disattached the label and threw it into the waste paper basket. And now, on second thoughts, I must perforce pick that label out of the basket, look at it tenderly, tell it what a nice color it is, how glad I am to have met it, and how much richer my life is because that nice bit of color came into this room this cold and rainy morning, and put it back into the basket with gentle and solicitous good-byes. The cause of all this was that in the railroad station yesterday a red-cap porter caught hold of my collection of little bags and put them on the train, and for that very small job spurned the dollar I offered him and demanded a dollar and a half, the while looking at me as if I were something that the cat had brought in. And here was I in mental pain at the sight of that little label, and increasing it by remembering that the porter had put tags on only half of my little bags and parcels, and cheated the railway company and made a fool of me, and so on, and venting it all on that little label. It was only a little piece of cardboard, eh? Yes, but it might have been a little bird, or even a child.

I hope I am not laboring this point, but I would like in this connection to retell a story that is commonly related to little children in India. There was a certain king of old time who once dreamed that all his teeth fell out. In the morning he sent for a soothsayer, who said: "Alas, your majesty, it is a bad omen. It means that all your relations will die before you." Much displeased, the king had the soothsayer's head cut off, and sent for another. The second wise man said: "Ah, this is indeed good. It means that your majesty will outlive all your relatives." And the king was happy, and heaped wealth upon the second soothsayer. So there we are.

I have just remembered about that rain which I disparaged just now—another pain in the mind! I thought I would go out this morning and enjoy the balmy air. But, on second thoughts, "Thank you, Mr. Rain, I am getting on with my writing." And that is a real pleasure.

Who was it who said: "A man does not understand anything unless he loves it?" I wish I could remember. Confound it, I said "I wish"—another pain in the mind, and all to no purpose. A little calmness and the name comes back—it was Goethe.

The present seems a suitable place in which to mention that our thought is always a servant (1) to our desires, which subject us to external impulsions, such as seeking food to satisfy hunger or gratify the sense of taste, or (2) to our moral or ethical impulses. Sometimes it serves one, sometimes the other, and sometimes both. If the moral or ethical impulsion comes into the picture the material desires become less urgent—they are at least kept within their natural sphere, and then, not becoming the subject of hot imagination, they do not govern the man. I have known quite a number of cases of persons who have died prematurely after much suffering on account of the human imagination, which became servant to desire for sense-pleasure, and drove them to excesses and follies in eating and drinking. This is immoral, that is, lacking unity. The immoral is also unethical when it makes a man an injurious piece of environment for others. The ethical motives, on the other hand, lead to co-operative living and the pleasures of companionship. In brief, the ethical feelings are combinative and constructive in social life, and thus manifest unity in their own sphere, just as thought produces examples of coherent heterogeneity in the course of its work.

The Second Discipline, described as not merely Uncoloredness, but, in its full form, as freedom from being colored by the things of here—this world—or hereafter—a pictured future life—is a natural consequence of the First Discipline, which is Discrimination between the permanent and the fleeting. Uncoloredness allows a true valuation of things for the real man, an emotional balance. It is not dislike for everything, which is only a contrast from liking, though it can be a sense of "enough," as when a picture is successfully painted or a piece of work is completely done.

CHAPTER 8

SIX THINGS TO DO

When the student has (1) discriminated between the temporary and the permanent—relatively speaking—in life, and has
(2) begun to be less swayed by the immediate impact of outward occurrences, and therefore has (3) begun to make his
actions less reactional and more dependent upon his own
calm decisions, he can take up whole-heartedly the business
of the third Discipline.

The First Discipline, it will have been noted, is the practice
of purified thought, the second the practice of purified feeling, and the two together produce greater freedom in practical
life. Now comes the third Discipline—the practice of purified will—the use of the will in daily life. This is divided into
six sections, as shown in our diagram:

WILL PRODUCES:—
1. Mind-Control.
2. Body-Control.
3. Cessation of dependence.
4. Endurance and patience.
5. Confidence and faith.
6. Steadiness of life.

Let us begin by understanding the function of the will,
always remembering that though will, feeling and thought are
distinct functions they always operate together, so as to act
as one, like the physical hand, heart and head.

First let us notice that will is not directly related to action.
It is not with our wills that we move our feet or hands.

Thought, not will, pulls the trigger of action. A thought-picture or idea in the mind produces action in the body. Psychologists have known for a long time that our bodies obey our thoughts. An old example of this is "walking the plank." If a nine-inch wide plank is laid on the floor from one end to the other of a long room and you are asked to walk along it, you will do so with pleasure and ease, but if a nine-inch beam is placed from a third story window to a third story window across an alley-way you had better not try to walk it, because you will probably fall off. The reason for this is that you think of falling; you picture falling in the mind—you imagine falling more strongly than you imagine walking. So you fall, even though you wish not to fall, but to walk the beam. Sometimes people have been considered to have committed suicide from the edge of high cliffs, when quite probably they had no such intention, but they looked over the edge out of curiosity and then the thought of falling took hold of them.

The reverse is also the case. Many people possessed of perfectly good legs are unable to walk, because they cannot—for some psycho-pathological reason—imagine themselves walking. If their physicians can somehow revive their belief that they can walk, they will then picture themselves as walking, and they will walk.

Swimming is another example. Once we have "got the knack" of swimming and are able to think of ourselves as swimming, we afterwards "put on the thought" (however easily, and almost, but never entirely, subconsciously), then go into the water and swim. One very good swimmer told me that on a certain occasion she fell from a steamer into the sea and was nearly drowned, because she sank twice before she collected her wits and realized that she was in the water. As soon as she said to herself; "I am in the water," she thought "Swimming," then began swimming and so was saved from sinking for a third time.

One could multiply these instances many times, and also give examples of the many common and also remarkable things that are done and can be done by the poised thought, but it is unnecessary here, if I have convinced the reader by the above simple examples. We are now concerned with another and more important piece of useful knowledge—how to govern our thoughts. It is here that the will comes in. Thought governs action, but will governs thought. You can say to yourself: "I will now think about cabbages and not about kings," or "I will think about walking the plank and not about falling."

Knowledge is power in this matter. If you know that your will can govern your thoughts, you have achieved the first step towards control of mind—or rather control of the contents of the mind, whether thoughts or feelings, or those ideas or pieces of knowledge in the mind which are compounded of both thought and feeling.

In this branch of self-study the first axiom is that will gives us power over our own thoughts and feelings, and the second axiom is that such power is relative freedom. The effect is twofold, because power over the contents of the mind leads to the enlargement of personal power in the external world, and also to the inner power that is both peace and poise.

I have used the expression "contents of the mind," just as I would "contents of a house," for ideas have precisely that character or nature. Ideas are pieces of knowledge in the mind, which have been acquired by experience or by reasoning or from the statements of good authorities. Further, like the furniture in a house, they are only for use. No one wants quite useless knowledge, such as to know all the numbers in the telephone book, with their respective names, any more than he wants to fill his rooms from floor to ceiling with unnecessary furniture.

Another point of importance is that we do these six things not to produce any outward effects, and not in order to influence the mind through the body, but to release ourselves from servitude to externals and to find out what our freedom feels like within ourselves. It is a new "learning to swim."

While putting forward the Six Things To Do, I must say, of course, that they are not compulsory orders. If the student wishes to plan for himself in an original set of "Things To Do," there is no objection. These were laid down by Shankara for his own pupils, and are handed on only in the spirit of brotherhood. We will explain them one by one in the following six chapters.

CHAPTER 9

CONTROL OF IDEAS

You have not to acquire the ability to control your mind [1] for you have it already. It is quite easy to observe this, in the following manner. Allow your mind to drift, as it often does. Let us begin with "cat"; it may go "cat—milk—cow—horns—ivory—elephant—India—raja—king—queen—woman—skirt—cloth—loom—factory—etc." Or perhaps: "Cat—mouse—hole (in the wall)—plaster—lime—stone—quarry—marble—tombstone—monument—Nelson—Admiral—etc."

At any point in this series of drifting thoughts you can say "Stop." If you stop, let us say at elephant, you are saying to yourself, "I want to look at this awhile; I want to dwell upon it; I want to think about it." Then you will find that a *fountain of thought* arises, replacing the *drift of ideas*.

When there is a play of thought upon a particular idea, such as the Taj Mahal, two processes arise in succession. First there is a review of the thing. You look at it carefully, both materially and mentally, at what you see before you and what is in your mind about it. Secondly, there is a new view of the thing, for you think about it, and if you are a thinker there will be a fountain of thoughts. Thinking about a thing does not exclude other thoughts about other things, but it relates them to the subject in hand, or rather in mind. If I think about the Taj Mahal, my fountain of thoughts begins at once to include other specimens of oriental architecture—various mosques and palaces and tombs that I have seen—but I find myself seeing these *along with* the Taj Mahal, and to some extent comparing them with it, noticing their similarities and differences.

[1] *Shama.*

My will can now go further, and say: "I wish to *complete* my thinking about the Taj Mahal." Then the fountain of thoughts will continue until the water is all used up and I have exhausted my stock of relevant ideas. This is not what usually takes place. Ordinarily, people go on "thinking about" something for a little while; then one or other of the fountain-thoughts catches their fancy. They thus shift their center of interest, and move over to that; the drift begins again, and they have soon forgotten the Taj Mahal altogether. This is failure to *complete* the thought and is due to weakness of will, lack of self-control in the form of concentration. Here may come in the *second act of will* with reference to the process of thought. You can say to yourself: "I want to think *all* about the Taj Mahal." You then complete your fountain, and still you hold on, hoping that something more will yet arise. This will complete your fountain, producing what is technically called meditation—a word which we can use in science and philosophy as well as in devotional religious practices.

So, mentally we can at any time, at our choice, (1) drift, (2) think, or (3) meditate.

People differ very much in their habits in this respect. Large numbers of people drift nearly all the time; some think fairly frequently—their thought dwells for a little while on particular aspects of particular subjects or topics; a few, very few, have meditative minds, which tend to dwell upon particular subjects or topics until they have brought together all their possible thoughts about them.

Many are the writers who give us one-sided or lopsided views in politics, science and religion, because they are thinkers but not meditators. Not that I wish to despise or disparage thinking. It has produced many good and useful things. But it is governed usually by a desire to produce some effect (like the fox and the hens) and stops when that end is achieved. For attainment of the best knowledge about anything, this, obviously, is not enough.

Ask yourself now which of these habits you want your mind to follow—(1) drift, (2) thinking for limited purposes, or (3) meditation, which leads to the fullest truth we can have about anything. Then cultivate the habit by using your will frequently in the control or direction of your own thought. After a little while your mind will take on the new habit.

Drift will not cease altogether, but it will become a deliberate act—comparable to relaxation in the body. We may have been working in the garden; we begin to feel tired and decide to take a rest; we may be over-tired and therefore nervous; so we tell ourselves to relax. Drift is relaxation for the mind, and is a good thing when it is voluntary, that is, when we intentionally permit it. Some people have found it an excellent preparation for sleeping, and even a help in insomnia.

Allied to drift is external mental entertainment in the form of light reading. Allied to thinking is reading for information. Allied to meditation is that studious research in which we endeavor to complete our knowledge on a given subject. To be beneficial to the mind all these require frequent breaks or pauses in which we allow our own drift, our own thinking, or our own meditation to play upon the subject matter of our reading for a while.

The object of this mind-control in the present enquiry—the purpose of this book—is the attainment of knowledge about ourselves and our relation to the world. The fact is that meditation—in which, it must be observed, the knowledge to be gained is not predetermined, as it is in mere thinking—provides the condition of mind for intuition, illumination, clearer, deeper and more inclusive conceptions than we had before. It is the positive, dynamic state of the pure mind, not being driven by any outside motive to work as a servant to produce an object of desire. Only into such a mind can truth flow; rightly has it been called a flawless gem.

Quite foreign to all this is any philosophy which tells us to stamp certain ideas upon the mind—"You must think only of so-and-so," or "You must think only good thoughts," or "You must affirm, 'I am so-and-so.' " These lead only to fixations of ideas already achieved; all such ideas block the free functioning of the mind, and halt their practicers at their standing-places, where the conscious being then gyrates in living mental slavery for a long time. It cannot be too strongly emphasized that we are concerned in our mind-control with determining the kind of mind-process that we will have, and not with any limitation of thinking or decision to have or to harbor certain particular thoughts. The habits to be cultivated are good habits of mind, not habitual thoughts.

Finally, then, let us observe that it is the action of the will, governing the mind, that leads to knowledge, which is not possible for a mind given over to drift, dullness and disorder.

CHAPTER 10

CONTROL OF THE TEN ORGANS

Control of the ten voluntary functions of the body constitutes the second of the six accomplishments of the will.[1] The ten functions appear in two groups of five each: five faculties and five powers, or five inlets and five outlets.

The five faculties are five inlets or openings for information to enter into us from outside, namely, the ears to hear with, the skin to feel with, the eyes to see with, the tongue to taste with, and the nose to smell with. The information about external things which we receive through these five organs is very incomplete. It informs us only of some of the appearances and actions of the objects of the world. We hear a sound, and say to ourselves: "That is a clock," or "That is a motor-car," or "That is a bird," but it is not; it is only the touch upon us of a set of actions of a certain kind. It is not even that; it is their effect in the deepest part of our sensory system. And even less than that, for it is that effect filtered through the mood of my mind at the moment—attentive or inattentive to this incoming impression, and, even then, attentive in a certain way only, according to what is interesting me at the moment. The cat became quite annoyed with me just now because I would not open the door for it, but gently stroked it instead. In another mood it would have purred when being stroked in that way.

So, when we are attentive to a sound and say, "What is that? Oh, that is the clock," it is not the clock; it is a sound. The mind, recognizing a sound and remembering that it is due to the action of a certain object, tells us that the object is there.

[1] *Dama.*

We do not hear objects, but we hear their sound-actions. Those sounds invade our ears.

But there is sight. Do we see things? How many people realize that the light rays carry pictures into the eye, which are seen only *after* their arrival there? In the daytime we do not look abroad into a large world any more than we do in the darkness of the night. But in the daytime light rays are being reflected by various objects, and when some of these enter our eyes we become aware of patterns of color and shade, and the mind says: "There is a tree"—or a person, or a cloud. It must be remembered that we do not even know the eye any more than we know any object looked at through the eye. We know the eye because we have seen it in mirrors and in other people. Even the detailed information obtained by scientific men about the structure of the eye is seen in the same external way. We thus become aware of the actions of things in reference to light; this one reflects yellow light, that one red light and so on.

Some thinkers go even further and believe that our experiences of lights and colors and sounds are due to ourselves— are mere sensations in consciousness; that a certain pulsation in the air is *converted* into sound in consciousness, another vibration of a different kind is converted into the color blue in consciousness, and so on.

The external world has only actions, it is said, such as when a leaf of a tree reflects "light rays" which, entering the eye, result in the sensation of green. The leaf is not green—it only reflects a certain vibration. Light rays in themselves are not light, and they have no color. Sound pulsations are not sound, and they have no tone. Colors and sounds exist in consciousness, it is said, but not objectively.

All this would be rather depressing to us who have been thinking that we are seeing at a distance and living in a spacious world of sound and color, were it a perfectly correct idea. But it is not.

Let us examine the sense of touch. With our eyes closed we can feel with hands or cheek the roundness of a ball, and we know that what we then experience as a sensation or sensation-group is true to Nature, that is, what occurs in sensation truly corresponds to what is in the world, for the ball will roll. If, on the other hand, we feel a cube, we experience a cube, and this which we thus experience, acts in Nature as a cube, standing on any one of its six sides and, if tipped over, falling into stance upon another. We can feel a thing as smooth, and it slides, or as rough, and it is harder to push along. Although sensation-experiences are within us, they are correct. Will the sense of touch alone have this quality of being true to the object, and not the other senses, which have grown up under the same laws and in the same environment? Surely not, so we may say we are justified in believing that the daffodil is in some way yellow, and sugar is in some way sweet, and light is light and has color. Is not all this analogous to a voice heard "over the radio." Although the means of transmission are not sound pulsations, we would not receive at our end the experience of a voice were the voice not there at the other end of the "line."

Inasmuch, then, as the outer and the inner harmonize, our feeling of living in a world of things in apparent space is true —that is, of course, each thing with its relative truth, for there is always room for imperfections and mistakes. In a chapter near the end of this book I will give what I believe to be the correct psychological explanation of this matter, when we have worked up to it.

Whatever that may be, the Discipline which we are now considering consists of the government, by the will, of the ten organs of sense and action. Body-control means that we are able to use these organs when we want to do so, and keep them quiet when we want to do so. A little training in this matter is one of the prerequisites for the attainment of knowledge. This is, behind the scenes, another form of mind-control, because the organs of sensation as well as those of action are activated by the attention. The hands and feet are usually well governed—we do not find that the body goes for a walk by itself without our consent. To learn to keep the limbs quite still for a while, and to relax sometimes, is, however, somewhat needed among the restless western folk.

The sense organs easily learn obedience, and do not trouble us with their ordinary messages when the mind is intent upon something else—a landscape painter at his easel out of doors may thus be quite oblivious of all the sights but that upon which he is intent, and all the sounds and scents which come to his ears and nose. A little reflection upon this fact shows us that we are very much the arbiters of our own destiny, inasmuch as by something we call the will we can and do activate or inhibit the ten sensory and motor organs of the body. With a little practice we can even learn to take short sleeps whenever and wherever we will. I do not think one could overestimate the practical value of these.

I think some attention to the body in general, in order to keep it in good serviceable condition, is in place within this Accomplishment. The world is full of teachers along these lines telling us all we need to know about diet, exercise and rest. In India the old Hatha-yoga system filled this need, with its postures and methods of breathing, and the exponents of these arts laid stress upon their usefulness to those who wished to go in for meditation. In teaching concentration and meditation—which I have done to a very large extent—I have always advised certain practices of occasional relaxation, balanced musculature, regularity of breathing, nerve-training, sitting perfectly still with head and spine well balanced, eye and neck exercises, and sense-training.[2] In these practices there is no intention to develop large muscles, but just enough. And when there is a proper *feeling* in the body in all these matters

[2] See *Practical Yoga: Ancient and Modern,* Ernest E. Wood. (New York: E. P. Dutton & Co.), 1948.

—which can be obtained only as a result of *doing* (compare my example of the feeling of swimming), and then the acquisition and realization of a proper *mood* towards the body, one can learn rest in action and proceed to the performance of concentration and meditation without any strain or noticeable effort.

All such training of the body, it must be noted, should be quite honest—not an austerity. It makes for happier living—to which there is no objection!—for, although it may limit certain sensuous pleasures, as dieting, for example, does, any loss of enjoyment in this way is far more than compensated by the feeling of health—unobstructed bodily functioning, ease, lightness and the pleasure of movement.

The present Accomplishment thus means not suppression of the body, but good government, keeping it in order, balanced freedom.

CHAPTER 11

CESSATION OF DEPENDENCE

To counteract any tendency to interpret the Accomplishment named Cessation of Dependence as a retreat from life, one may take especial notice of the general tendency of the whole training. We began with Discrimination. Discrimination did not mean "Don't think"—quite the contrary. The second Discipline was Uncoloredness. That did not mean "Don't feel"—again quite the contrary. The third Discipline, containing six Accomplishments, similarly, is quite the reverse of "Don't live," or "Don't act," or "Don't use your will."

So, when we have Cessation,[1] what is meant is living without dependence upon things, but using them for our purpose. If you possess something and you have no use for it in your plan of life—dispose of it. This is not proposed in a spirit of monkish austerity. It is sanity of living. It is the application in practical life of the operation in the mind whereby we instinctively cast out of our memories what we no longer need. It takes an effort to recall what we had to eat yesterday, and as to last month—the memory seems to be totally gone. Sometimes we hear people who believe in rebirth say: "Would it not be nice if we could remember our past lives?" to which the answer is "Certainly not. You should be thankful that you do not." To clutter up the mind with useless memories can only take away from the vigor of our present living. It may be asked: "What about the case of old people, who live so much in their memories?"

The answer to this was well given by one old gentleman I know, who said, when questioned as to why he kept going

[1] *Uparati.*

over old experiences, "But I get so much more out of them now than I did then." There was still value in them for him; but no doubt he will let go when he has got all he can out of those pictures.

That is quite different from turning to past memories because present conditions are intolerable, or from doing so in order to decide from precedent what to do in the present, when we ought to make our decisions with our present qualities of character. Also, it is not at all the same case as that of those who talk about the past to bolster up their fading self-esteem in the present, or to force into other people's minds an excellent picture of themselves, so that in the mirror of other people's praise they can respect themselves. In such cases there is utility of memories. But when the utility of a memory goes, the memory itself goes, and that keeps our minds clean and sane for present living.

Cessation of Dependence means that we do the same with things. Look round your room. Out should go everything that has not a good reason for being there. This does not mean that we should expel the useless objects because we consider it a good thing to do. We ought not to need such a "moral effort" if we simply looked at those things as we have looked at our thoughts or rather our ideas in the mind, and said to ourselves: "That is a correct idea; that is a wrong idea; that is a fancy; that is a memory." We can say with regard to the chair or table that it is useful, or an ornament, that it is just a fancy, or has the utility of beauty for us, or whatever may be the case. The point is that there should be no self-deception about these things, and then the tendency of the living-that-we-are is to flow along its proper channel without being dammed up or distracted by useless things. We just do not want those things, but as they do not themselves fade out, as memories do, we have to give them the order to go.

In older days, in classical times, when most people lived the simple life, they still had plenty of merchants to sell them

things they did not really want. Those merchants allied themselves to religion and sold the people numerous ceremonies
related to life after death and to social, personal and business
success in this life. In India people had to perform prescribed
ceremonies when a person was born and when he died, and
numerous times between; when the seeds were sown and when
the crops were ready, when a house was begun and when it
was occupied, when a person got up in the morning and when
he went to bed, and even in some cases when he had a shave
or a hair-cut. A dictionary of such ceremonies would make a
very large book; and generally people were led to believe that
something unpleasant would happen to them if they omitted
the acts and recitations, and the frequent contributions to the
priests that they involved. The merchants of ceremonies emphasized the Unseen[2] and claimed special influence and special
knowledge and powers in relation to the Unseen, and they
even set up castes and clans, and hereditary or salable suc-
cessions to support and maintain their trade, which they
sincerely regarded as an essential contribution to social and
individual welfare.

So, when we read about Cessation in the works of Shankara
and similar reformers, we often find it particularly described
as "Cessation of belief in the efficacy of rites and ceremonies."
Cessation of dependence means cessation of all superstition,
which is putting something over on life, imposing something
unreal, or unnatural, or irrelevant, upon our process of living,
and thereby rendering the stream of our decisions impure.

At every fork in the road of life which way do you go—
to the left or the right? Is this to be decided by you, a living
entity, or are you to be moved this way or that by a decision
previously made by someone else, quite possibly by someone
else who has his own interests, not yours, at heart, and plays
upon your timidity or some other weakness of yours?

In modern days a great amount of superstition is foisted

[2] *Adrishta.*

upon us through aggressive advertising, with its array of veiled and often open threats—if you use someone else's brand of tooth-paste and not ours you will have your throat injured, or at least you will not be included among the "best people," who all use ours!

We must revolt against these attempts to put blinkers upon us and drive us, because our own acts of decision are as precious to us as our life. Indeed, they are our life; our very living is composed of our own voluntary thinkings, feelings, and willings. Perhaps we will decide that next time we come to a ladder leaning against a wall we will walk under it in a spirit of freedom—first glancing up, of course, to see that no one is splashing paint about up there.

Every little problem is really a fork in the road of life; the way we turn in these seemingly small matters may ultimately make an immense difference in our lives. But more important than the outward result is the inner condition. In making our own decisions we are *conditioning the will*. This fact points to the secret of success in life, which is primarily inward, in the character of the man rather than the event. So important is this self-living as a preparation for real knowledge that I will venture to quote here what I wrote on this matter for students thirty years ago in a little book entitled *Character Building*, now long out of print.

Why should you deliberately aim at the development of character? First, because you will never be satisfied or happy till you do, and secondly, because the game of life requires it of you as a duty. You are alive for a purpose, and somewhere within your consciousness you have a dim inkling of that fact. You are either seeking or expecting something, the lack of which leaves you without complete satisfaction. Your procession of little destinies, from tomorrow to next week, to next year, and to the end of life in this body, and your larger destiny, whatever it may be, in the future beyond that, all lie in your own hands, and the coming of future satisfaction may even now be accelerated by the efforts that you make.

No one can eat, learn, feel or think for you, nor develop your will power or any other part of your character, though you may find environment a source of help or difficulty in your growth. As the power within a tiny seed determines the form, even to a detail, of the mightiest tree, so is the power within you a mere seed of what shall be truly a man and even a god; and as no one can grow an oak tree from a mango seed, so no one and nothing in your environment can make you grow into something that you are not destined to be. There is something marvellous in the power within a seed, and when that seed is the human soul, containing the powers of will, thought and love, no one should dare to measure its possibilities by a puny and undeveloped imagination. With such powers within him, man must not depend upon external accidents for the food, water, and sunshine necessary for his unstinted growth—it is for him to be his own gardener, to understand his own destiny, and to make his circumstances assist him in its swift achievement.

It has been determined by your inmost self that you shall develop character, the powers of the soul, through effort and experience, and the quantity as well as the quality of your conscious life will thus ever increase until it is too great for human limits. Abundant life is not chiefly to be found, however, in material quantity. You do not need enormous physical riches, any more than you want a huge body, like a giant in a story book; but you desire abounding health, physically, emotionally and mentally, for these are the spiritual riches of freedom, love and truth. The spirit within measures its things by quality, not by quantity, and what will give you permanent joy will be not greater wealth, nor power over others, nor the spread of your meaningless name in what people call extended fame, nor longer bones, nor more abundant flesh, but more character—realization of freedom, love and truth in all their ramifications and modifications.

For those who aim at these things success is certain, for the power within the seed is on their side, while those who aim otherwise have their life-forces sapped by a constant struggle to hold what is perishing. And there is always this help—that what you have attained in character will soon reflect itself in your outer life. Material opportunities of all kinds will soon come to him who has determined to make the right use of his powers. Each thing that comes before him will be more significant and more useful to him than it would be to others. Life is a matter of degree, and there is as much difference between one man and another as there is between a fine horse and an earthworm which is blind and deaf. The external world is also different for each of these. Character deals with circumstances and in the long run makes its own opportunities.

In the course of life your character undergoes constant modification. Every experience adds something of strength, insight or feeling. Every feeling or thought, however transient, makes its permanent mark on the growing character. But, as environment plays upon it, there is no such thing as the passive reception of modifications in consciousness, so that the mark that is made in the character by any experience is compounded of two distinct things—the outer event and the inner character that meets it. The result of the reaction between these two (which we call life) produces two effects—a modification in the character of the man and some change in the outer world.

It is the modification within, not the effect in the outer world, that we have to consider in our present study. You and I may go for a sea voyage, be wrecked in the same vessel and be rescued from the same boat. We may have had the same hunger and thirst, and buffeting and fatigue, but our experiences have been widely different, because of the difference of character within. And one of us may have gained much more benefit than the other, more that is, of strength or understanding or love built into the character, or rather brought out into it from within.

What is in the heart of the seed, in the depths of the soul, beyond anything that we are able to define as the character of the man, we can at present know little about, so for all practical purposes it is the character that is the man, and the soul powers become known to us only when they appear in that. It is the character that is the man, and the only thing that can be called progress for him is its development.

Life will give you no permanent happiness until you recognize and obey this truth, and realize that life is for the development of character towards some destiny glorious beyond all present imaginings. A spiritual hunger will give you no rest, but will drive you on to this goal of human life. Success will follow success as you develop your character in the material world, but ever new realms to conquer will open their vistas before you, and spiritual hunger will drive you on till you obtain the greatest fruit of life that human experience can grow, and beyond that something greater still.

It is the human destiny to achieve happiness not by the method of forgetfulness, like the sheep in the meadow, which enjoy their simple pleasures and do not think of past or future, but by the method of will, of understanding of life, and love. We cannot go back and become sheep; it is ours to go forward by our own will-power and become gods.

Glance over the world of human endeavour with the question what it is for. Ever since the human form appeared upon earth men have worked with their brains and hands, and with infinite labor have turned over the dust of the ground. They have scratched the surface of the earth, gathered stones, smelted metals, built cities and monuments, constructed languages and policies. All these have endured for a space, and then gone for ever. But Greece, Rome, Chaldea, Peru, Egypt and all live now in us. Their material triumphs have turned to dust, their old languages are dead, but the gain of character that was achieved by those ancient labors is ours now and for ever. It is not the work that matters, except for the sake of the workers, individually and collectively. All that exists does so, as an ancient Hindu writing says, for the sake of the soul or the self within. Character is the important thing, and the development of character is the important work.

The world is a school for all of us, but it is not a cramming institution. In it games play the greatest part, and most of its objects are educative toys, however seriously grown-up people may regard them. Even knowledge is not valuable for its quantity, but only for its appositeness to the needs of your character or of mine, or as leading us to a realization of the truth about life. I knew a young man who had a great thirst for knowledge, and it was his habit to frequent a large reference library and study all kinds of subjects, in which he found absorbing interest. But after a while he grew despondent, for he realized that he could not gather the treasures even of this one library in less than four hundred whole lifetimes of close reading. That little calculation taught him that it was not the business of life to acquire knowledge of external things, except such as is necessary in order that each of us may live truly, kindly and actively.

The toys of knowledge are endless in their variety, but realization of the truth comes through the use of our powers of thought upon that bit of the world that happens to be ours, and living a life of love and activity according to that thought. Thinking about life is not living, and the thought that does not find some positive use in my definite scheme of life is not of great benefit to me.

Each one has his daily destiny to fulfill; certain knowledge is very important for him, and it is wisdom for him to seek the knowledge that he can best apply to his own life and to concentrate his mental power upon it, so that, like the fabled swan of the Hindus, he may separate the milk of wisdom from the waters of knowledge. I have known little boys to boast that they had walked through every street of their particular town; I have known travellers, or rather tourists, to rush on wheels through every celebrated country of the world; but I am sure that he has learned the lesson of life best who has pursued his quiet occupation and moved abroad occasionally as a corrective and a change. A realization of the truth about life may be had everywhere, and the means to its attainment (the very purpose of life) is indicated in that coarse old proverb which says that a fool cannot learn even from a wise man, but a wise man can always learn, even from a fool.

From another of my older writings I will quote another passage, showing the importance of voluntary decision in our daily lives:

The habit of definite decision favours the intuition of the will. There are few things more fatiguing than the habit of indecision in small matters. Sometimes people wear themselves out in trying to decide how they will enjoy themselves, where they will go for a holiday, whether to the seaside or the country. I knew a lady who used frequently to tire herself by trying to decide what dress she would wear, and sometimes, it was said, she would array herself for going out, and then suddenly at the very last moment rush back and change her stockings or even her entire dress. Once, when she was going on a voyage of several weeks, a friend advised her to make a time-table of dresses, and they sat together and made an engagement book of her wearing apparel; the dates were written down, with morning, afternoon and evening in the horizontal columns, and in the vertical columns dress, shoes, stockings, and even underclothing, were set forth. The lady kept to her programme, and afterwards declared that she had never before felt so free and happy; she seemed to have four times the nervous energy which had been hers before.

This is a matter in which we may well take a lesson from the Stoics, who had a formula for both peace of mind and success in life. They said that when any problem comes up in the course of life we should look at it dispassionately, and ask ourselves: "Is this a matter within my power, or not within my power?" The second step in this practical philosophy was not to waste time and energy on things or occasions not within our power. The third part of the process is to realize the importance of using our own will and making our own decisions with regard to what *is* in our power. It is raining—all right, it is raining, and that is not a matter within my power. But it is in my power to decide whether I will go out with an umbrella, or sit and write indoors.

Such decisions become very smooth and easy when we are used to them. In fact, we shall realize the great truth that the will is the quietest thing in the world. Putting this into practice, one discovers the peace that inhabits the emotion of strength, the inward sensation that no effort need be put forth, and that it is excitement that is negativity, indicating dependence upon something outside. It is not will to exert force, to push and scramble, to shout, or to bully oneself or others. When machinery is perfected, it also will be quiet. The flow of electricity, the expansion of steam—these are quiet, but they are the power. It is the imperfect machinery through which they work, which can scarcely bear their power, that makes the noise. He who in his own life, hearing the racket of the machinery in motion, thinks that to be the will, has not found the will, for, as I said before, the will is the quietest thing in the world.

CHAPTER 12

ENDURANCE AND PATIENCE

In the last chapter we learned the proper manner for a human being to act with reference to any matter that is in his power. It was: "Make your decisions and act upon them," or "Act with independence, not with dependence," or, in other words, "Use your own faculties as far as they are usable." There was no suggestion that one should not obtain information from others to help oneself to come to a decision, but that information has to be digested by oneself and be treated with discrimination and uncoloredness before it is used.

We come now to the question what to do about the things which press upon us, but over which we have no power, and therefore with respect to which we must submit. For example, I must eat, if I want to stay alive, so I submit and eat, though I may not want to eat for the pleasure of eating. I do not want to go to the dentist, but I do so occasionally. "I would like to go to the office in pyjamas or a bathing suit on a hot day," a man may say to himself, or his secretary may say to herself, but they do not do it, because they are up against the stone wall of other people's prejudices against those costumes in those circumstances. So they submit. We are carried round by the earth, so there is day and night, and we submit. The train goes at 11:00 A.M. and not at 9:00 P.M. as we want; we submit. It is raining when we planned to go and sit in the garden in the sunshine—we submit. We decide on a day's outing in the car, but it breaks down, and we submit. There is a war on, and bombs begin dropping round about; we must submit, and go into a shelter, if we want to live. Many times every day we have to do what we do not directly want to do.

What matters in these circumstances? The manner in which we submit, and the feeling with which we submit to these things which are stronger than we, which we have not the power to change. In general, the situation comes to this: difficulties, dangers, injuries, problems, come trooping along. When it comes to the point, "We can take it." But now the question is: "How do we take it?" Shankara says, "With endurance." [1] That is another way of saying, "Do not kick against the pricks." With regard to such things, another wrote: "Have patience, as one who doth for evermore endure." Do not try to rationalize your "troubles" away. A formula does not help us if it only soothes us, and it can be harmful if it sets up a conflict between us and the world. Our attitude must be positive in all these cases. We must be masters of ourselves, even when we cannot be masters of our circumstances. One old book distinguishes between (1) the conditions in which we find ourselves which are the immediate product of our own efforts, and (2) the things which come to us without effort. Briefly, these are (1) the makings, and (2) the happenings. The attitude then prescribed towards the latter is contentment. Do not fume, or fret, or wish. Take the situation calmly, accept it agreeably, without any emotional conflict. Do not class things as good and bad, but go ahead in full strength, and see what you can do in the matter.

Different translators of the word which describes this Accomplishment have rendered it as endurance, patience, resignation, submission, tolerance, forbearance. One writer goes so far as to call it cheerfulness, regarding that as the logical meaning, although the original word comes from a verbal root which means to endure or bear a difficulty or a burden patiently. The implication of cheerfulness is drawn from the observation that patience contains impatience—inasmuch as we would never think of being patient unless we were impatient. The successful aspirant will, however, have patience

[1] *Titikshā.*

when he has lost his impatience, and does not think of it. The Accomplishment really implies honest untroubledness.

It is important to realize that the teacher is not advising us what to do in any given circumstance, but to meet all things in the right spirit. He is not setting up a rule, but warning us to preserve our high quality of living. We have constantly to remind ourselves that life is not life, a sort of invisible something that lives, but life is living itself. We are not life, but we are living. Do not say that if there is living there must be something that lives. We have no justification for such a presumption. We know we are living, and when we are not living we do not know ourselves at all. To assume something-that-lives is unjustifiable, and it distorts our experience. Is it not a thousand times more important to live with all our faculties of thought, affection and the will than it is to have a set of rules such as "Thou shalt not kill," etc.? If we always act with thought, affection and will—not one of them, nor two of them, but all of them, and all together—surely we will know when to kill and when not to kill. Not all the law books in the world can tell us what to do and what not to do on all occasions, or indeed on many occasions which will arise in our experience within the very next day of our lives. At any rate, it is very important that in the conflict of duties and in the conflict of our own desires, which frequently arise, we must make our own decisions.

There is a tendency, when a teacher sets up a rule, or when we set one up for ourselves, for that rule to obstruct some of the thinking, affection and willing with which we would otherwise act, and also to obstruct our experience. If we have rules for looking at a tree, they may be good as far as they go, but we must remember also to go beyond them. If they control our looking we shall be obstructing our reception of what the tree has to give us. These rules have been set up according to our old standard of lookability, which should be superseded in our every new experience.

This talk about rules applies to the feelings also. We have too much of a habit of setting them up automatically. We become resentful, indignant, impatient, angry, envious, jealous—there is an immense brood of these things, and all of them are impediments to living—unless they themselves become for us mere matters of experience (objective, not subjective), so that we are not immersed in them, and do not go on being swished about by their swishing, without even realizing that we are being swished, as is very commonly the case. The connection of feeling with idea is often casual and quite irrational.

There is a great danger in trying to put life into words, to make a picture of it, so to say, for the mind. The mental propensity to try to make a mental picture of life, when mentality is itself only a part of our conscious living, is a way of obstructing our own full conscious living—first our experience, and then our action. Any system of philosophy of this kind is bound to obstruct our living.

Let us consider an example of a portion of philosophy which has been accepted as true to the facts of Nature by nearly all the classical and modern teachers of India, and also many other countries, and most of the modern "theosophists." I speak of the doctrine of karma, which can be briefly expressed in two ways: (1) What you do to others recurs to yourself, or (2) You get the results of your own work.

Under (1) various teachers say that anything that occurs to a man if it is not the result of his present efforts, comes to him as a result of actions that he did to himself and others in previous lives. In this way he obtains a certain kind of body and brain, with their material heredity, certain social conditions and opportunities, certain incidences of apparently good or bad luck, certain personal and social contacts and relationships, etc. Although each person has his own karma in this way, it is recognized that people also do actions together or collectively, so that a great amount of the karma, as it is called, is also received collectively. There is also the principle of exchange, whereby I make a chair for you and you make a shirt for me.

The teachers of karma then go on to say that this law of karma must be regarded as a natural law, just like gravitation, or the circulation of the blood. It is not a law made by a ruler of some kind. If it is called a moral law, that only means that because of this law human morality or ethic—the golden rule —is common sense, is not merely a virtue but is in accord with the world, which will reward goodness with goodness, and punish injury with injury. Reward and punishment, however, are not the correct words. It is regarded as the restoration of a balance of forces, and as these forces are rooted in "lives" the restoration of balance is between the "lives," and so it constitutes a moral, not a material law.

They next say that knowledge of this law of karma is very useful to us, because it relieves us of bad feelings towards experience, resentment, impatience, discontent, anger, greed, jealousy, envy etc., because there is no thing or person to complain against except ourselves. Things and people are not restricting or hurting us, as it may seem, but we are doing all this to ourselves, inasmuch as we have done it to others in the past and it now reverts to us. In this view there is no caprice in life, and no danger hanging over us, and no "chance" in what occurs to us. So there is no need to fear the Unseen,[2] a term which covers everything which we cannot take into our mental calculations. Let us, therefore, its exponents say, begin now to act with only kind regards for others, and our goodness to others will henceforth be repaid in goodness to us. It must be remembered, however, that we still have some "bad" karma to come to us from the past. When it does so come, we shall be able to bear it more bravely and cheerfully because of our knowledge of the karmic law; at least we shall not be wondering how many more dreadful experiences are impending, and may occur to us totally without reason.

[2] *Adrishta.*

At this step in the argument there is a divergence of teaching, according to the dispositions of different teachers, which shows that people use philosophy or science just as they use anything else—one man will defend me with a gun, and another will shoot me down. So one exponent of karma says: "Wait patiently and as bravely as you can until the clouds roll by," and thus makes it a doctrine of fatalism. A second says: "Karma is opportunity; everything that comes to us in a world of law must be an opportunity for useful experience, and the very fact that you have brought it upon yourself shows that you need the lesson, so make the most of it." This is the doctrine of self-reliance. A third says, "It is your good karma to have been brought into contact with me, for I am the agent of your good karma, and I can even convey to you great opportunities and benefits—for a consideration." This is the doctrine of mutual exploitation. And all are called the doctrine of karma!

The point I have now to put to the proponents of karma is as follows. If we accept the position that karma is not a doctrine of fatalism, but of opportunity, does it remove the fear of the future that hangs like a cloud over the present enjoyment of thinking beings, an anxiety that agitates them so that they are in no condition to get the best out of the present experience, but which disappears if the world is viewed as always the friend of man?

It is only fair to study everyone's belief at its best, not comparing the best interpretation of our own "religion" with the worst of our neighbor's, as some missionary-minded people are inclined to do. At its best the doctrine of karma says in effect; (1) you need not fear, (2) every experience is an opportunity, and (3) the height of human attainment is achievable in the materially small conditions our karma brings to us, whatever they are. The last point gives relief from the bugbear of material greatness, and tells the student that in one small fully accepted experience, or in one small bit of common work perfectly done, he can reach the top of living, and in that top of living he will attain the fulfillment of his being, which is the discovery or rather realization of his own self, pure living.

Shankara does not talk about karma in connection with Endurance (or shall we say patience, or better still, peaceful action?) in the numerous books in which he briefly mentions and describes it. But it is known that he accepted it, and he does tell the student that if he fails now he will have future opportunities until he does succeed. It is clear that the student can succeed only in "a present time," though that time may at present be in the future, so the present time is tacitly extolled in the prescription of Endurance as a necessary element in successful living. However, it is only when the attitude of Endurance is achieved that that future present will become a present present, and life or living will have its fulfillment. So the teaching simply is: "Do it now."

Endurance, then, is not bearing with things while we wait for better things to come, to make things easier for us; it is not merely putting up with present circumstances while waiting for better karma. It is, on the contrary, our fullest living attention to present experience, whatever that experience happens to be. It is meeting that experience with all the living-power that we have—not merely thinking about it. There can be no tinge of resentment, impatience or discontent in this. This state of mind cannot be described, but certainly can be achieved. It is not merely contentment; it is joy.

In general living, Endurance means the acceptance of things and people as they are, with no wish that they should be different. It means remembering that the living is all-important. It has not quite the usual meaning of the word endurance, which conveys some feeling of dislike or disapproval, nor is it quite the same as our word patience, which contains as I have said before, a feeling of impatience. Perhaps the expression "active peace" comes a little nearer to the meaning. In this matter of translation there is always this difficulty of satisfying both the form-content and the feeling-content of the original word.

Finally, this Accomplishment is to be practiced until it is felt and understood.

CHAPTER 13

FAITH AND CONFIDENCE

There is no getting away from ourselves, and there is no getting away from the world. The Accomplishment that we are now considering is the clear recognition and the practice of this fact. Fact is not a very good word for this; indeed, we lack a proper word in the English language. Fact indicates something that is made by something else; it contains that flavor or feeling of objectivity. I will therefore call it experience. In speaking of ourselves, we are easily caught in the toils of the word "fact," so we say to ourselves and others that we are something that knows, whereas the real experience is only that knowing is present. This "presence of knowing" *is* our consciousness; we call it "I," we feel it as "I," and it has power as "I." The reality is "I," yet the I is not "a fact" but is the *being of knowing*. If we say "I am," we are already slipping into error, if we attribute to the word "am" some character of being which is other than the knowing. We have to ponder on this matter until we get a sense of the I as mere knowing. It is *knowing* that I am. The acceptance by our minds of this reality as truth is Confidence. It is reliance upon direct experience.

Essentially, confidence is Faith.[1] When we look at this matter with our mental machinery we seem to be merely revolving words, for we say "When I am conscious, I am," but if we look at the experience of being conscious directly (and do not think "I am something that is conscious," which is not direct looking) we find that the consciousness that we are is present and is holding all our other experiences.

[1] *Shraddhā.*

If we know a tree, the reality is that the tree has floated into the I, that the fact of the tree has entered the knowing or consciousness. This is a matter of direct experience for every one of us, and it is worth while to spend a little time now and then to have a good look at this reality, which is fundamental. Each one who does this will become aware that, in doing so, he is for the time being shedding something of an illusion—which he has heretofore taken for granted—having the nature of a memory of something seen before, somewhere else. For example, a tree: "I am like a tree knowing." Have you not been doing this; if not a tree, then something else? This is the super-imposition[2] of fact on the knowing or consciousness. Realizing this, we see that the process of knowing is the climbing out of the tree into the I. We say that we are not satisfied with the tree, and that we must know more about it, so we study the tree in all its relationships (its qualities or attributes and actions) and come a little nearer to a unified picture of it, which we call understanding. In full understanding I shall be less calling myself a sort of tree, and therefore shall be more myself. Understanding is a progressive attempt to expand my knowledge of the object with which I have identified myself until that knowledge leaves nothing out. There then comes a point in the maturity of understanding when the tree yields up its secret, just as there comes a point in the maturity of body when the child can walk. In what we call knowing the tree, or thinking about the tree, we are only maturing the mind. When the walking comes we shall no longer compare details, as in thinking, but shall have the freedom of the tree, like the freedom of a city. One man says "I saw a walking bird walking just now, and I swear to you that I enjoyed the real freedom of that walking." We must trust ourselves to these experiences; that is what is meant by Confidence.

There is a new adventure here. If life ceases to be a plant and becomes an animal, it leaves its root and goes out on a

[2] *Adhyāsa.*

dangerous adventure. Becoming man is another adventure.
Going beyond the stage of the ordinary man into the life of
affection for others, we embark on a further dangerous adventure. And next beyond that is the adventure into free life,
which we are proposing now. A plant may have thought:
"What? Give up my root? Why, it is my only security!" Later
we will give up our "human root" quite naturally, and find
the "I."

Faith, as distinguished from Confidence, may be taken to
refer to the constancy of facts. When it is established that a
certain object has certain constant qualities and actions in relation to other objects, the recognition of that constancy is
faith in its reliability or character. This becomes faith in the
world. Without such faith we could not walk or talk or lift
a hand. When I come to think of it, it is a matter of surprise
to me to find things where I put them; here in America I open
a box which I packed in India, and there I find the old pyjamas
and that colored handkerchief which someone gave me and
I never used, just as I folded them and put them there months
ago. It is astonishing; it is marvelous; but it is a fact. Yet I
know it is an illusion, and the fact is only that the tempo of
the change of the pyjamas and the handkerchief is slower than
my tempo of change. If we could come back to the familiar
world after an enormously long time, I think we should find
that everything was a little bit changed—even carbon, oxygen, and hydrogen would not have *exactly* the same properties
and actions that they have now.

It may seem to us that the stars are steady in their courses,
but they too are unpredictable to some extent, are playing
their own little game in their own slow way. So faith in the
steadiness or reliability of the world is not faith in reality, but
is the knowledge of the slower tempo of our subhuman companions on the road of life. It is accepting them as they are.
And what in Science we call "the laws of Nature" is nothing
but the presence of great masses of attributes and actions of

these companions of ours. When we look through the attributes to the companionship we can walk with our companions, and in that walking there is unity of living, fellow feeling, and philosophic love.

The books say that this Accomplishment called Faith is confidence in the scripture, the teacher, the path and yourself. The teacher, or *guru*, teaches us that all things are our teachers. He tells us to meditate on experience. Then we find out that meditation is nothing but pure experience, but that hitherto we have not been allowing ourselves to experience things properly and fully. We have been shoving the experiences aside as they come, and asking for excitement instead. That was all right in its place and stage. We have been asking to be stirred up, not yet being mature enough for the calmness of meditation-experience. So the *guru* as Nature has plunged us into light and darkness, into honey and boiling oil, so that by these alternations we may be awakened and finally matured. Then the *guru* as scripture, or some fellow man, comes in with this testimony about this calmness, and we follow the calmness, not the *guru* or the scripture, just as in college we go into the chemistry class to learn chemistry, not to hear the professor or devote ourselves to him. If the scripture and the *guru* are not to our liking we do not accept and follow them.

I do not wish to turn anyone against belief, but only to warn the student that his beliefs should be well grounded. If a man has a genuine belief in the law of karma, for example, and a sound understanding of its meaning in life, there is great gain in confidence that the world will treat him reasonably and properly. To *rely* on such a belief, however, is unsatisfactory, and a failure to face experience—any experience—in the fullness of our own strength. It is a failure in *full* responsiveness to experience. You see, we can, and sometimes do, cover up or hide away our fear of an experience by finding a mental reason why it can never occur. In doing that we are preserving our fear, and shrinking from life. We are not afraid of going to sleep, are we? Or of going through the stages of life? Or of a possible future life?

Allied to fear is impatience. The mental picture of time and a goal then stands as an obstacle to full experience. But we are warned—do not be afraid of being afraid, afraid of impatience or goals—or again there will be the old panic and running to and fro.

One piece of mental excitement which frequently comes up is the classification of things as superior, equal and inferior. Thus hot water is superior in hotness to cold water, and one man is superior to another in the attribute of courage or kindness or skill in music or drawing. Sometimes people think this when they consider the accomplishment called Faith; they say that we must have faith in our superiors. We must have faith in the "good man" rather than in the elephant or the tortoise. He will show us what to do better than those. If a man is superior to a mouse, or a *guru* is superior to the average man, it is because of a greater capacity for the unification of experience, both in learning and doing, which are the two exhibitions of knowing or consciousness. But in the last analysis the teacher can only announce the qualifications and accomplishments and so advise the student to pass from excitement to meditation-experience.

When we pass from consideration of mental appraisement of relative factual superiorities for particular purposes, to the *feeling* of our own superiority, equality and inferiority to others, we are in danger. Superiority and inferiority are modes of mental appraisal, not of love. We can argue that we are superior to a flower—we can walk and talk and it cannot— but if we *feel* superior when we are in the presence of the flower we will not receive what the flower has to give. It will spoil the companionship, and bar the experience of beauty. We must give ourselves in companionship, without the bar or wall of superiority or inferiority, in order to have that companionship and to receive what the flower has to give. If a pupil says, "I am inferior to the teacher," he similarly shuts out the flow—if that is what it can be called—of what he has to give. If, however, one makes another mistake, and says, "I am equal to the teacher," one means something by the equality, and that fixation also shuts the mind. The truth is that companionship is just companionship or affection, or philosophic love, not to be subjected to the system of values brought in by thought.

CHAPTER 14

POLARIZATION OF LIFE

The sixth Accomplishment of the will has been translated steadiness and one-pointedness. The original word [1] comes from a root which means "agreement." All our life, instead of being composed of a series of non-cohering experiences, must become orderly and uniform in direction. Our life is a line of contact between what comes in (that is, objects) and what goes out (that is, mind). Polarization of life is perhaps the best term to describe this Accomplishment. All our activities must *agree*, and not conflict or carry us off in different directions, or point in miscellaneous ways.

I may take an illustration from the elementary course in the teaching of magnetism. The teacher takes a test tube, fills it half full of iron filings, and lays it on its side on the bench. He then brings a small piece of iron near to it, and finds that it is not attracted. This means that the test tube of filings is not a magnet. His next procedure is to stroke the test tube a number of times with one end of a bar magnet, always in the same direction. As he does so we see the filings stand up on end, following the movement of the stroking magnet, and then lie down—all now lying in one direction, although they were higgledy-piggledy before. The bar magnet is now put away, and the small piece of iron is again brought near. This time it is strongly attracted, showing that the test tube of filings has now itself become a magnet. It exerts a magnetic influence upon all pieces of soft iron that come near, and tends to bring them also into line.

The iron filings illustrate what we suppose to happen in a

[1] *Samādhāna.*

bar of iron when it is magnetized or converted into a magnet. There is some sort of polarization of internal parts or particles, which were conflicting and so neutralizing one another before magnetization, but have now been brought into line, and operate as a magnet. The term for this process is polarization. On this analogy, the sixth Accomplishment may be called Polarization of Life.

There is a very well-known word to describe the fulfillment of an act of meditation. It was given by the famous teacher Patanjali, who said that meditation is a continuous flow of thought in one field, and then added that the fulfillment of this arrives when all the ideas in the mind touching on this matter come into agreement, and so allow an unperverted or undisturbed perception of that ground. His word is *samādhi*, which means agreement. I have translated that word as contemplation, as several pandits have already done, because that is what we find in our own experience of meditation. Contemplation is a sort of waking trance, is it not, in which there is no conflict of mixed thoughts, but a perfect one-pointedness of experience of the object or ground. This example is taken from the well-known process of meditation, but in the sixth Accomplishment it refers to our living.

It is well known that we do ordinarily polarize our lives to some extent. Let two men walk together along a street in a town, one being an architect, the other a physician. The architect will notice and remember the structures and appearances of the buildings, while the doctor will notice the physical condition of the passers-by. These selective tendencies become directional in their effect, enabling the respective observers to extract from their collective environment the experiences, information and opportunities useful in their specialized lives. The Accomplishment called Polarization has this effect in the life of anyone who is intent upon "knowing the One Reality" —he finds the One Reality everywhere.

Another illustration of Polarization is the mood of concentration which I have described in an earlier chapter. First there was the practice of concentration to be done until the student gets to know what concentration is by experience of it, then there is the feeling of it, and finally that feeling can be applied as a *mood* which will exercise a polarizing influence upon all incoming thoughts or perceptions. The mind is now in order, with all its ideas or thoughts in agreement, and without the need of any of that intro-mental fighting for agreement which we know as ordinary human thinking.

It will be seen that the six Accomplishments which we have been considering in the last six chapters are intended to produce wise living in the world of makings, or of action. In our relation to the world we unconsciously select our path. We are selecting both what we see and what we do. It is not a deliberate selection, item by item, but one that results from pointing our faces always in a certain direction. However varied the things we meet there is then an equality of experience. There is a sameness of everything for us, and an instinctive valuation. I may again mention the standard example of the fabled swan which can separate milk from water, dipping its beak into the mixed drink and always taking out the milk. It is said that the wise man has this quality of taking the milk from the water of practical experience. That is why you sometimes find the title of *Hansa* or Swan bestowed upon spiritual teachers, or even *Paramahansa*, that is, Supreme Swan.

The material side of this matter is also important. There always is some milk present, however watery the experience of the moment. People have a tendency to undervalue present things in their craving for other things. But clay is as good as gold, and an enemy is as good as a friend, to the wise man. There is therefore an equality of experience in all circumstances, and the opportunity for equanimity of content in the mind. Everything is useful to the wise man, because he is appreciative, not being blinded by dislikes. One of Emerson's verses is very apposite in this connection:

Every day brings a ship,
Every ship brings a word;
Well for those who have no fear,
Looking seaward, well assured
That the word the vessel brings
Is the word they wish to hear.

This verse has no doubt been very much misunderstood. It could be taken to mean that something comes to us every day and we are very lucky if it happens to be the thing we want. Would Emerson have written a verse on that banal topic? The teaching that I find in it is quite different. It is well with us if we understand the value of all things, so that whatever comes to us today will be something wanted by us, something appreciated, even loved. With such an outlook upon life we could have no fear. Emerson believed in a divine background to life, whereby the thing that comes to us has some special relation to our need. To apply this philosophy is to find that "it works."

Intentness on the knowledge of the One Reality will polarize our mood to our life, and our life to our mood—thus governing the outer life of events as well as the inner life of the mind.

A concluding instruction of great importance which I must give to the student in regard to the last four of the six Accomplishments is to cease from wishing. This is to be practiced whenever he remembers it in daily life, and it will help greatly to confirm his understanding by experience. This is another of those matters about which I have written with insistence and emphasis in the past, so I will quote myself here, from an old book of mine entitled *Concentration:*

You must give up wishing, for you cannot both wish and will. The two things are utterly incompatible. It should be understood that indulgence in wishing is not only a waste of time, but also an invitation to harmful emotions. It is like slouching along the road instead of walking erect. The only proper attitude of the positive soul towards things, events and people is to accept them for what they are—not wishing them to be different—and then decide what to do about the matter. I am not confusing wanting with wishing. As a result of calm judgment and not mere wish you can want to have something or to do some act. Even when you have said: "I want this," again you ask, "Do I?" And the wanting that comes out of this thoughtful intuitive poise will be a clear strong feeling, useable for polarization of a mood.

This matter of calm judgment is important, so I will introduce it with a statement, illustrate it with a diagram, and elucidate it with a question.

1. *The statement.* Impressions from the outside (through hearing, touch, sight, taste, smell or telepathy) strike upon us, and we react to them *after* they have penetrated into us to a certain depth. These processes are called afferent and efferent by some psychologists. There is a point however, where the afferent ceases and the efferent begins, and in that I am or you are.

2. *The diagram.*

A, represents an animal which reacts from emotional habit; B, the animal-man who does the same with the addition of memory, imagination and cunning; C, the man-man who considers what likes and dislikes to encourage, in accord with "natural law"; D, the good-man, or philosopher, who feels for others, and reacts from the depths of intelligent love, or intelligence in service to love. For those who do not immediately see this as a natural and necessary fact, I will merely quote Emerson's statement, to be reflected upon: "I see that when souls reach a certain clearness of perfection, they accept a knowledge and motive above selfishness. A breath of Will blows eternally through the universe of souls in the direction of the Right and Necessary. It is the air which all intellects inhale and exhale, and it is the wind which blows the world into order and orbit." This contains something of a still deeper depth, of which we will become aware in due course—a spiritual intuition of the purpose of our being in the present moment, as though the future tree were talking to the seed or at least the seedling. Enough said. I hope we shall all experience this before long.

I must prevent a possible error by pointing out that we are not to become desiccated men, without likes and dislikes. We have flesh and blood and a heritage of emotions and ideas; but impressions from all these will be carried inwards on the afferent stream, and dealt with according to their true worth as seen in the depths, and brought out again in full strength, but purified.

3. *The question.* In which depth will you establish your mood? I beg you to think again and again about this, and to explore and re-explore those depths until they become familiar ground. Give yourself leisure for thought.

Be brave then, and face the world with clear thoughts, intelligent love, and enlightened will.

There will be a new policy in your life. Consider it practically. What will it mean to you when you rise in the morning, when you eat, when you lie down to sleep? What when you meet your companions, your friends, your so-called enemies? What when you lose your appointment or money or meet with an accident, or fall ill, and your family suffers? Sit down, and think over all the disagreeable things that might happen within the next week, and see in each case what it would mean to you. You would not wish them to be otherwise; you would say to each of them: "What are you for; what use can I make of you?" You would not sink down weeping; nor rise up in thoughtless battling. There is not hoping in this mood—but there is certainty, inherent steadiness of power.

There is no expectation, but there is knowledge. There is no fear, but confidence in the true law of life within you and in all things.

Every morning for a week, before you begin the day, spend five minutes in thinking over this strong outlook upon life. Every night before you go to rest, spend a few minutes in glancing back to see how you have maintained your spiritual dignity during the past day. Do not ask yourself especially: "In what have I erred?" but: "In what have I succeeded?" Each day will tell its tale of achievement. Do not wish, nor regret, nor hope. But when you are about to go to sleep, whisper gently: "I will." And when you wake whisper gently: "I will."

CHAPTER 15

REACHING FOR FREEDOM

It is written that when the student has carried on the previous Disciplines to some extent he will find himself loosened from the old desires of stimulation, and beginning to move and act from desires that rise within himself. The "world of making" ceases to rule him, and the "world of growth" now opens.

What I call the world of making is that universe round us which is full of forms which have been made by living beings. This classification is familiar in our everyday civilized life—there are houses, furniture, clothing, appliances and machines of many kinds, roads, bridges, gardens, and many other things. In that world, too, there are our living bodies, which have gradually been indirectly built up into their present form on account of the pressure of our minds within. This applies to all living things and all the forms for which they are responsible.

In the long course of our making of all these things we have not been so much interested in the making as in the things. We have made the "world of our desire," which turns upon us, so to speak, and envelops and enslaves us. This condition is something like that of a certain British soldier fighting in the Crimean war of the nineteenth century. He captured one of the enemy, who were Tatars. His companions heard him calling, "Come and help me; I have caught a Tatar." They shouted back, "Bring him along here." "I can't," he replied. "Then let him go, and come without him," the companions called. Came the pathetic reply, "I can't. He won't let me!"

So men are caught in the things of their own making—products of their own desires—which, made to be possessions, become their possessors. Thus desire leads to slavery, based on the desire to continue what we have made. We are caught in our own bird-lime.

The Disciplines, if self-engendered from the principle of growth within him, gradually awaken a man to the unsatisfactoriness of this condition. The things that he has made in the past can never be equal to the intent of his being, and so can never fully please him. The impulses of the "world of growth" within him impel him from within to a new set or series of desires. It is a new sunrise of desire, coming into the mind from the beyond; or, rather, it is the stirring of a spiritual will.

IMPULSES OF THE WORLD OF GROWTH
1. Desire for understanding
2.   "   "   companionship
3.   "   "   freedom

These desires give rise to new interests. The satisfactions now wanted are within the mind itself—much more in the feeling of the process of making than in the enjoyment of the things made. In this degree the artist does not cling to his old pictures, but is intent upon making new ones.

The man who has developed a big business and has put aside a million or two of dollars—quite enough to satisfy his material needs and capacity for material pleasure—nevertheless goes on with his business because he enjoys the inside sense of power in his work. No doubt he then develops a very strong mental capacity. He becomes "a hard man." He outgrows this, and begins to take an interest in living beings as such—in his fellow men especially. He begins to work quite genuinely for their welfare—sets up workers' welfare and community centers, etc. Quite apart from the question as to whether such doings really benefit the people, he *thinks* they do so and his feelings and motives are what we are now studying. I am assuming a man who is not doing these things to satisfy his own personal pride. He really has sympathy for the sufferings of others, and a capacity to enjoy their happiness and welfare. Sympathy, affection, and love for his neighbor really arise in his being, and appear in his mind. He becomes "a soft man." This is not dependence on companionship, but real feeling for life.

In time, however, he outgrows this enjoyment of companionship and love; it ceases to give him full satisfaction. He will also have discovered that indiscriminate love—love responding merely where sympathy calls for it, does not produce the welfare and happiness of the people he loves. He feels that it is, after all, only "directionless love," and it leads to thousands of confusions and a multiplicity of troubles, for himself and even for the people he loves. He finds that all his mental and material planning does not relieve this situation, because the people are really suffering from their own slavery to things— born of their own desires—as he was himself not so long before. The mentality and love which act in the world of making have now to give way to another power arising in the "world of growth" within him.

The secret of the situation is that we are gardeners, not builders or sculptors. We may try to build a satisfactory world, or we may try to sculpture our companion's lives into happy form, but such efforts are foredoomed to failure, because we must give up those unnatural efforts and become the gardeners that we more really are. No gardener will try to make a rose; he will not even try to open a rose from bud to bloom. But in his action to the rose he will be concerned with his thought and his love in providing, as far as lies in his power, those conditions in which the rose can fulfil the intent of its being. This is not a matter of giving thought, or giving love, but giving freedom. Freedom, in companionship with both people and things, has a greater height of joy than either thought or love. So freedom is the great desire of those who desire the One Reality, the Free—if it can be called desire. Really it cannot be called desire; it must be called the joy of harmony with the intent of our being.

Is it not perfectly clear that in the world of making and in the world of growth we are subject to some universal principles which we cannot gainsay? Can a man by taking thought return into his mother's womb? Let us not fool ourselves with human pride. There is a growth taking place, as with the rose. We are inexorably bound in that pulse of life. Can we feel harmony with that? Can it be *our* purpose, and the heart of our desire? Surely that is so, and when we have cured ourselves of the fevers of unharmonized thought and love we shall live in the joy and freedom of that harmonious life.

This is what the candidate longs for in the fourth Discipline. The word which describes it means literally: "Desire for release." [1] It refers to all the releases indicated in the previous chapters.

It can also be called "the higher uncoloredness." [2] In the second Discipline we had a state of being uncolored by all those "Tatars." But there is a higher uncoloredness—the state of not being colored even by the desires of the world of growth—of the mind and heart. We want the deeper wisdom, which is found in our consciousness called "I," as will be shown in our following chapters on the *Song of Praise to the South-Facing Form*, which can lead us to the threshold of the sanctuary of true freedom.

The fact is that growth is not forever. No particular growth is forever—not that of the rose, nor of the human body, nor of the human mind. The flower falls and gives place to the seed. The mind will reach its maturity—through self-gardening. It will slip into what I must call freedom, beyond even the

---

[1] *Mumukshā.*
[2] *Paravairāgya.*

harmony with growth, the all-covering and underlying cause of all that looks to us like process, when that Sun is seen through the cloud of thought. Call it nirvana, *moksha, parabrahman*, truth, freedom, anything—we shall reach it through "I" beyond the clouds of "you" and "it."

CHAPTER 16

FROM HEARING TO KNOWING

We will assume that the student is trying to carry out the four Disciplines mentioned in our previous chapters, and is succeeding to some extent. He is now ready for the three mental steps towards knowledge of the One Reality.

These are: 1. Listening
2. Reflecting
3. Contemplating.[1]

Listening means paying attention to the statements of the Scriptures with reference to the One Reality, and also to the words of seers and sages on the subject. It is held that no man would be likely to think greatly on this matter all by himself. Everyone whom I have questioned on the point says his interest in this idea dates from an occasion when somebody told him about it, or he found it in his reading. All the religious teachers and philosophers have had something to say about it —a mixture, no doubt, of truth as far as it can be put into words, of error, and in some cases of downright self-deception.

The student will no doubt have sought out such teachers as he could reach, in the form of books and persons, because he wants to hear all the important things that have been said about the One Reality. This applies to all religions or any religion. It is a matter of collecting the appropriate references and allusions from any scripture.

So the reception of testimony is the first stage.

[1] *Shravana, manana* and *nididhyāsana.*

The instructions next are: The aspirant must think, consider, reflect and reason upon the statements to which he has listened. It will be seen that there is no suggestion that he should merely believe what he has heard; it is required that he shall submit it fully at the bar of reason. Indeed, one cannot merely believe in these matters, even if one wishes to do so, because belief relates to something already mentally grasped, whereas in this matter we are going on to experience something beyond that. Thus reasoning is the second stage.

Thirdly, he must make a repeated and profound meditation, passing even into contemplation, on the subject of what he has heard. Meditation is the completion of one's thought on the subject in mental view. It might be a sentence such as the following; "Being is one, though named variously," that he has heard. In meditation you bring out from the mind every possible thought about this statement, at the same time seeing the cogency of each thought in relation to the statement. Such a meditation will, when the thoughts are exhausted, become an alert expectancy without any mental clutching, and so will pass on into Contemplation. You are looking at the idea without ever remembering who you are, although you are so fully conscious. In this way, the student obtains direct experience.

In a letter from an Indian spiritual teacher the following passage occurred—a very clear statement about this condition:

Believe me, there comes a moment in the life of an adept, when the hardships he has passed through are a thousandfold rewarded. In order to acquire further knowledge, he has no more to go through a minute and slow process of investigation and comparison of various objects, but is accorded an instantaneous, implicit insight into every first truth. Having passed that stage of philosophy which maintains that all fundamental truths have sprung from a blind impulse—it is the philosophy of your Sensationalists or Positivists; and left far behind him that other class of thinkers—the Intellectualists or Skeptics—who hold that fundamental truths are derived from the intellect alone, and that we, ourselves are their only originating causes; the adept sees and feels and lives in the very source of all fundamental truths—the Universal Spiritual Essence of Nature.

It may have been noticed that these three stages of a student's knowledge follow the course of the three means to right knowledge given in Chapter 6. The three were direct knowledge, inference, and testimony. The aim is direct knowledge of the One Reality, and the process begins with the hearing of testimony, goes on to reasoning, and ends with direct vision of the truth of the statement or experience being pondered on.

In a work entitled *Direct Experience*[2] Shankara has given a very careful account of what he calls the fifteen aids to Contemplation,[3] which is yoga. I will translate the verses dealing with this in my next chapter. This group of verses may be called the Vedantic yoga.

[2] *Aparokshānubhūti.*
[3] *Nididhyāsana.*

CHAPTER 17

THE FIFTEEN AIDS

The following is a new translation I have made of the fifteen points of Contemplation given in verses 102 to 124 of Shankara's *Direct Experience*. Where the great teacher of yoga, Patanjali, in his aphorisms, prescribes eight limbs[1] or aids of yoga, Shankara lays down fifteen limbs or aids of that yoga which is direct knowledge of the One Reality, attainable through Contemplation.

> *Verses 102 and 103:* The following are declared to be the aids (of yoga, according to the nondualistic system), in the order given:
>
> 1. Restraint
> 2. Regulation
> 3. Renunciation
> 4. Silence
> 5. Solitary Place
> 6. Proper Time
> 7. Posture
> 8. Root-Control
> 9. Straightness of Body
> 10. Steadiness of Vision
> 11. Regulation of Breath
> 12. Withdrawal from Sensation
> 13. Concentration
> 14. Meditation
> 15. Contemplation[2]

[1] *Angas.*

[2] *Yama, niyama, tyāga, maunam, desha, kāla, āsanam, mūlabandha, deha-sāmya, driksthiti, prānasanyamanam, pratyāhāra, dhāranā, ātmadhyānam,* and *samādhi.*

Verse 104. Restraint is that poise of the village of sensations which arises from the knowledge that everything is Brahman; it should be practiced again and again.

This verse deserves a long commentary, because it contains the secret of peace of mind in this world. It tells us that somehow everything is Brahman. We have constantly to remind ourselves of this piece of knowledge and then we shall value our present experience. Everything that occurs is worthy of our most appreciative attention, since it is in some way Brahman. There is no need to seek somewhere else for what is worth while. If our present experience is worth while, let us poise upon it. Poise means that we stop the mental running about which goes on constantly like a panic. Is your mind like a person shut in a room which has taken fire, dashing at this door and that door and banging upon them, beating upon the walls, stamping and shouting? Look into this matter. Is there peace of mind?

But if you believe that what is contained in your present experience of drinking, let us say, some carrot juice, is supremely and inherently valuable to consciousness, you will naturally become so poised that there will be a great release from mental feverishness. It will be an experience in itself, not a preparation for some other experience. This is not a mere relaxation of mind. It is a perfection of mind. It should be practiced every now and then, until one really has caught the experience of the feeling of the poise. It will afterwards be present along with all the successive activities of body and mind, at all times.

In the beginning this has to be done as a kind of exercise, because the old restlessness and anxious condition of the mind has to be overcome, and it keeps on coming back until the poise is properly caught and known and enjoyed. I have described the poise mentally—only such description is possible—but in the practice one empties the mentality out of the experience and takes the experience only; just as when we have a sight, we do not mentalize—when I look transfixed with delight at the snowy heights of Mount Everest, I do not say: "That is Mount Everest, a 29,000 feet high pile of rock; think of that; how beautiful!" I do not even say: "How beautiful!" Even that much mental chatter takes something away from the pure experience.

We ought not to look mentally for beauty, or goodness, or truth, or freedom, or anything else in the present experience, whatever it is, but we must find the poise that is our true life in relation to the experience—and without even seeking for that. It awaits us, but we cannot seek it, because we do not know it. It is perhaps the secret of pure being—but again I spoil it by naming, which provokes seeking. I beg every reader of these lines to try out this poise for himself or herself. It is what in the present work is technically called Contemplation.[3]

In this verse I have translated the expression "village of sensations" literally, because it is so very expressive. When one looks at a village with all its varied activity—its shopping area, homes and gardens, fire-brigade and what not—one sees a great resemblance to a human mind. And a perfectly harmonious village would seem to be the very embodiment of really peaceful active life.

> *Verse 105. Regulation* is flowing with the harmonious, and bending away from the confused, which is considered by the wise to be the greatest joy.

Here we are told of the joys of simplicity—the simplicity that is harmony, not paucity. In harmonious action and thought, without clouding, without jaggedness, there is poise, and incredible delight.

> *Verse 106. Renunciation* is the letting-go of the forms of prolixity as a result of seeing the true nature of consciousness; it is valued by the great as a means of instant liberation.

[3]*Nididhyāsana*, or *samādhi*.

This verse is put in by the Vedantic teacher to emphasize the importance of inward nonattachment to things, and to minimize the crude idea of renouncing the world by merely casting aside possessions and responsibilities. It is only what happens in consciousness that is important, and the casting aside of material things may sometimes be due to a jagged and jerky condition within. Smoothness of possession and action is possible when there is true renunciation. Once I met a little girl carrying a cat, and asked her if it was hers; the unconscious wisdom of her reply rebuked the thoughtlessness of my question, when she said, "It is mine sometimes." I learnt that there is nothing that is mine always, and that there is nothing that is not mine sometimes and in some way.

> *Verse 107. Silence* is that state, unreachable by thought, in which speech falls away; the wise always aim at this goal of the yogīs.

This verse points out where silence really lies, and implicitly deprecates common vows of material poverty and of silence, severe austerities, and similar practices. Various old books launch out vigorously against these common perversions of the ancient spiritual teaching which are all too prevalent in the world. The following, from *Garuda Purana Sāroddhāra*, which I translated for "The Sacred Books of the Hindus" series in 1909, is a case in point:

Donkeys walk about among people, in forests and among houses, quite naked and unashamed. Are these free from attachment? If men are to be liberated by earth, ashes and dust, does the dog which always lives among earth and ashes become liberated? The jackals, rats, deer and others, which feed upon grass, leaves and water, and always live in forests—do these become liberated? The crocodiles, fishes and others, which from birth to death, dwell in the waters of the Ganges,—do these become Yogins? Pigeons at times eat stones, and Chataka birds do not drink water from the earth—are these observers of vows?

Therefore this class of practices is a thing which merely makes pleasure for people, but direct knowledge of the Truth is the cause of liberation.

Fallen into the great well of the six schools of philosophy, the brutes do not understand the chief good; bound in the snare of animalism. They are tossed hither and thither in the dreadful ocean of Vedas and Shāstras; caught in the six waves they remain sophists. He who knows the Vedas, the Shāstras and the Purānas, but does not know the chief good—of that imitator all this is as the speech of a crow. "This is known; this must be known,"—thus bewildered by anxiety they read the scriptures day and night, turning away from the highest truth. The fools, decorated with garlands of poetry constructed of forms of speech, miserable with anxiety, remain with senses bewildered. Men trouble themselves variously, but the highest truth is otherwise; they explain in different ways, but the best purport of the scriptures is otherwise. They talk of the highest experiences, not realizing them themselves. Some have ceased preaching, being engrossed in egotism. They repeat the Vedas and the Shāstras, and argue with one another, but they do not understand the highest truth,—like the spoon the flavour of the food. The head bears flowers, the nostril knows the smell. They read the Vedas and the Shāstras, but find impossible the understanding of the truth.

The fool, not knowing that the truth is seated in himself, is bewildered by the Shāstras—a foolish goatherd, with the young goat under his arm, peers into the well. Verbal knowledge cannot destroy the illusions of the world of change—darkness never disappears by talking of a lamp. Reading, to a man devoid of wisdom, is like a mirror to the blind; hence, for those who have understanding, Shāstras are only a pointer to the knowledge of the truth. "This is known; this must be known,"—he wishes to hear everything. If one lives for a thousand celestial years he cannot reach the end of the Shāstras. The Shāstras are numerous; life is brief; and there are tens of millions of obstacles, therefore the essence should be understood—like the swan taking the milk which is in the water.

Having practiced the Vedas and the Shāstras, and having known the Truth, the wise man should abandon all the scriptures, just as one rich in grains abandons the straw. Just as there is no use for food to one who is satisfied with nectar, so is there no use for the scriptures to the knower of the Truth. There is no liberation by the study of the Vedas, nor by the reading of the Shāstras. Emancipation is by knowledge alone, not otherwise. The stages of life are not the cause of liberation, nor are the philosophies, nor are actions—knowledge only is the cause.

The allusion of the goatherd peering into the well is the old Hindu equivalent to our modern: "The old gentleman searches for his spectacles, when they are upon his forehead all the time." I have elsewhere explained the proverb of the swan, which is reputed to be able to extract milk from a mixture of milk and water, and is therefore emblematic of the wise man who, by discrimination, can extract the essence from the scriptures and from life. The "stages of life" mentioned near the end of the quotation refer to (1) childhood and youth, which are the student years, (2) the period of family responsibility, (3) the period of retirement, considered as characterized by much thought about life, and (4) the renunciation which is proper to the last part of our personal life-history. In modern terms we could indicate the same idea on a large scale by saying that there is no evolution into liberation, but that sooner or later each man must awaken to the truth, and proceed thence to his own liberation.

Continuing on the subject of Silence, the teacher states in verses 108 and 109 that no one can describe that which is beyond verbal description; so the real Silence is that which is *inborn*, while the silence that is merely the restraint of the tongue is childish. This emphasis on the inborn silence is immensely significant. Words are only symbols for things, like the letters in algebra. Even things are known to us only as sensations in consciousness. You cannot describe the color red or blue to persons who have never had those sensations in conciousness.

Our inborn condition of consciousness is vitally important. Yet we cover it up constantly with the noise of the mind.

Verse 110. The Solitary Place is that which is present in every part of this whole world, in which people do not exist at the beginning or the end or in the middle of something.

Tradition says the sage is not only silent, but also solitary. In the present verse the teacher shows what solitariness really is. He declares that it is in the consciousness which is present everywhere, which we have discussed in the first part of this book, which is only one, without a second.

Verse 111. The Proper Time is when there is the unbroken joy, that which is without a second—that is the meaning, because it is the source of all the activities there are, of Brahmā and all the rest, even in the shortest period, such as the winking of an eye.

In this verse there is a play upon words, which is difficult to reproduce in English, but the meaning is clear. There is a proper time, just as there is a proper place—the solitary place mentioned in the last verse—for this practice. The proper time is that in which the one pure consciousness, which is also joy, is present. As it is in the pure consciousness that every event in the sequence of things arises—whence the joy of life in each being—the pure consciousness can be reached "everywhere in time" that is, at all times. So he who wishes to practice need not select a special time, such as in the morning, or in the afternoon, or on a Sunday, as being preferable to other times. Brahmā, here mentioned, is regarded as the creative aspect of the universal life. There is a trinity of Brahmā (creative), Vishnu (preservative) and Shiva (destructive) in Brahman (the totality, or rather, the One Reality). Brahman and Brahmā have to be distinguished when we are reading Sanskrit books.

Verse 112. The Seat or Posture is only that in which contemplation of Brahman can be comfortable and continuous; that should be adopted, not others which interfere with comfort.

This counteracts the statements of some minor exponents who prescribe particular postures. There are eighty-four well-known postures prescribed in later books dealing especially with what is called Hatha-yoga. Like Patanjali, Shankara does not approve of prescribed postures for meditation and contemplation. All the same, it must be mentioned that there is no objection to practicing postures for health and suppleness of body, and to relieve the mind from the depression caused by bad body-habits, provided that it is done with adequate knowledge of the body and the bodily effects of particular postures. It is desirable to practice some way of sitting for meditation, for the sake of health of the body and nondisturbance of the mind.

In anticipation of the next verse I must explain that in the Hatha-yoga system there are various practices intended to awaken a force called the Coiled One[4] or, in a less direct way, the Serpent-fire. Shankara selects a typical one of these practices called Root-control.[5] The "root" is near the base of the spine, and a certain practice of contraction or pressure there produces heat, and this heat rouses the Coiled One, which is ordinarily regarded as a latent or potential force, which then runs up the spine. Shankara emphatically states that this practice should not be taken up by those who follow his course in these matters. It is very dangerous. He probably held to that school of thought in which the belief was that this force is released slowly and without being noticed whenever the mind achieves a suitable degree of meditation.

> *Verse 114. The Root-control* which is proper to be practiced by the Raja-yogī is always that which is at the basis of all beings, and is the source of mental bondage.

In the next verse the teacher again refers to a practice very much distorted by some misguided persons who think they

[4] *Kundalinī.*
[5] *Mūlabandha.*

can free themselves from bodily desires by self-maiming,
which they mistake for mastery. Extreme cases of this kind of
practice are to be seen now and then—such as men who have
blinded themselves, and others who have held up an arm until
it has withered. Sir Edwin Arnold speaks of these in his beautiful poetical biography of Buddha, "who made our Asia mild,"
The Light of Asia. He relates how Buddha approached a
group of such men, and said:

> Will ye, sad sires,
> Dismantle and dismember this fair house,
> Where we have come to dwell by painful pasts;
> Whose windows give us light—the little light—
> Whereby we gaze abroad to know if dawn
> Will break, and whither winds the better road?

The story goes on to tell how the men would not heed
Buddha's words, and then:

> Onward he passed,
> Exceeding sorrowful, seeing how men
> Fear so to die they are afraid to fear,
> Lust so to live they dare not love their life,
> But plague it with fierce penances, belike
> To please the Gods who grudge pleasure to man;
> Belike to baulk hell by self-kindled hells;
> Belike in holy madness, hoping soul
> May break the better through their wasted flesh.
> "Oh, flowerets of the field!" Siddartha said,
> "Who turn your tender faces to the sun—
> Glad of the light, and grateful with sweet breath
> Of fragrance and these robes of reverence donned
> Silver and gold and purple—none of ye
> Miss perfect living, none of ye despoil
> Your happy beauty. Oh, ye palms! which rise
> Eager to pierce the sky and drink the wind
> Blown from Malaya and the cool blue seas,
> What secret know ye that ye grow content,
> From time of tender shoot to time of fruit,

Murmuring such sun-songs from your feathered crowns?
Ye, too, who dwell so merry in the trees—
Quick-darting parrots, bee-birds, bulbuls, doves—
None of ye hate your life, none of ye deem
To strain to better by foregoing needs!
But man, who slays ye—being lord—is wise,
And wisdom, nursed on blood, cometh thus forth
In self-tormentings!

Shankara was at one with Buddha in this matter, and indeed with all the great spiritual teachers. In the next verse he writes:

> Verse 115. *Straightness of limbs* occurs when there is resting in harmony with Brahman,[6] not if there is only straightness like a dried-up tree.

The next item is *Steadiness of Vision*. In this case the same principle is maintained. It is not to be regarded as fixity of gaze on the tip or in front of the nose, as is often thought:

> Verse 116. Having achieved knowledge-sight, one sees the world as composed of Brahman—that kind of seeing is the highest, not the gazing in front of the nose. Or when there is the cessation of (the distinction of) seer, seeing and seen, there is the *Steadiness of Vision*.

That the whole world is constituted of the One Reality has been the theme of the early chapters of this book. It is one of the essential principles of Vedantic thought. However, the unity of seer, seeing and seen now comes up for the first time in this book.

The proper way to understand this is by experiment, by looking into one's own mind and seeing what is going on. Commonly, in the world, people say there is (1) someone who sees, (2) the act or function of seeing, and (3) something that is seen. We are thinking here not merely of seeing with

[6] *Same brahmani.*

the eye—or hearing, touching, tasting or smelling—but of being conscious or knowing.

In this triple classification, what is really known, and what is assumed? To answer this, each one of us must inspect what is going on in himself. What I find, when I do this, is that there is only one, not three. It is simply that consciousness is going on. If we are careful in this process of observation, we find that when we say "I" we mean this consciousness, this action of seeing. We are not directly aware of somebody who possesses or who performs the act of seeing. That is purely a mental assumption. One witness to an accident will testify, "The car ran into me, and I was unconscious for three hours"; another witness, less sophisticated, will put it quite differently, "The car ran into me, and knocked me out." When the first witness said "I," it was only a mental assumption. If we complete the idea, it will amount to "only a mental assumption in consciousness." What then is a mental assumption? Nothing but a certain act of consciousness. It is a kind of slowing down of consciousness; the runner reduces himself to a walk, lingers, pauses, but does not entirely stop. Or, a train going at sixty miles an hour rushes through a country station, and one passenger says to another: "What was that place?" The second says, "I do not know. I saw the sign and the name on it, but we flashed by so quickly that I could not read it." A mental operation becomes possible when consciousness slows down. Another name for this slowing down is "concentration." The point of our present argument, however, is that we find that we *are* consciousness, or, in other words, our very being *is* consciousness.

So we have reduced the three to two. We have eliminated the knower, and left consciousness and its object, or the seeing and the seen. Now we are on the common ground of the common or unsophisticated man, who regards his day as a succession of meeting-points of consciousness with objects. What are these objects? One after another the philosophers have told us: "Objects are only known in consciousness." The common man (who is never very wrong) replies, "We know that, and it is not interesting; they exist even when consciousness is absent." This question then becomes a scientific one to be settled by material experiment, not by conscious reasoning, since consciousness is capable of error, as we have seen in the assumption that the personality is "I." The common man is clearly right in his observation when he says, for example, "The volcano Krakatoa blew up, not as an act of consciousness, and some of its dust travelled in the atmosphere four times round the world." Similarly the milk went sour in the night, but the housewife knew it only in the morning. We cannot say that such objects are an assumption.

On this point our ancient Aryan thinkers were scientists as well as philosophers. They said, "As a matter of fact all the forms in the world and all the clashes of forms *are* acts of consciousness. We defy you to find one form that is not. There is consciousness acting humanly, plantly, animally and minerally, and even sub-minerally, and producing all these forms, with their qualities and activities, and their clashes. The forms are merely outposts of the consciousnesses that made them; it needs them, makes them, uses them. They express their maker. So when consciousness has experience with forms, it is viewing itself in the mirror of Nature, and the form is thus not something entirely different from itself. So, objects are operations of consciousness."

We have now resolved the object also into consciousness, and thus removed the erroneous idea of the triplicity of "seer, seeing and seen," and produced the Steadiness of Vision proposed in the verse. Emerson put the matter in a nutshell when he said, "Everything is fluid to thought," and "Nothing is more fleeting than form." This which I am putting forward as the deepest of thought about the self is thus not only the wisdom of the ancient forefathers of the branch of the Aryans in Asia. It is also good, sound, American sense, and basically it is the philosophy of life that has made America what it is, a land of fearless endeavor and unlimited confidence in the power of man—with all its faults nevertheless free from hole-and-corner cowardice and servitude to *things*.

We come now to the last five "aids to yoga" or "limbs of yoga" familiar to students of Patanjali, but described here in their deepest philosophic significance—the practices of regular breathing, withdrawal from sensation, concentration, meditation and contemplation. I will translate the verses here without comment.

> *Verses 118-120. Regulation of Breath* (the pulsation of life) is the control of all events through pondering upon the mind and all things only as of Brahman. The warding-off of the complex world is the breath breathing out; the realization "I am indeed Brahman," is the breath drawing in; and then the unchangingness of that realization is the poise of the breath within. This is the way of the wise; troubling the nose is for the ignorant.
>
> *Verse 121. Withdrawal from Sensation* is to be understood as immersion of the mind in the vision of all things as of the Self; this should be practiced by those desiring liberation.
>
> *Verse 122.* The highest *Concentration* is that concentration of the mind in which it sees Brahman wherever it turns.
>
> *Verse 123. Meditation* means stability in the idea of true being, not dependent upon anything, which is expressed as "I am indeed Brahman." It gives the greatest joy.
>
> *Verse 124. Contemplation* is that knowing in which there is the complete forgetting of ideas, by taking on the form of Brahman without any modifications.

I have written at some length in *Practical Yoga: Ancient and Modern* upon the meaning and practice of Concentration, Meditation and Contemplation, but the subject is so important that I must give a chapter to it after this one. Here it will be enough to say that contemplation means a state in which the mind becomes poised on something without mentally working upon it, and without thought of self, drinking in the experience without distorting it by anything coming from the past.

After describing the fifteen steps ending in Contemplation, Shankara says that the aspirant no longer needs the practices once he has acquired the capacity to go at will into the desired condition. This is a state which can then be his whenever he wants it, and it will to some extent permeate and color all other activities with its calm qualities of being, and knowing and joy. He tells us, however, to look out for and set aside various difficulties and obstacles likely to arise now and then, including missing the point, laziness, sensuous pleasures, sleepiness, heaviness, excitement, wrong eating and drinking, and emptiness of mind.

CHAPTER 18

PRACTICAL MIND-POISE

The object of this chapter is to explain some of the technique of concentration, meditation and contemplation. People may say, "But there is no need for that. All we have to do is to pay attention to things and thoughts. It is all very natural, just like walking or breathing or eating." There is much truth in this statement, yet it is also true that most of us would be the better for a term in a good school, conducted by competent teachers, which would train us to better ways of walking, breathing and masticating than we now have. In all those three activities one does not find that people improve year by year, by simply continuing in the same old way. By going to a teacher, or by reading and thinking and practicing by one-self, one can make improvements—not otherwise.

Let us not think that training, whether physical or mental, is going to make us artificial, stiff, stilted or overconscious. Once we have learned to walk with good balance, using the right muscles for each portion of the act, and have practiced sufficiently to educate and develop those muscles in proper degree, we can take our minds off the matter—except perhaps for an occasional inspection, to see that all is well—and allow the new habit to carry on without attention. After we have changed an old, rather poor, habit of this kind into a new, good one, we shall find that it is not a superficial and unimportant matter. Somehow, all these common things touch the very root of our being. They are spiritual. Nothing is more so. I think it is only laziness, which is lack of will, which has induced so many people to accept the thought that ideas are more spiritual than acts. Is memory better than experience? Has it more quality of living? When it has, ideas will be richer and more spiritual than acts!

Earlier, I explained that man adapts his environment to himself. This tends to cause him to neglect himself—his own body and mind—until suddenly he awakens to the fact that these are part of his environment, not of himself; although, it must be added, the most intimate part. Then, quite instinctively, he begins to adapt them to himself—to study them and work upon them so that in their moderate and relative sphere of operations they will function with ease and harmony.

When training the mind, let us remember that we are only correcting bad habits, inducting it into the art of "walking and breathing and eating" properly. When we have put it right, we are not going to operate it by certain rules or laws—that is not at all the idea. We are only going to develop its muscles and restore its balance.

Mental health begins with observation. It is the very secret of life and joy. We may look at a flower casually as we pass. We have not been much aware of its qualities, but only that "there is a flower there." Or we may pause, attentively, and say to ourselves: "That yellow color is really nice. How yellow it is! And the shape is beautiful, as the petals turn this way, then that way! And the scent is delicious! And to the touch—the texture of it is heavenly!" I do not mean that we should start the mind working upon the flower with all these adjectives, brought out like so many yardsticks and thermometers, but that we should have this experience. When I thus pause I bring more of myself to the flower. In this moment I am wedded to the flower, without reservations. It is a moment of rich living.

All life is such, is it not? Sometimes we experience something, sometimes we think about it, and each of these empowers the other. Even the high point to which philosophy and religion call us will be a looking, a communion, as with the flower. Nothing different. And a flower will then be enough, for we will no longer be passers-by.

It is not only the study of the components and qualities of a thing that informs us about what the thing is. Incidents of its relationships—stories about it—play a great part. Here is a story I have used when teaching these subjects. One day, Diogenes, the Cynic, visited Plato, the Greek philosopher. When he came into the room, he saw the table covered with a rich cloth, shelves glittering with silver cups and other vessels, and other sumptuous furniture. He took hold of the cloth with force, dragged it onto the floor, and stamped upon it with his feet, saying, "I tread upon Plato's pride." Plato quietly answered: "And with greater pride!" This story tells us a great deal about Plato. Our lives are made up of such stories, in action and thought, some true to fact and some fanciful. It is the richness of the stories that makes the richness of our lives, and it is the richness of our minds that makes the richness of the stories. Fact and environment give opportunity, but living has strength, color and richness only on account of what it brings to opportunity. The natural is the rich, and can always teach us.

I could ask myself now whether I have truly tasted the richness of a yellow envelope—a common thing—which lies upon my table and catches my eye as I write these words. I look at the envelope because of this question. I close my eyes and think of the color of that thing. I open them again and see the richness of that yellow color better than before. It feeds my mind. I feel a new delight and enhancement of life—the immediate result of this small but fruitful act, and I acknowledge with thanks the beloved companionship of that common yellow thing.

Now to a little training. First, concentration, so that you may, when you want, dwell upon something without restlessness of mind. This is poise, balance. Take a very large sheet of paper; draw a circle about two inches in diameter in the center of it; write in the circle the word "cat"—or draw a cat. Then draw many arrows radiating from the circle. You have now our diagram from Chapter 1 on a larger scale.

Next, look very peaceably at the word cat, and note what comes up in your mind. It may be milk. If so, write "milk" at the point of an arrow. Do not think about milk, which would lead you on to cow, dairy, and so on, but slide your attention back along the arrow to the cat. Then ask yourself: "What next?" Perhaps it will be "mouse." Do not think about a mouse; give the mouse only a moment's clear attention, and then slide back along the arrow to the center. Repeat the process, filling as many arrows as you can. When it seems that you can think of nothing more, still hold on, looking most peaceably at the cat. You may have fifty or sixty arrow-words, including the nature of the cat, the parts of it, the qualities of it, cats you have known, and many other things.

Usually people's minds wander. They have a habit of dissipation and diffusion. Some people never look at anything properly, so their observations of both things and thoughts are very shallow. This little practice of concentration could soon rectify that. As you perform this practice of recall, you will notice that you begin to know what recall *feels like*, you will develop a *feeling* of concentration. When you have acquired the *feeling* of concentration you will discover that you can have a *mood* of concentration. This mood of concentration you can then switch on and off, just when and as you like.

Concentration will now be natural and easy. You will not even call it concentration. You will not be thinking, "I am concentrating; I am paying attention," any more than you think of walking when you walk. It is simply a power of the mind.

The word concentration is in some respects unfortunate. It makes people think of force, effort, control, compulsion and other such ideas. And these thoughts cause people to feel tense and become tense when they want to concentrate. But there should be no tension anywhere in the body during concentration, and no thought of force, or of gripping or holding an idea in the mind. It is simply looking. It is as light as a feather in the hand. One does not plunge into it. One floats into it, like a person floating on water. It is a poise.

We come next to thinking and meditation. If you are thinking about something, your mind does not wander away to something totally different. Or perhaps I ought to say that it does but it should not. Thinking thus contains concentration. And meditation is thinking fully about something. The best elementary exercise for thinking and meditation is done with the same diagram as before. Open your chart again. Take the first arrow-word—let us say milk—slide back into the cat as before, but bringing the milk with you. You then dwell on the cat and the milk together. You think about the cat with the milk—the whole story, as fully as you can. You have thus appreciated the cat, understood the cat, known what the cat is, better than you did before. When you have told yourself all of that story, you move on to the next word—say mouse—and repeat the process. And so on.

Meditation on a thing or an idea consists essentially of keeping your attention on it while you bring up one by one all the ideas you can bearing upon it, and assimilate them into it one by one. Observe all the relationships between them. This applies not only to external things, such as cat and milk, but to the parts—cat and its claws, whiskers, nose, tail, etc.— its qualities—cat and its smoothness, softness, independence of character, etc.—and it cogeners—tiger, leopard, hyena, etc. —and even other animals, such as elephant, horse, dog, etc., etc. Take one thing at a time, and combine it in.

Both the exercises—on concentration and meditation— can be practiced without the written chart, but it is desirable to use it in the beginning. They can be applied to simple or complex, and concrete or abstract, subjects. They can be used in study or in writing—whenever you want to deal with a subject accurately and fully.

After a month or two of this practice for a little while each day, the mind will be much renewed and enriched. Take the analogy of morning exercises, by which in perhaps fifteen minutes you tone up all the muscles, some of which would otherwise have been totally neglected, for the whole day. I mention this so that you will not think that concentration and meditation are to be a task. Quite the reverse—they are a refreshment.

The third point of mind-poise is contemplation. This is really the perfect observation that results when concentration and meditation have done their work. When you have completed a meditation, do not cast your mood away, but poised in that condition remain gazing expectantly, like a person at an open window who does not know what is going to pass by. I need write no more about contemplation here, as it is so often mentioned in different connections throughout this book.

PART III

THE MEDITATIONS ON THE SOUTH-FACING FORM

CHAPTER 19

THE FIRST MEDITATION

The following nine meditations—the subjects of the present chapter and the eight that follow—constitute a translation, made by me in 1950, of one of the most prized of the *Stotras* or Songs of Praise written in Sanskrit by Shankara Āchārya, the famous exponent of the nondual outlook upon life, which he termed the *adwaita vedānta* philosophy—or rather outlook, for philosophy usually implies a system of thinking, but outlook indicates an attitude towards the world and life. Instead of writing Shankarāchārya, all in one compound word, as is usual in Sanskrit, I have kept the two words separate, a practice commoner in our language, and written Shankara Āchārya. The word āchārya means "teacher." We may then use the name Shankara in brief, with no less respect for it than we have for the similar name Plato, or Socrates, or Shakespeare.

Such songs of praise are numerous in Sanskrit. The present one, entitled Song of Praise to the South-facing Form, stands out among the rest for its brevity, and its close adherence throughout to the assertion of One Reality.

It is based on the belief that man *can know* that one reality —that men have known it in the past and can do so now— that in fact any man can do so if he has a mature mind, and follows the procedure described in the "song." To fulfill this purpose, it is held, there is no need for special greatness of mind, or anything approaching the mental power of genius; it is the right-facing that will procure success. One teacher emphasized this when he wrote to an enquirer: "Nothing draws us to any outsider save his evolving spirituality. He may be a Bacon or an Aristotle in knowledge, and still not even make his current felt a feather's weight by us, if his power is confined to *Manas*." *Manas* is the thinking mind.

Let us proceed to the first stanza:—

MEDITATION I

Devotion to that Glorious Presence,
Infinite Instructor,
Who,
Seeing the universe as if outside,
Though it arose in himself,
Through maya,
Just as in a dream,
Or like a city being seen in the inner
            depths of a looking-glass,
In the awakening,
Discloses his own nature,
Than which there is no other.

The above translation contains exactly the statements of the original stanza. I have added nothing of my own "to make the idea clearer" or in the spirit of "This is what was meant or intended by the writer," except in the case of the terms Glorious Presence and Infinite Instructor, for which exceptions I will now give my reasons. What I have given as Glorious Presence—that to which we are addressing our thought and devotion—is in the original "the South-facing Form." [1]

[1] *Dakshinā-mūrti.* Following the meaning of the word *dakshinā* further back, we come to "on the right-hand side." When the ancient Aryans moved eastward and came through the mountain passes into the north-west of India, they occupied the large territory in that part, and then, flowing onward,

In our first three chapters we have tried to think of a primary Principle in all Nature, which is the basis of everything and is therefore the essential nature of everything, and we have realized that it cannot be anything, cannot have the character of anything in Nature, whether form or force or law —cannot be one of the known things. The assumption that one of the known things is the basis or substance of all the others is the mistake of modern "Materialism" on the one hand, and of anthropomorphic religion or nature-worship on the other. The conception of the whole converging upon and present in every part, and being the essential nature of that part, is what we have been aiming at.

Yet we all acknowledge that responsiveness to Nature— the whole world of experience, including man—the lending of ourselves in a companionate spirit to the lessons of experience, gradually brings us enlightenment in the direction of realization of the basic Principle, the essential nature of ourselves and all. By a kind of natural devotion we all acknowledge our allegiance to this whole field of experience called Nature, while recognizing our special relation to the parts of it by an intellectual process of practical companionship, which we call practicality, or being sensible, which is nothing but the acceptance of our part-ness in nature along with our wholeness of essentiality. We are conscious of the point of reference and response in ourselves, which we call "I," to which all part-experiences are submitted, and which confers temporary unity or integrity upon the aggregates which we consent to deal with in our lives.

Each one of us finds himself in a certain position in Nature. I—for one—sit now in a lovely garden. It is on a gentle slope. The house is built to enclose a portion of the slope. The bank has been cut and supported with a five foot rough stone

turned to the right into the lands of central South India, which then came to be called dakshina-patha, the right-hand or southern journey. To this day a large part of the country is commonly referred to as "the Dekkan."

revetment, so that the garden may be a level ground, which is partly grass lawn and partly flagged as a patio. There are flower beds and a fountain along the wall. There are bushes and not-too-big trees judiciously planted in the angles, and on the bank there are bigger trees and flowering plants, which enclose the peaceful scene. In the patio section are a table and chairs, lounges and a garden umbrella—the heavier pieces being on wheels.

Here I am, writing in this enclosed portion of Nature, which was not thus framed off from the rest of Nature by accident, but by design. It was the doing of an intelligent friend of mine, who owns this property, and has—though unintentionally—stamped his own well-ordered and pleasing personality on this plot of ground which somehow "has been given him to till." Sitting here, in delightful acceptance of this situation, in happy companionship with this portion of Nature, and even for the time being forgetting that there are other portions of Nature outside this garden, I am being made aware that it is a unity—it is the source of my delight—which, when I think of others, I know to be the same kind of unity which some other persons in some other gardens may be enjoying at this moment, in some other parts of the total unity which reflects itself into all gardens, all parts. My garden—it is mine sometimes, is it not?—is my window into the infinite; my delight has for its core my resting in that infinite.

Recognizing then, that the particular can be our window into the infinite, I proceed to explain the South-facing Form. It is a mental "garden." It is a particularized infinite! *Dakshinā-mūrti* is pictured as like a man, sitting away up in the Himālaya mountains, and looking southwards over the Indian mainland and peninsula. Of course, everybody knows that there is no such man. But it was maintained by the Hindus —by Shankara, at any rate—that without intelligence no man can know the infinite; that even with intelligence, if it is in service to desire for particular temporary pleasures, no man can know the infinite; and that even with intelligence and the desire to know the infinite, but without Nature-forms, still no man can know the infinite. This is so because Nature is the window to the infinite. Intelligent meditation—dwelling on the form with full fellow-feeling—leads to a mergence in which companionship slips into unity.

The make-believe is good as long as it is known to be make-believe. That a little girl plays with a doll is good—the "meditation" of that experience assists the awakening of her latent love. The little girl knows that the doll is not a real baby. And when we turn our thoughts and feelings to the South-facing Form, we know, and indeed are reminded again and again in the Song of Praise, that it is no "particular" or entity that we are dealing with, but the very infinite itself. On such points I must leave the meditations to take their own course, and not anticipate them here.

However, to suit the Western world, I have translated South-facing Form as Presence. This idea is not wrong. It is in fact very exact, because the Form is regarded as a special presence of the divine being, although belonging to the region of māyā, and although even "Presence," even "Omnipresence," is only a "particular." All our words are dolls, which we will some day forego, but mere foregoing is not the gateway to the infinite.

Why glorious? This is a translation of the word *shri*, which is used as an honorific prefix to the names of deities, eminent persons and celebrated works. It carries always a meaning of richness, magnificence, splendor, or fullness of any admirable quality or attainment that is specially applicable where it is employed. The original says *Shrī Dakshiṇā-mūrti*—the glorious South-facing Form. *Murti* means form.

We come next to my second, and last, "liberty with the text." I have written: "Infinite Instructor." *Guru* is the word, and a *guru* is one who gives instructions in "spiritual matters." India is full of *gurus*, very many of them having much deep wisdom, whose words are worthy of the most profound and respectful consideration, but none of these *gurus* are thought of as greater teachers than Shankara—just as none of the yogīs claim to supersede Patanjali. And Shankara writes this song of praise to the South-facing Form, as to both the Truth and the Teacher. Shankara bows to the one Presence as the *guru* or Instructor. Again the prefix *Shrī* appears, and I have this time taken it to mean infinite. We shall see how this applies in each of the meditations.

So much for my two derelictions from literal translation, if such they are. Let us now proceed to consider the first stanza. I will try to explain some of the less obvious of its expressions.

It is the infinite itself that sees the universe, as if outside, inside itself. Here indeed is something to dwell upon. Dualism is cut away at its very root. There is not something else that is seeing the infinite wrongly. The error or illusion of particularity—if it be such—is of the infinite itself. The point of this must be that error is a particularity, and particular is looking at particular when it says error to itself, but all the time the very particular is based on the infinite.

What we are really taught by this difficult statement that he sees the universe "as if" outside is that our *thinking* will not reveal the truth, because it is only a limited mode of knowing, is in its very nature only the knowing of particulars by comparing them. It is the common mode of knowing that we employ in our daily affairs. But it is not the mode of knowing the infinite. That must be a kind of contemplation in which there are no comparisons and classifications, but a replacement of particulars by unity.

Meditation is that process in which we pay our fullest attention to something—we give all we have to it, forgetting other things for the time, so that it has all our thought and feeling. It leads on to the point—though not intentionally, for that would spoil it—at which we forget even our "selves," forget that there is someone who is meditating and something that is being meditated upon, and then there is the rapture of the new consciousness.

After such an effort, we sooner or later fall from this, and think: "I am having the experience; I am in contemplation," and then the new consciousness is shattered, but there is still joy, for we remember it, or, rather, it has become a living point of joy, which occurs again and again and is shattered again and again, but visits us ever more and more if and when we love it better than any other "interests" from which our pleasures are derived.

"Though it arose in himself, through *māyā*." I keep coming across this word in quite popular literature. It is becoming acclimatized into the English language. I have discussed it to some extent in earlier chapters, and it will come up again in various contexts. I have shown that it is not "illusion," that if it were to be taken as such its meaning would become self-destroyed, because, all particular things and words being illusion, illusion would also be an illusion. Two negatives can hardly make an affirmative in this case.

As I have stated in other places, I believe every question of this kind must be approached from where we now stand, from the position and condition in which we find ourselves. We cannot jump and keep our feet on the ground. We cannot leap into infinity. Surely that way unconsciousness would lie—not knowledge within the mind-sphere, and not the new knowledge of the new consciousness. What we do find in practical life and in thought is that we ourselves reduce ourselves temporarily from time to time, from a less limited to a more limited sphere of attention. When you are reading this page or this chapter you are not reading page 140 or Chapter 14, though you could as well read those as these. This is a voluntary self-limitation, is it not? Yet out of the self-limitation, at the end of the period of your reading a page or a chapter in a book, has come some enrichment of your field of thought. When you revert to your less limited conditions there is more delight there than there was before. You descended into hell, dwelt a while there, and thereby ascended higher into heaven—to use another simile. It cannot be too much emphasized that every time we act or think we begin with a self-limitation; then the better the doing or the thinking the better will be the illumination afterwards.

It must be seen that even material creativeness belongs to this process, and could be described as "action-meditation." The carpenter working at a chair, or the artist painting a picture, or my friend planning and making his garden, or the musical composer getting a ditty in his head and running to the piano to work it out—all of them are thinking something out and helping themselves in their self-limiting or concentrative efforts by the aid of hands and the material things which stand up boldly before them and help to hold the wavering mind to its purpose. The work itself is an expansion or completion of something within the self-limitation, the self-imposed "ring-pass-not" accepted for the time being. Each such practical or mental meditation will have proved its windowness-into-the-infinite if it passes on to its fulfillment in a contemplation, already described. So the meaning of *māyā* is self-limitation. That is not self-denial. It is not *total* error. It is self-initiated, acceptable and fruitful ignorance[2]— ignorance as a means to knowledge—something to be valued, cherished, understood, and consciously applied.

This *māyā* is always spoken of as having two functions— covering-up and expanding.[3] That is what we do. First we cover something up. The carpenter comes to his workshop in the morning and, after a little consideration of all the things he could make, decides to give his attention to a chair, thereby covering-up or forgetting all the tables, stools and other things

[2] *Avidyā.*
[3] *Āvarana* and *vikshepa.*

he could do; then he expands by going into all the details of what is to be done about the chair. Finally, the chair is finished, and the man turns to something else.

So, with some such process of *māyā*, why should not the Glorious Presence, to whom I do not propose to apply any limitations, see the universe "as if" outside, though in fact it arises in himself?

And if you and I are also addicted to doing this, even if we do not know why, are we not thereby receiving an intimation that in our essential nature we are not different or separate from the Glorious Presence? And if we pursue these meditations, may there not come a glorious moment—and more than that—when we shall pass through them into a contemplation which shall set its seal upon our consciousness for evermore?

But do not ask for it. It is pure grace, beyond any "making" of ours. Then: "In the awakening"—in himself, in us, "discloses his own nature."

"Than which there is no other." This gives us another concentration, and meditation and, let us hope, contemplation. I have nothing here to add to my remarks on this subject of nonduality given in Part I of this book.

I must now make a statement about the background of our lives. It is not to be supposed that these meditations which are now proposed, or any similar ones, are merely separate things in our lives, and not part of a unitary fulfillment. Every single mind-meditation or action-meditation produces its effect, which goes into the all-ness or background of our consciousness. This backdrop is present with us on all occasions, so that when one act is on, and we are performing something— doing a practical or a mental "meditation" under the spotlight in the center of the stage—the whole background is still there, exerting its total influence on the scene.

In human life this is what is called our character, distinct from memories and precedents. Our character of the present day, from which we act spontaneously before we think, or from the platform of which we begin our thinking on any given occasion, contains in some way the distillate or essence of all our past, incorporated and consolidated into this entity we call self. Our knowledge, for example, of the planetary and starry systems, is not merely an odd and casual thing that we know. We are different on account of it; it has something to do even with the kind of cheese and the kind of bread we may buy in the market this afternoon, and it will speak its part in the conversation at the evening party.

The nearer to perfection any one of these meditations may be—the completer its seclusion and the fuller the internal reciprocity of all its contents—the more will its essence provide an ingredient in character, which will assist unseen in future meditations. This means not an accumulation or collection of habits, but a progressive awakening of power—of affection, thought or the will. The past and the future thus co-operate in living, and the power of *māyā* comes to be more and more wielded by us in voluntary living, and less and less a mere covering and dispersion of the light.

When embarking upon this meditation the student may be expecting something interesting or novel to happen the very first time. It is with reluctance and regret that I must now tell him not to start off in that spirit, for in doing so he will be blocking his own way. It is like this: We look over the ocean at something floating in the distance, and ask ourselves: "Are those dark things boats or are they lumps of seaweed?" We take it for granted that they are something that we can and will recognize. There will be in our mind what Hindu friends call device.[4] If on looking more closely we find that the objects are mermaids, we may not believe our eyes, at least not until we have explained away the impossibility of such a thing, by the thought that there is a movie location somewhere about that is staging this phenomenon.

[4] *Vikalpa.*

The spirit of expectation of something contains a psychological implication of recognitiveness—it is within the "device," even if one expects the bizarre or the preposterous. It will lead to psychic visions colored by our own thought, missing the unitary principle, or to a feeling of disappointment at the terminating of the meditation, when the time is up, or perhaps we must go and feed the cat.

It will probably be necessary to go into this meditation many times, without the expectation of finding anything that is within previous experience, or within previous mental classifications. The mind will not be trying to recognize those dim objects, so as to say: "Ah, now I know; they are boats." This is not to be a meditation in which there is any determinable expectation in the result. If you take it up as such, you will still be imprisoned within the limits of the ordinary thinking mind, and will be excluding yourself from the new state of consciousness which will admit you to the Glorious Presence.

Do not strive; do not make efforts; do not drive yourself hard. Float yourself into your meditation as lightly as a little boy launches a paper boat upon a pond. Do not ask for success. You are not making something. You are not going to see something. Perhaps you are awaiting the dawn, and in the darkness you are growing eyes!

This attitude will, incidentally, enable you to enjoy the non-devising meditation at odd times. It will become a pleasure, and every occasion will bear its unseen fruit.

Set meditations at fixed times tend to carry with them the feeling of a special task for a special purpose, but the unset meditation will lead to a condition in which all our life becomes action and meditation occurring together at the same time. This is a condition we shall arrive at without intention, and without particularly noticing it, just as the convalescent becomes fully well again only after forgetting that he was ill, so that he catches himself, with surprise, saying to himself, "Why! I'm not ill. Isn't that strange?"

CHAPTER 20

THE SECOND MEDITATION

Our first stanza asserted the nature of the unitary basis of all things as being present in action or change as much as in the relatively static phenomena of the universe. It showed how the production of a world of forms is like the arising of a dream-form within—and its dissolution occurs at an awakening in which the reality is disclosed.

The reality which is the basis of all this has been stated. Now, in the second stanza, the action rather than the presence, comes into view.

MEDITATION II

Devotion to that Glorious Presence,
Infinite Instructor,
Who,
By donning space and time, produced by maya
Like a conjuror, or rather a great yogi,
Opens up and spreads out this world,
At first formless,
Like a sprout within a seed,
And afterwards wonderful in its diversity.

"Space and time." It is here necessary to realize that the words "space" and "time" belong to the class of words of discovery, not to that of words of definition. If we speak of marble or concrete the words are themselves as definite as marble and concrete; we speak of the precisely known. In the meaning of such words there can be no variance. But if we speak of God or of space or time, we are voyaging in a boat of words on an uncharted sea. Like Columbus we do not know where we are going, though, unlike Columbus, we hope to know where we are when we get there, and where we have been when we get back. But, as in his case, the boat is necessary.

Consider a known solid object. It has length, breadth and thickness—measurable dimensions. In these and other particulars it can be compared with other objects—not in itself, but only as regards such qualities and actions. To space we must not attribute such dimensions, however. Space is something we infer from the objects. We say that because these objects do not touch one another there is space between them. But we cannot say that the space occupies space, that in itself it has dimensions—length, breadth and thickness. These things are a denial of space. Their presence is an interference with space. So space is a limitation of the one reality, and things are a limitation of space.

Time, too, occupies no time. It has no measures, and has no inherent unit. But mind-process and change in the world are measurable occupants of time, and as such are denials of time.

So these two ideas, of space and time, cannot be formulated as "thingly" or "changely," but are donned as a garment or covering in that process of *māyā* which brings objects and minds into our world. It is the act of will which is concentration, which is a self-limitation and covering-up of the light.

The coverings are multitudinous. This act thus opens up and spreads out the whole world. There is a good example and illustration for this. Let us set the stage with a block of marble, a sculptor friend and myself. The friend asks what I would like him to make for me from this block of marble. I say, perhaps, a little horse. At once he sees the horse-form within the marble, and he will cut and chip away all the material that is not within that form and leave the horse standing there in its beauty. The form was really there—otherwise he could not have left it. I might have asked for a flower. In that case he would have seen the flower-form, and would have revealed that form—which was also really there—for me. So, little horse and flower—and how many other things?—were within the marble, all really there, and all existing together, without interference, until my friend, denying the flower and the other things, gave me the horse, or, denying the horse and other things, gave me the flower.

Such is the infinitude until *māyā*, the sculptor, steps in and covers up or denies all the reality except that little horse that is desired. Such is the nirvanic world, or state of unobstructed consciousness. Can you think of this as a possibility?—the annihilation of space and time as the concomitant of liberation into the new state of unobstructed consciousness?

If not, let us speak of memory and ideas. Perfect memory is as good as direct vision. If we look back to yesterday's meeting with a friend, will it not be that that face and form will be vaguer than those of the actual experience? Yes, but that is because present things and present other thoughts occupy part of my attention, and obscure the memory. Memory depends upon forgetting, inasmuch as all else being denied and forgotten it is there undimmed. In perfection it would not be what we call memory, but a re-living of the experience as undimmed as it was when lived. Old people get near to this. Hypnotized persons also attain or nearly attain it sometimes. So also the yogī who has nearly perfect control of mind. Even a dream gives clearer pictures than do efforts of imagination.

My point is that ideas are real; we embody them in things; we then recover the ideas from the things. So all life can be ideally, that is really, lived without space and time, like the existence of all the forms at once within the block of marble.

"Like a great yogī." The mark of the yogī is control of mind. He can concentrate when he wills, and produce his world of limitations, and can contemplate when he wills, not reversing the action, but using the finite things as a gateway

back into the infinite. But in this stanza we are studying "creation," which is limitation, the opening-up and spreading-out of
things, as it appears in this world of *māyā*.

"At first formless, like a sprout within a seed." How interesting! Shall we look within the seed for that little sprout,
smaller and smaller in its ungrown-ness, within and within,
almost to an infinite origin? Or to the revelation of an idea in
form, operating from within the life working through the seed
—an idea which produced it in the first place and can now reproduce it again and again?

The tide of the life or mind process flows on. There is
a shuttle action between the manifest (as we call it) and
the free, between the impermanent form and the permanent
presence. These are not a pair of opposites, like hot and cold,
or big and little, or bound and freed. There is only one
reality there, but it contains all, and in self-reduction it is still
all there, but the whole is there attending to a part of itself.
There is the expansion and contraction of one heart.

CHAPTER 21

THE THIRD MEDITATION

In the second meditation we have seen how the Glorious Presence produces the world by the inverse proliferation of concentration. It will have been noticed by now that concentration is a natural process, not something special that we do for a special purpose. The cycle is: concentration, meditation, release. Even breathing follows this law: inbreathing, pause, outbreathing. Walking also follows the law; step, poise, push. There is nothing unnatural in meditation, which is applied knowledge of the processes of life, and has its natural technique and growth.

In the third meditation we see the Glorious Presence returning from his concentration, which produces in this universal being wonderful variety all at once (an immense grasp in one act, an unlimitedly powerful concentration), back into his all-presence, a release from the forms.

Really he does not do this, except as being all of us, for in that fullness of unity the whole is fully present in the part, as we have seen by the example of the block of marble.

MEDITATION III

Devotion to that Glorious Presence
Infinite Instructor,
Whose coming forth reveals the nature of true being,
Amidst the objects produced in false being.[1]
To those who turn to him,
He gives direct knowledge,
By means of the wise saying "That, thou art."
As result of that experience there is no return
To the ocean of things.

[1] *Asat.*

167

We have now to think of the Glorious Presence as shining forth everywhere, in everything. If we look at a leaf, the whole is there; or at a grain of sand. It is shining there, and if we do not see it, it is because we do not truly look, but shut ourselves into the prison of concentration which we have not fulfilled into its meditation and contemplation. This may seem to be a matter of thought, but there is feeling also. We have some positive or negative desire for a limit—a desire that produces the concentration and imprisons us in it, positive if it is something I want to have, negative if it is something we want to avoid. We may recognize this as a prison, and be annoyed with ourselves, but the only way out is through fulfillment; we have jumped into the pond and entered the race, and must now swim to the other side. In the ripeness of experience we shall find release, not in frustration or repression; but since things are only there to help thoughts, meditative thought can always reduce the need for things, for experience, to its minimum—which will some day become a zero, through the gateway into the infinite. There is no need for such a great amount of experience, and so many repetitions of it, when we have learned to meditate. And when we go on into contemplation we shall not need that kind of experience at all again. Not needing it, there will be no internal vacuity, producing a hunger of desire.

If you enquire what is the difference between yourself and the Glorious Presence, you will find that it is this vacuity that you have, which is an inability, and yet a hungry desire for the ability to be all in all. When you enter into the new consciousness you will find that you can sustain it, because it sustains you, and with one glimpse of it you will weep with unbearable joy. But let us turn to the meditation.

"His coming forth reveals the nature of true being." That is what we have been talking about. Do not miss anything in these meditations; the teacher's every word is potent. So there is great significance in the addition: "Amidst the objects produced in false being." This thought should do away with all expectations and desire for release or escape. In the midst of the prison we shall be free. Every one of those things that confined us before now manifests to us the Glorious Presence of all-being. It is only in concession to our need for the idol that we call these things limited, imperfect, unreal, false being, for we know there is not, and in thought we cannot picture, any unreality. The unreal is in some way real. It is classifiable within the real.

"To those who turn to him." This "turning to" is to be thought about and felt. Some may say "resort to." That is all right, if we do not think of any sort of running to a refuge or to something or someone to give us protection or strength. To "take refuge" in the supreme *guru* is a denial of the Presence. Let us argue: If I have a *guru*, will he stand between me and the impacts of my experience, to soften the blows of fate? Surely not, for those are my need. Or will he pour his strength into me to deal with them more effectively than I can? Certainly not, for these are my instruments of self-development and realization; they call for my thinking, and love and will. This is my meditation-job. If someone else does it I am out of the picture. No real *guru* will consent to such silliness. So the "turning-to" that we are doing is nothing but a sort of revolution on our own axis, whereby we are facing the light, instead of turning our backs upon it, as we were doing before.

And then—"he gives direct knowledge." It is a grace. This is nothing of our doing, It is no work of our hands, nor thought of our minds, nor love of our hearts, nor will of ours, that produces this new knowing. It is like light. We do not make light; we accept it—or else we shut our eyes and say, "I refuse to see." But do not ask for it, because you can only ask for something that you know. But this thing: eye hath not seen, nor ear heard, nor hath it entered into the heart of man to conceive.

If we would dare to make a picture of this in relation to

our evolutionary march, we would describe the evolution as bringing the mind to a maturity of meditativeness, standing on the threshold of contemplation, and peeping through into that "world of unobstructed life." We could imagine all the human beings of the past who have run their race and entered that world. We would not find toys there, such as we have in this nursery. There the very sands of the seashore, and the drops of water in the tumbling rivers, would be living Buddhas and Christs, every one of whom would be not less than the whole. We must not picture a negative state, less than this, but a positive one, more than this. For the atom is not our all, and the vacuum is not our all, and even that partial vacuum called man, and even perfect man (saving the paradox!) is not our all. And surely we must not think of that world as separate from ours, but as pressing always around and upon us as really as the atmosphere that we breathe and feel upon our skins.

"By means of the wise saying." What I have here translated "wise" is, in the original, vedic—belonging to or from the Vedas, which are the sacred lore of the Hindus. In naming their bible, or sacred library, those people use this term which means wisdom, that is, knowledge about life. Common knowledge is information about things, but wisdom is knowledge about life. The wise person is one who knows how to deal with himself and his neighbor as living beings.

The sacred lore contains many wise sayings. These are themselves often called the Vedanta, that is *veda-anta*, end of the veda—the high point of understanding and purpose to which all the rest of the lore is only leading up. Wise men of the past collected these sayings together, commented on them and thereby produced vedantic literature. And those of them, including Shankara, who see in these wise sayings a statement of only one reality, call that reality nondualistic,[2] and themselves nondualists, referring constantly to the one than which there is no other.

[2] *Adwaita.*

We come then to the saying "That, thou art." [3] This is what that infinite instructor is saying to us everywhere and through everything. This is the key to the kingdom, the gateway to the infinite.

First notice it is not "Thou art that," but "That, thou art." That is because we are to meditate first on the Glorious Presence, not upon ourselves. And the devotion is a glad surrender of this to That.

Yet, in the second step, it is a meditation on this thou. What is this "thou" that each one of us says he is? Is it what I really am and you really are? I have seen this thing built up, and I know its history. There was a baby, without guile, but full of desire and feelings, with no memory but a strange and puzzling maturity of character, as though some elder person had somewhere lost his body, and could not find it again, and had somehow got into this babe. Then the baby grew physically, and mentally, and began to "get ideas." It entered into danger, for "getting ideas" usually results in ideas getting us. It reminds me of a provincial father, talking to his wife about their adolescent son, and saying with anxiety: "I am afraid our 'Erb's beginning to get ideas.'" It reminds me also of Emerson's warning: "Beware when the almighty lets loose a thinker upon this planet."

That baby got an idea, and then the idea got it, and the idea was "I am so-and-so." And this so-and-so idea kept on growing for a good many years, until suddenly I saw through that trickery, and I laughed, and knew that I was not this dummy, this so-and-so. Not that there was and is no person there, but I know him as a sort of puppet of mine, and I try to keep him clean and useful. He is the only puppet I have in this world, so I take care of him, and I admit he has a considerable grip on me, for, as with all possessions, we are possessed just as much as we possess.

What is this thou that you are? Is it not the same sort of a

[3] *Tat twam asi.*

thou that other people are? Is not the world full of these thous? And are they not mental things, that we can look at mentally? We can almost see that Mr. Jones is composed of certain proportions of this and that quality of character, and has collected a quantity of mental furniture in the shape of memories and more or less fixed ideas. With all that, Mr. Jones is not entirely predictable, as an umbrella is, or even a leg. That thou is not all dummy. There is an I in there, who has a hand on the steering wheel.

It is a question whether this I is in bondage to that thou, whether it has given its main allegiance to the pleasures and pains of the body, and to the prides and fears of the thou-self, or has given it to something that it has found in contemplation as a result of some meditation upon self. If my thoughts about myself have reached the point of a meditation peeping through that gateway into infinity, I shall know myself as That, not as this thou.

This is not an experience that can be described. But it can be said that the I is released from the thou, so that we see the thou in ourselves and call it thou with exactly the same thouness that we apply to other persons. And we then do not make the mistake of calling the thou "I." Then—what joy— when the *guru* says "That, thou art," to us, we know that he is meaning I, and I am aware of my allegiance and devotion to the Glorious Presence which is the same I behind all the thous.

So the process of meditation on this wise saying is clear. First, "That." We must be aware of that Glorious Presence; we must be full of it inside and out, as some of our Hindu friends put it, "like a pot dipped in the sea." Next, we must look at the thou in which we have formerly been submerged, and know it for what it is, a piece of concentration. And then —if this is our happy day—we shall fulfill the *guru's* teaching in our own experience in the spontaneous declaration of an- other of the wise sayings: "That, I am."

This is the pupil's response to the *guru's* teaching, but he has to be careful to avoid any mental content in the assertion. There can be no objectivity on either part. It is a declaration of unity.

A piece of information is now given: "As result of that experience there is no return to the ocean of things." This, too, is to be dwelt upon and understood in all its bearings. The ocean of things describes the world. In several places the sacred lore makes the statement that all the objects in the world are mind-produced, being the outcome of the thoughts and actions of all minds. The ocean of things is thus really an ocean of beings, all of whom in their meditation-actions are producing outposts of themselves. This is very apparent in modern human life; for all the clothing, furniture, buildings, roads, books, etc. are man-produced, and would not be in the world but for him. They are outposts of himself. And if the shape and form of the body has itself resulted from the pressure of the central urge in man, in relation to his environment, in that also we find a man-produced form, as I have previously explained. Add to these the animal-produced objects, plant-produced objects, and even (as I argued in Chapter 2) mineral-produced objects, and we have spread out before us an ocean of things which are not intrinsic being, but depend upon the ways of life. Secondly, all these things are action-meditations; they lead to experience; they are educative toys; all dolls. Thirdly, when any one of the toys has satisfied the need for which we made it, has filled the void whose hunger is our desire, and thus fulfilled for us the purpose of its temporary being we turn from that thing to another. This is where we find what our preachers often call the divine discontent of man, and indeed of all embodied beings. So "there is no return." I will make him a pillar in the temple of my God, says Revelation, and he shall go no more out.

In vedantic thought this teaching is linked with the belief that the human soul returns again and again to rebirth, until the true Self is realized. This is not to be regarded as a mandate. It is understood that it returns under the impulse of unful-filled desire. Theoretically, if a man has become mature in body, and in mind, and he then turns to the Glorious Presence, he should realize the truth of "That, thou art," and then he will not return to the ocean of things. Such a return would mark our failure to live truly, the result of our addiction to unseasonable and immeasured material pleasure, and our con-sequent failure to turn with devotion to the Glorious Presence. If there is rebirth, however, still there is nothing lost, and ex-perience will ultimately carry us, even if will does not, to the point where we peep through the gateway and say "That, I am."

CHAPTER 22

THE FOURTH MEDITATION

In the last meditation we have raised our outlook from the thou in ourselves to the I, and come to the point of saying that this I is one with that Glorious Presence. It is the I in all, but not the thou. How easy it is on reflection to see all the people around us as thous! As such they are not I, but are objects of our knowledge. When my thou (that bundle of ideas and thoughts and loves which are integrated into one thou by service to me, just as the trees and grass and flagstones and water and walls that are here make one enclosed garden on account of their service to the owner, one gardener) is thus distinguished by me from myself, and becomes objective to me, like all those other thous, I shall be overcoming an old error—the instinctive imposition of the thou upon the direct knowledge of myself that is I. This is a matter to be known in I, not to be pictured in thought.

I, thou and it are important words, and if for a while I confine my attention to the little world of this body, I shall find the whole trinity there—God, man and the church—as I, thou and it.

This I-consciousness cannot be an object of meditation, as can the thous and the its, but the reflections upon which we have become engaged can pass over into contemplation, in which there is a new kind of knowledge, called sometimes self-knowledge, which really is not knowledge but is knowing. This knowing is not additional to being, but is in the nature of being itself. This is not something erudite, difficult, to be attained. The whole "secret" is revealed every time we say "I," but we shall know it only when we stop deceiving ourselves, and cease to impose upon it any shred or attribute of the thou. The knower is self-known by direct knowledge. Knowledge is what it is, not what it has. Indeed, knowledge is not the right word for it, but consciousness.

The theme of the fourth meditation is that my I and every I is that one I, the Glorious Presence. After I have said "That am I," my next discovery is that those others are also That—not those thous, but those I's, and then we face the mystery of mysteries, the joy of joys, the presence of all in each. And in the understanding of the thous we see that the practical result is that wherever "I" operates through a thou it makes an outside pseudo-I, an object, in which there is variety mysteriously governed by unity. This is the principle of the whole—the ultimate self-existent power—which governs evolution from within.

MEDITATION IV

Devotion to that Glorious Presence,
Infinite Instructor,
Whose consciousness,
Brilliant as the radiance of a big lamp,
Stationed inside a pot pierced with many holes,
Spreads externally
Through the agency of the eye
And other organs of sense.
Only after that shining as "I know"
Shines this aggregate, the world.

What this stanza tells us is that there is only one Principle of being and it is at the same time the Principle of Knowing. Nothing else sees. And you can rightly say "I am That." This is a matter for your direct experience—not knowledge by thought, if you do not find this fact immediately in yourself, look for your error, in a wrong appraisal of yourself.

Do you think the eye sees? It is not so. Light comes into the eye, carrying with it a picture, and if the eye were a camera, with a sensitive film or plate inside, the picture could be recorded there. But the film or plate in a camera does not *see* the picture that is on it. The kind of limited knowing which we experience as seeing with the eye is found on examination to be only an acceptance of the light-picture in the eye by the knowing "I." This is a true piece of knowledge in its limited sphere, but it is possible only because of the existence or being of the pure I. I can accept the eye-consciousness only after accepting myself. "If the eye could see," wrote an old thinker, "the eye of a dead man, if uninjured, would see."

Having realized this fact we may go on to examine the whole personal consciousness. There is not only the eye, with its peculiar material operation in relation to light, but also the ear with its sound-receptions, also the skin for touch, the tongue for taste, the nose for smell. These, aggregated and unified by the mind, make the personal "self." That mind does not know, any more than the eye sees. Every one of these things in the universe shines with knowledge only in subsidiariness to that which is itself essentially knowing, that of which it can be said that knowing is the nature of its being.

In our meditation, or deep, full and complete thinking on this point, we can pass into that contemplation beyond mentality, in which the "I" is known in the knowing of itself. We can directly know, but first we must think. The mind thinks itself thus into surrender. Or rather, the I releases itself from that more elaborate eye which is the mind— releases itself from the voluntary error of the limited mind-condition.

In this stanza we have come to the root of our being-knowing. The student is advised not to strain his brain by trying to grasp this truth quickly. There is to be no forcing or pressure —but only the quiet continuity of occasional and then more frequent thinking. There is an unseen "growth" going on within, analogous to the growth of the root of a little plant.

This thinking fosters that growth. Do not look for results, but quietly go on, mingling this thinking with your ordinary life, and some time all will come clear.

There comes a time, it has been said, in the life of the student, when his efforts are greatly rewarded, and he sees truths quickly and clearly, no longer needing to go through a slow and laborious process of investigation and comparison of details. Indeed, he will have implicit insight into the truth of the "wise sayings," because he sees and feels and lives so near to the heart of Nature, so much more within the depths of true Being.

Subsidiary to this, but on the way to it, is the thought of the world as the mingling of lives. Let us have done with that old stupidness which makes us see the world as a collection of *things*. All these things that are made one way and another are the little games of the lives that make them, so that in every act we are dealing with lives—something that we do not and cannot make. We are participating in one another's lives, all the way round—that is all. Each person participates because he is a part. Wherever we look we should see and feel the *life* at work.

With this vision of life established, we can next face the most wonderful and supreme thing—the fact that we are all together. To think on this is incredibly rewarding. This person then becomes ready to see in all the other portions of the divine life those perfections which have not been and cannot be vouchsafed to himself. Superior and inferior disappear. Mouse and elephant are equal. The Glorious Presence is at hand.

CHAPTER 23

THE FIFTH MEDITATION

In the fourth meditation we dwelt upon the "I know" consciousness, and read how it is only because of the shining of that one (like the sun reflected in many pools of water—to use another familiar illustration) that there is "I know" in each conscious entity in the whole world. The lesson of it is that the "I know" in us is true and direct knowledge, pure consciousness, though naming it as such sets up a mental condition that we shall have to overcome.

"I am" follows easily upon this. That "I am" is dangerous will be seen in the fifth meditation, which shows how people find that they have slipped into "I am the body" and other such thoughts, or at least given some mental picture to the "am."

The fruitfulness of this meditation will arise from seeing the Glorious Presence as the Destroyer. In Stanza IV it was the producer of the truth "I know"; now it is extolled as the destroyer of "I am this."

MEDITATION V

Devotion to that Glorious Presence,
Infinite Instructor,
Destroyer of the great bewilderment
Sportively produced by the power of maya,
Whereby extremely misguided thinkers assert:
"I am the body"
Or—"the vital functions,"
Or—"the senses,"
Or—"the moving mind,"
Or even—"mere nothing,"
Thus resembling many women, and children,
Or unseeing the dull persons.

Of all objects in our experience, the most difficult to understand is oneself. It is most bewildering. I have explained several times that the act of knowing a thing begins with paying particular attention to it—that is concentration upon it; goes on with examining all its details of material, qualities and actions—that is, meditation upon it; and ends in a capacious but simple idea in the mind, which contains unitedly particulars we have seen to be essential to it. Now I want to draw special attention to this capacity to simplify the complex which indicates the growth of the mind.

In the cat experiment in concentration and meditation we easily found fifty or sixty other things that contributed to the full idea of the object. In making this statement I do not mean that there is merely a mental contribution. Mice have helped to make cats what they are; so has milk. The knowing of the cat's action towards mice is part of the knowing of the cat at the present time. I have dealt with this most fully in Chapter 1.

If there are fifty or sixty things to be known in order to know a cat, how many are there to know ourselves—five or six thousand? But a young child notices only three or four things about the cat—that it is soft, moves about, and has claws. Three or four stand out, and the child is interested in watching the cat, because it is finding more things, increasing its knowledge, which is the chief ingredient in its idea of self. The child is being itself when it is knowing—it is not doing knowing—like doing eating, or doing walking, or doing talking. Knowing is different because it brings quantities of experience together in one mental act. Knowing has more capacity than doing. There is, however, in each mind a certain limited capacity in this knowing; the child has not acquired the ability to unify fifty or sixty things in the cat, but the man has. When we say that many people still have a child mind, this is what we essentially mean. The condition is to be seen in the popular craving for novelty; the child mind cannot dwell long on one thing because its capacity for unification is small, so it absorbs only a few superficial features of the object, and then turns to something else.

Therefore many people know very little about themselves and accept without thought "I am the body," or—a little further on—"I am the vital processes, living, breathing, hungering, thirsting." There have been schools of thought—if we may so call them—among primitive men, among whom a belief in ghosts arose because they felt that "breathing, hungering and thirsting" could not be attributed to a merely material body.

A little further and we have, "I am the senses," and "I am the mind." There are two arguments which show that most civilized people think of themselves as the mind, not the body. If you point out to a man that his body is diseased and advise him to consult a doctor, he is not offended, but is pleased that you are interested; but if you say: "Look here, my friend, it seems to me that your mind is out of order, and I think you had better go to a psychiatrist," he will be deeply hurt—because he feels that in the latter case you have found fault with *him*, but in the former case only with his body.

The second argument takes the form of a question: "What do you fear most, or what would you most abhor—to be injured in an accident, to be ill, to lose your money, to lose your loved ones, or to go mad?" The answer invariably is: "If I must meet with such a disaster, let it be anything but madness."

Finally there is the further thought along the same lines: "The I is not any of these things; it is therefore just nothing at all, but a fancy in the mind."

Such a summit of thought arises from the conception of I as an object. People talk of "I," or "the Ego," or "the Knower." But careful observation of what is going on would convince them that there is no knower, and the conception of any such thing is pure assumption, or fancy. I may as well speak of the horns of a rabbit. The fact is only: "I am *knowing.*"

Look at the facts. If I walk from one end of the room to the other, and someone asks me: "What are you doing? Are you walking?" the proper answer is, "No, I am watching the body walk." If I have puzzled over a problem, and am asked: "Were you thinking?" again the answer is, "No, I was watching the mind think." Of course, in popular speech we say "I walk," and "I think." This is a concession which we have to make among the comparatively unobservant people. But the fact remains that *I* am not involved in this. Sometimes instead of ego the word "self" is used. By those who know, it is used as a concession to the ignorance of others; for those who do not know, it is a word-idol, an object where there is no object. For those who are in between, it is a symbol. Such a symbol, too, is the Glorious Presence. It can be known only through "I."

This is an appropriate place to talk about the Destroyer. It is well known that in popular thought in India, and in the books called Purānas, that is, old traditions, deity is described as three-fold, or three in one, as creator, preserver and destroyer of the world. Creation, preservation and destruction correspond to the three processes of concentration, meditation and contemplation, which three taken together are the essence of yoga practice. When we have finished thinking or meditating upon an idea we see it whole for a moment before we put it aside into the storehouse of memory as done with for the time being. Life is a succession of such processes of attention and withdrawal.

Withdrawal of the mind is indeed destruction. In some of the cities we are instructed by the authorities to burn our rubbish or pay someone to take it away. If we did not do something like this with it, it would accumulate about us and ultimately suffocate us. Creation or production has to have its complement in destruction, which, however, in nine cases out of ten is useful, as when our waste paper is taken away and converted into packing paper and bags.

In Nature, with our superior intelligence, we build a house; then preservation begins. This too requires the application of our intelligence, in repair and repainting, and it is all the better if this work is done continuously, as each little necessity crops up. Let the human intelligence be withdrawn altogether from the house and the inferior intelligence of sub-human Nature will soon destroy it. There are whole cities in every continent which have been overgrown and broken down into ruins by the wild growth of the jungle.

In our mind operations, there will be an immense clutter of rubbish if we do not destroy it. Do we not now and then examine our old beliefs and scientific theories, and deliberately and consciously throw some of them into the discard? If we are today thinking on some theological subject we do not bring in as data a benevolent and all-powerful old gentleman living in the clouds, or a devil carrying a pitchfork and delighting in fire and brimstone, as we might have done in some remote past. I remember that, when I was a very little boy, I was much frightened by something called a "bury-hole" to which somebody told me I would be consigned if I was not good, that is, obedient to them. I remember too another dreadful two or three days of apprehension, when I had swallowed by chance an orange pip, and some undiscerning elder had told me that a tree would grow up my throat and out of my mouth. Sometime, I destroyed those beliefs.

We cannot overestimate the value of intelligent destruction. I am all for the God who destroys when he thinks fit, as well as creates. And I admire that intelligent woman who goes through her rooms now and then, and throws away or gives away or sells the things which do not serve her, and she is not likely to need in the reasonable future.

For the enlightenment of what one yogī called "our superstitious masses"—with no trace of contemptuousness, be it emphatically stated—the Puranas relate many allegorical stories about Shiva, that aspect of the triple god which is especially concerned with the destruction of the rubbish of life, the things no longer useful to us. It is understood, of course, by the more thoughtful, that deities work through us, not upon us, so Shiva becomes the patron and object of special devotion to all those men and women who have resolved to destroy or get rid of all the possessions—objects in the world and ideas in the mind—which obstruct their pathway to realization of the Glorious Presence, their attainment of the knowledge: "That, I am." Shiva is thought of as perfect in freedom and in the fulfillment of yoga-meditation, that is, knowledge of "I." He is depicted sometimes as dancing on a dwarf. The dwarf is called the "man of forgetfulness." He is that person we erroneously think ourselves to be when we have forgotten "That, I am." In union with Shiva, the devotees say, we too will dance with joy upon the back of that old dwarf.[1]

Shiva is always depicted as holding various symbols in his hands. The figures vary in different temples, but destruction is emphasized, and he is associated with fire and skulls and cremations, not to inspire dislike for the body and the world, but to inform us that there is triumph over these things, while his dancing indicates that being and knowing are also accompanied by joy. This principle of destruction is the liberating member of the trinity. Of the three, Shiva is especially joy. In many pictures he is represented as sitting up in the Himālaya mountains, looking over the world—in this resembling our South-facing Form—with the new moon as an ornament in his long hair, from the meshes of which the Ganges (a goddess) comes tumbling forth, a third eye in the center of his forehead, a blue throat (due to drinking up the poison of the

[1] See *Song of Praise to the Dancing Shiva*, translated and commented upon by Ernest Wood. Published 1928 by Ganesh and Co., Madras, India.

world—another idea of the divine sacrifice), wearing snakes and tiger-skin, carrying a trident, a sword, an axe, a flame, a diamond, a noose, a drum, an elephant goad, etc. and making signs of protection and enlightenment. One can imagine what a lot of food for thought there is in the pictures of this symbolic personage.

The use of the word sport in connection with the action of māyā is deliberately intended to remind the devotee and aspirant not to read mentally-understood intention into the covering-up and the spreading-forth, which we have found in the human mind as concentration and meditation, and in human action in the production or making of any article of a pre-determined kind.

We must not let the mind come in and formulate a goal. This is the worst sin on the path of yoga; and the worst of it is that you will get what you ask for and miss the better thing that you cannot know in advance. We are not coming to something which is a glorified copy of what we know; heavens full of glorified American girls, or harpists sitting on golden seats with crowns of merit upon their heads, not even the society of *gurus* and deities. Even when we go to a sculptural exhibition, we cannot pre-determine what we are going to see. But when we get inside, we catch our breath and exclaim: "I never knew that the curve of a child's head is so beautiful!" In yoga, everything that we meditate upon will give us something that we cannot in any way predict. Every lesson in life brings something that we shall miss if we allow the mind to step between and say that this is to teach me so and so, thus pre-determining the result. And in that greatest meditation, the experiencing of "I," shall that trader on the sidewalk, the thinking mind, be allowed to pick up from his stall a piece of soap or a candle, and tell us that this is the sort of thing to look for when we seek the self? Indeed, if Shiva speaks within us he will say something very different:

"Divest yourself even of the thoughts of seeking and of self. See through the clouds; the Glorious Presence is there, and that thou art."

Speaking of pictures and images—and the whole world as composed of such things—Shankara gives a warning. Buddha too, in the words of *The Light of Asia*, by Sir Edwin Arnold, warns the aspirant:

"Sink not the string of thought into the fathomless; who asks doth err, who answers errs. Say nought."

In this respect, Sankara and Buddha are at one. There is something of the same depth also in the scripture which says: "No man hath seen God at any time." I put the emphasis on "man," for realization of the Truth will be ours when we transcend the mind.

If we say, with Kant, that the moral principle in man is testimony to the presence of the divine, even though the argument be sound, we are still only in the region of mental inference, which is a situation not altogether pleasing to the religious devotee, who will be satisfied with nothing less than direct knowledge, for which inference cannot be regarded as anything more than a temporary deputy or scaffolding.

So there is great meaning in this nonapplication of purpose to the process of māyā. It is not purpose as we think purpose. Life is more like a dance or a piece of music than the painting of a picture, and none will say that the last movement of a dance or the last note of a melody is the goal of it, or its purpose. Our meditation is an opening of the mind and heart, to be and know.

CHAPTER 24

THE SIXTH MEDITATION

In meditations four and five, we have looked at the two processes of *forthcoming*, like a light shining from inside a pot pierced with many holes, and of *withdrawal* from the mistakes that obscure the light, so that the light shines full even in our darkness.

We are now in a position to say that the "shuttle action" of conscious life, or the succession of contractions and expansions, is not a pair of contrary actions, like a man going out of the house into the garden and then back again. The light of "I know" shines, is absorbed by the darkness, but not wholly absorbed, grows stronger and purer, overcomes the darkness, and shines again as pure "I know." The destruction is not of the light, but of ignorance.

This is a good example of enveloping causation—like the enveloping causality of the sun in relation to the rotating earth, in the production of day and night—not to be confused with succession-causation. The succession-causation that we speak about in science has no foundation in experience. No one has ever seen such causation at work. We have only seen "invariable sequence," and formulated the statement that if and when the same prior group of events recurs, the same posterior events will arise—that consequence will always be the same when presequence is the same! This "triumph of logic" resembles a great amount of other so-called thinking in the world in which the conclusion is implied in the premises and does not add to our knowledge. The result being the same when the cause is the same implies "all the causes"; and that means the enveloping cause, which must remain the same throughout the result, and be there to sustain that result, like the sun which is present all the time.

In life, however, the same situation never recurs exactly. Life is always to some extent unpredictable; it is, in fact, the unpredictable in Nature that we call life. Those men who claimed to be able to take liberties with lions because they knew the psychology of those animals very well frequently lost their lives in the end. Among all the creatures that we know the human is the most unpredictable.

This understanding of the process of knowledge disposes of the question: "Why should consciousness envelop itself in ignorance and then work its way out again?" The answer is: "Observe what takes place in human life. The thing you see limits you in the beginning, not in the end. In the end the thing can still be there but you are not limited by it. You see through it." As I have said before, everything is a gateway to infinity. Experience tells us that at the end of any process things will not be exactly the same as at the beginning, but this does not authorize us to say why or how, because even sameness and difference themselves will not be the same to us at the end as they were in the beginning. The only practical good sense is to wait and see, and not try to pre-determine the end in the means. Remember too that in this case the end is the envelope—the whole dance, the whole piece of music— not the end one of a series of things. As we grow older we take more things into account, and are less hag-ridden by the application of succession-causation to a goal.

Let us put it another way. A cat may look at a king, but does not know what a king is. Only a king knows a king—how uneasy is that head that wears a crown. In the process of human knowledge we are kings; we know what is taking place. It is the nearest thing to us, and therefore the best norm of reality —the "lo, here," not the "lo, there" of so-called material and efficient causes, which are less enveloping than what we directly know.

A curious thing happened this morning. My wife and I are staying at present in a house away up on top of a hill, two miles above the town. We have a car. Yesterday we decided that it was high time to have the car properly cleaned and polished, so we spoke to a service station executive about it, and he said: "Tomorrow morning I will send a man up to bring the car down, and we will return it to you in the evening." Last evening, my wife and I spent quite a little while speculating as to how the man would come up. Would he walk? No, indeed, being an American. Would he come up on a motor-bike, or in a car, and leave it here all day? Quite possibly; but would not that put the bike or car out of action when it might be wanted for some other purpose? In the morning the problem was solved. Two men came up in a service car and one of them drove it back! The executive's "meditation" on the subject was better than ours. Our minds were blocked by the statement, "a man." A great many conjuring tricks are seen to be perfectly simple when you know how they are done, but perfectly baffling before. These reflections remind me of a story about a truck driver who, going under a viaduct with a high load, got his load wedged against the roof, so that he could drive neither back nor forward. He had been scratching his head over his problem for quite a while when a small boy came along, looked the situation over, and said: "Hey, mister, will yer give me a dime for ice-cream if I tell yer how to get loose?" The driver agreed, and the boy said: "Let some air out of yer tires."

I am tempted to tell here my little story about Isaac Newton —which, I fear, has recurred too often in my lectures in various places. There was in his day a constant question: "Why do apples fall to the ground?" One day the youth was lying under a tree, puzzling this over, when it suddenly dawned upon him that apples do not fall to the ground, but the apple and the earth attract each other, and fly into each other's arms. Only when the error in the question disappeared could the truth flow in. This discovery of the "principle of gravitation" is one of the best examples of intuition that I have come across, and it shows a mind-movement towards enveloping cause.

If you cannot solve your problem, probably you have shut the answer out by a piece of self-inflicted ignorance. This is a kind of mind-blinding, which the art of contemplation will help to allay.

We are now in form for the sixth meditation.

MEDITATION VI

Devotion to that Glorious Presence,
Infinite Instructor,
The real man,
Who,
Because of being hidden by maya
Resembles the sun or the moon
    caught in an eclipse;
Yet, all the senses being withheld,
When he was in deep sleep,
Was constituted of pure being itself,
Which, at the time of waking
Is confirmed by the knowledge,
"I was sleeping just before now."

In the alternation of waking and sleeping it is in the waking state that our consciousness meets with most resistance. It is blocked at every turn by the objects of the senses. The senses themselves bring us into this servitude. "Is it not a good thing that we have eyes," people say, "for with their aid we can see?" But strictly, the eye is as much a limiting as an enabling instrument, for it is geared to the light rays only.

There is a sense in which it can be said that we see because we cannot see. If the eye were geared to the rays that pass through the walls, such as those used in the radio or wireless telephone, we would see right through the wall. It would be transparent to us, and therefore unseen. So perfect sight would be no sight at all.

The next point of interest is that the obstructiveness of things is beneficial to us, because it anchors and ballasts our minds, and thus produces conditions in which we can very definitely think. If our minds were open to receive pictures of the whole world of things, they would come pouring in upon us overwhelmingly, but as it is, we are assisted by the limits of the senses to receive just about as much as we can at present grasp.

The ballasting effect is well seen when we want to work something out in our minds. The musical composer, having a new tune sounding in his mind, runs to the piano to get it pinned down so that it does not elude him, and also in order to fix it while he works at the improvement of details. Where would we be without our note books, address books, telephone books, account books? We would be mentally flopping about like persons without bones. In a word, we would be in a dream.

That is the state of dream. Some people daydream or drift most of the time. We describe them as persons who have very little control of mind. Nothing but the insistence of external events compels sufficient of their attention for even the minimum of thinking. Night dreaming is mostly of the same kind, with even less ballast, and less control, than daydreaming. In daydreaming there is at least a little rationality to take the edge off the play of fancies, and to tone them down. Yet we must not overlook the important fact that in the dream state the visualization of the pictures thrown up by the mind is far clearer than that of our daydreaming. There is nothing to inhibit its incoherent exuberance, but also there is nothing to inhibit its clarity of vision. For example, the other night I dreamt that I was taking a long voyage on a luxury steamer; we had on board the Himālaya mountains, with their wonderful snowy peaks, and also a splendid oriental garden, with palm trees and all the rest! Fantastic as this may seem, it was a valuable experience, because of its clearness and detail, and because of an educative value which I hope to explain more fully in Chapter 28.

It is interesting that we do not feel any actual pain in dreams, though we may have plenty of mental pain in the form of fear, terror, hurt pride, despondency, disappointment, frustration, helplessness and what not.

It is noteworthy also that when this state is induced suggestively in the practice of hypnotism, some kind of external control is exercised by the operator, who is able to guide these "dreams" and give them some order and purpose. He can even give directions to the mind as to what to remember and what not to remember in the subsequent waking state.

Another thing that is revealed to us, sometimes in ordinary dreams, and often in those hypnotically induced, is the perfection of memory when it is well held and not allowed to branch away into the irrelevant. Only today in the newspapers the case is described of a woman in New York who is now 29 years old, happily married and the mother of two children. Nine years ago, it is recorded, she found herself walking dazedly along a highway in Pennsylvania, with no memory of her name, or home, or childhood. To support herself she took a post as waitress, and afterwards she married and settled down. A few days ago, however, a psychiatrist, using hypnotism, succeeded in breaking through the block in her memory, so that she now remembers her girlhood, and has made herself known to the parents who thought she was irretrievably lost.

Our memories of dreams are usually very fragmentary and imperfect at best. They are difficult to capture when we wake, and usually the harder we try the more quickly they fade. The best condition for their reception is one of very quiet watching, without search or thought. Recollection thus being so imperfect, we must acknowledge that we have very little reliable knowledge as to what the dream state is really like.

But we know enough to assure us that it will be very well worth while to try to know more.

First you should observe for yourself by an inspection of your own dreams how much clearer your dream-images are than those you try to picture in the waking mind, perhaps in meditation. Neglect the quality of irrationality and discontinuity in the dreams while observing this fact. Think of the value of this clarity of vision and how useful it is when brought into the waking state. Many thinkers deliberately sleep on their problems, and come out of their dreams with ideas far clearer than they had before. Because of the absence of rationalizing in that state we are honest with ourselves—if a man is a coward, he acts the coward in that state; though he may have many devices for saving his face to himself in the waking state. The psychopathic conflicts of our waking state are often resolved in the dream state, because of this clear seeing.

There is a practical utility in this knowledge. If you have dwelt a little upon your memories of dreams, quietly and observantly, without shattering them by thought (and without trying to interpret them), but sufficiently to see that their honesty is equal to their clarity—you will have a new respect for the dream state and a new confidence in it. In future, then —this is a bit of practical yoga—you will every night slip smoothly into sleep far more peacefully and happily than ever you did before, because you will feel that you are going into a deeply good and effortless house, wherein there is balm and healing. From such dreams or sleep you will wake renewed in your depths of body and of mind.

The ancient Aryan Vedantists insisted that the three states of waking, dreaming and deep sleep are three distinctly different conditions of the real man that we are. In the first, he is fully attending to limited sensory experiences which enable him to obtain clear ideas, in the second he has dropped that ballast, and is letting the mind look freely at the pictures collected with the aid of ballast in the waking state, and in the third he has dropped even mind—or, I should say, almost dropped it—and so is described as pure consciousness, knowing "I know."

"I know—what?" you will ask. "I know myself"—provided we make no error in the definition of that self. When, nine years ago, the lady found herself walking along an unfamiliar road with no memory of who she was, was she or was she not the same thinking and feeling entity that she had been a month before? She most certainly was the same, but with her lapse of memory she had lost one of her ideas, with all its connecting links—the idea of Miss S. Is not a person the same sufferer of toothache who was suffering toothache before he went to the dentist, though he does not try to recall that suffering in memory just now?

This is a most important thing to realize—that we are not our mental pictures of ourselves, but are pure "I know." If then, in deep sleep I am experiencing something which I cannot remember in my waking state, because it has no parity with my experiences in the limitations of my waking state, that is no reason for disbelief in such a state. We have reasoned, have we not, quite convincingly, that our present waking state is one in which we are subject to great restrictions upon our possibilities of consciousness, and when we add to that the terrific block in memory caused by the mental production of a false ego with a mass of associations in which we have become more interested than in anything else, what hope is there for even a glimpse of the true "I know" while in this state?

But, someone will ask, why assume such a thing? First, when there is consciousness it cannot become unconsciousness, though there can be absence of the false ego, with all its memory-associations. In deep sleep, then, there is experience containing the absence of the limitations of the waking and dreaming states, but not the absence of that central core "I know," and not the absence of being and the joy of knowing and being. At that point there must be some "environment" also, but it is an object of contemplation, not of concentration, or even meditation.

Secondly, this has been declared to us by mystics, as they are called, of both East and West. Mystics are so called because they see "with the eyes closed." They see what can be seen without eyes, and hear what can be heard without ears. Their testimony should be received, not, I would say, with mere belief, but with serious consideration.

The proposition before us is that this world is not like a triangle with its apex at the top, $\triangle$, broadly based on material foundations, and narrowing upwards to spirituality, but, on the contrary, is like a triangle pointing downwards, $\triangledown$, broadly based in spirituality, and becoming less and less complete and more and more limited as we descend to materiality.

The claim is that self-recognition, or "I know," is the most fundamental thing in our existence, and it does not depend upon any particular memory or group of memories for its support or sustenance.

In the present stanza there is an indication that the same principle applies to the Glorious Presence and to ourselves. What can be said of the one can be said of the other, if, indeed, the two be not regarded as one.

The clue to the central power in our lives is in the word "I." I am only really I in myself when the false ego, the mental idea of self, is looked upon as one of the many "thous" in the world. I must recognize the "thou here," as being of the same nature as the "thou there." All these thous are different in particulars. However, if I think of an "I there" (in another person) as I do "I here" (in myself), again I must recognize them as of the same nature, but I must add that I can think of no difference between one I and another I, as I can between one you and another you, or between one it and another it. All these I's are the same.

There is a third sort of evidence for our being conscious in the deep sleeping state. When we wake, we can remember that we slept, and that we enjoyed that sleep. It is not: "I feel happy now, so I *infer* that I must have slept happily," but there is a definite memory that we slept happily, that we were experiencing something then, though not the things we meet in the waking and dreaming states.

An impatient voice now seems to speak to me in my imagination: "What is the use of all this, even if true—this talking about experience outside our reach?" It is not mere talk. It is thinking, the kind of thinking that cracks the carapace of cramped ideas. Knowledge is the way to realization of new widths of consciousness as well as new material liberties. And if the weakening of the grip of the false ego is attained through knowledge, we shall less fear its fading, and will be the more ready to enjoy the wider consciousness obtainable by overcoming it now, or by finding release from it in death, which, after all, may turn this grub into a butterfly. Knowledge itself will make us free; we need not *do* anything in the matter.

One last matter. I may have given the impression that this release from the false ego involves something totally out of this world. It is not really so, for the same "I know" is present in all three stages. The prides and hopes and fears of the false ego, bent upon its own preservation and enhancement, give us a piteous time. To know it for what it is leaves us freer for the present adventure of living and more conscious of the powers that we even now enjoy, which are easily obscured and inhibited by its prides and fears and hopes.

When things and even the false ego are set aside in deep sleep we receive our best healing for both mind and body, and some say that from there also they receive also their best leading, that it is the well-spring of the essential motivation of our body-life and our mind-life. Sages and saints in their self-induced tranquillity[1] of mind and body similar to sleep outwardly but fully conscious within—have declared their expe-

[1] *Samādhi.*

rience of a new and higher life, which they cannot describe because its content is different from our bodily and mental experience, but which nevertheless brings back a sort of radiant peace and poise even into this.

So there is in this practice no devaluation of our life at the surface of things. Experience will still have its effect. But a deeper motivation will be at work in us, and will have its way.

CHAPTER 25

THE SEVENTH MEDITATION

In the seventh meditation the over-all thought is that in any state or condition that may arise the "I" is present. I remember that one Vedantic teacher in India once said to a would-be pupil: "Your consciousness would not be any the worse if it were put into the brain of an ant." "I" would still be there; but not the human personality-picture, of course.

Even though there is a covering-up of the light of consciousness, or what we have called a self-limitation, in an act of concentration, the "I" is still fully there.

MEDITATION VII

> Devotion to that Glorious Presence,
> Infinite Instructor,
> Who,
> By means of the auspicious hand-sign,
> Makes clear to the worshippers
> His own real nature
> Always shining within as "I,"
> Following into all the successive states—
> Those beginning with childhood,
> And those beginning with waking.

The Auspicious Hand-sign is made by joining the tip of the first finger to the tip of the thumb, forming a circle, and leaving the other three fingers loosely extended, thus:

It is a symbol which has been called in Sanskrit literature by various names, such as the symbol of wisdom, of study, of teaching and of consciousness. Here it combines all these four meanings. When the Instructor is pictured as using it, there is wisdom, teaching and study, while the symbol in itself represents the consciousness, or "I," which is the same as "I know," or "Knowing, I am."

I have already explained the three essential ways to obtain knowledge about the world: by seeing or sensing, by reasoning, and by being informed by a reliable witness. However, this knowledge by which we say "I" is not obtained by any of these means, but directly. It is the very being of knowing, now and always, just as much as it is the knowing of being. As a symbol of this, the Auspicious Hand-sign reminds the erring mind of this truth, which comes into view as the background of all our thought or study, as soon as the instructor or *guru* raises his hand. He is saying, in effect: "This is at the back of all our thought, the basis of all our knowledge, taken for granted as affecting every piece of knowledge."

We must go so far as to say that no thinking about the "I" can prove its presence. To assign any character to it is to deny it, and tend to shut it out. It is present as the background of error as well as of truth. As it is beyond proof, so it is beyond memory. But it is the power in the will.

In its aspect of wisdom, instruction and study the hand-sign has much to tell, by symbolical teaching which is simpler and fuller than the use of words. It has the extra advantage that while it holds for the student what he has been taught in words or what he has discovered, it still stands before him as full of suggestions for further thought. A sentence is a closed thought, but a symbol, if well-appointed, is an open one.

The circle made by the thumb and forefinger may be taken as a symbol of unity, of the boundless all, of space that is never empty. The three fingers declare the triplicity which is present always in the world (matter, energy and natural law) and in the mind (will, feeling and thought). The triplicity at the back of things also appears in the two sets of successive states which are mentioned in this meditation—the states of waking, dream and deep sleep, and the states of childhood, maturity and old age. It is there also in every act and thought as concentration, meditation and contemplation, bringing each act to full cycle.

There is, to judge from experience, a three-fold cyclic impulse within us and in the world, whereby changes take place in which our mind has no say, and for which we see no cause. It is something beyond the mind. It is responsible for the phases of life. Although evolutionary forms can be ascribed to the conscious mind, behind and beyond both forms and mind there is the cyclic process, including childhood, maturity and old age, also waking, dreaming and sleeping, and concentration, meditation and contemplation, which take place whether we think them or not. I know that some have said that old age comes on when we expect it, and even death is produced by thought. Cessation of all interest in anything could lead to death, no doubt, but before we credit too much to the human mind, we had better observe that even the animals and the trees go through the same course, and thus present us with examples disproving the argument.

The cause of the successive states is evidently something enveloping and inclusive; we certainly cannot say that waking is the cause of sleeping, or childhood of old age.

Knowledge of the presence of "I" (I ought not to say "the I," for might I not then be inviting the reader to think of it, when really he must not think it, nor feel it, but only "I" it?) in all the three states is not to be confused with the mistake of superimposition[1] about which Shankara and many other teachers and commentators have so fully written. "I" is present in its own right in all states. We know this by the direct experience of being conscious,[2] which is independent of all modes of knowing things, such as perception and inference, and independent of memory.

The mistake of superimposition is described as follows in the *Mānasollāsa:* "On account of ignorance, the attributes of the body, which is insentient, unreal and finite, are ascribed to the conscious self, and (conversely) reality, consciousness, and joy (which are the very nature of the self) are ascribed to the body." This is how the false self "I am a man," and what is more, "I am a man of such and such a kind," is set up in our minds.

So importantly is this matter regarded in the eyes of Shankara and other ancient Aryan teachers that I must not dismiss it briefly here, without some further play of thought upon it. I therefore now offer a free translation of Shankara's own statement upon it in his *Commentary on the Brahmasūtras,* keeping exactly to Shankara's ideas, but not to his sequence. I have numbered the thoughts that come up, to facilitate a full grasp of the whole idea. Although this is put forward as an argument, not as a meditation, suitable pauses, in which there is some pondering on the meaning of the items successively brought in, will help.

[1] *Adhyāsa.*
[2] *Pratyabhijnāna.*

1. As regards the connotations of "you" and "I,"

2. Which are object and subject,

3. It is an established fact that it is inconceivable for one to be the same as the other,

4. Their very natures being opposed,

5. As are, for example, those of darkness and light.

6. Still more inconceivable is it for the qualities also of one to be the same as those of the other.

7. It therefore follows that the superimposition of the connotation of the "you," that is, of the object, and its attributes,

8. Upon the connotation of the "I," that is, of the subject, which is of the nature of consciousness,

9. And conversely, the superimposition of the subject and its attributes on the object,

10. Is correctly called false.

11. Still, there is in the world a common instinctive custom of saying "I am this," and "This is mine,"

12. Mixing error with truth,

13. Due to false knowledge,

14. Which, by lack of discrimination of objects and qualities which are totally different,

15. Has superimposed mutually, one upon the other, the nature of one upon the other, and the attributes of one upon the other.

In the foregoing argument the word "you" applies to everything in the world; both the things in the category "it" and the living beings in the category "you." Previously I have spoken of three kinds of things, its, yous and I, but here Shankara lumps together the its and the yous in one group for simplicity and convenience.

And now, what is to be done about this? One person will say, "I don't care if there is an error. I am willing to go on living in the same old way, which on the whole I enjoy, only trying to get more comfort and security for myself and others than we have had before!"

To this, the old vedantist would reply: "Very well. There is no harm in that. In course of time, we believe, all men will slowly grow into a maturity which will cause them to want to spread their wings for a higher flight, but in the meantime,

all will go well with those who are good to others, fitting harmoniously into the collective life."

But to those who wish to pursue this meditation further,
a warning must now be issued: do not regard the I and the you
as contraries. Do not leap from one error into another. Contraries, or "pairs of opposites," as they are frequently called
in the old books, are always similars. They are opposite poles
of the same thing, opposite ends of the same stick. Examples
of pairs of opposites are: hot and cold (both temperatures);
big and little (both sizes); man and woman (both human beings); mouse and elephant (both animals); mind and body (the
two opposing and contrasting features of our ordinary life).

"I" and "you" are to be thought of as totally disparate.
They have nothing at all in common. They do not contrast.
They are not a pair of opposites.

So, in meditation, to pass over from the you-error in myself
into the I-truth, I cannot negate the common errors "I am a
man; I am this; This is mine"; by saying "I am not a man; I
am not this; This is not mine." These negations set me over
against the states denied, but they are still of the same class.
Though negations in words, they remain positive in thought.
In such a case I put myself in new categories of the same kind,
on the same old level. I am really then saying: "I am a non-
man; I am a non-this; I am a non-owner of this."

The discrimination required involves such a cherishing of
the I-consciousness and I-nature as such, such a frequent opening of ourselves in contemplation, beyond thought and feeling,
to which we naturally trend in the fulfillment of thought, that
the gate is bound to open. I will not say it calls for meditation
on "I," but for I-meditation. True, the meditation will begin
in thought about what the I does in our lives, but it will be fulfilled in contemplation and the arising therein of the new experience—*the I-ing of I*. Analogous to thinking and feeling
is I-ing.

And then, may I say, we shall more and more understand

how the greater can be in the lesser, but not the lesser in the greater, and how the All can be in each? We shall be on the way to a true grasp of pure consciousness, free life and the infinite, which cannot be put in contrast with anything, such as finity and bondage. It is no wonder, is it, that those who have attained these heights cannot tell us what they know?

CHAPTER 26

THE EIGHTH MEDITATION

Do not forget, Shankara seems to say in the eighth meditation, that the Glorious Presence is still here in the midst of all the pairs of opposites of the world. We were prepared to understand this by the seventh meditation, especially by the warning not to fall into the error of regarding "you" and "I" as a pair of opposites, or contraries. The fact is that the relations of those pairs are usually seen from a strictly personal point of view. It may seem to me that Mr. Selby is the owner of the dog "Blackie," and in the eye of the law and the tax-collector it may be so, but a perfectly impartial observer might equally see the cogency of Blackie's thought that Mr. Selby is his master, from whom as such something is due. Even in ownership in which no moral obligations are involved—as they are in the ownership of a fellow-being like Blackie—there is a mutuality of possessiveness, whereby a man is the servant of his house, his automobile, his tools, and even his clothes, not to speak of his body and his mind. Released from such possessiveness—I am not advocating the full practice all at once of this counsel of perfection—a man can enjoy his neighbor's enjoyment of his car; speaking for myself, for example I know it gives me great pleasure when I see the pleasure of that young couple across the street and their children—all so full of energy—when they pile themselves and miscellaneous belongings into their car on a sunny morning to whirl away for a day on the beach.

In the appraisal of things, much depends on the point of view. And then—an important matter—the way of looking out from that point of view, for in accordance with the state of our own minds the appearance of things can change within a very wide range. Then our actions will change. Then our view-point will change. Then our viewing will change again.

So it seems that it is not by giving up our point of view as definite persons—that we shall attain release from the bondage of possessions, but by a new poise of mind on the edge of infinity, in which thought has become servant of love, and love has become infused with that deep purpose of the will which makes this living what it is. By contemplation of the Presence, given admission by us to ourselves, freedom will be found.

In the eighth meditation there is a return to look upon the world again, with the thought in mind that in the midst of it the I can still be itself, and the gateway to the All.

MEDITATION VIII

Devotion to that Glorious Presence
Infinite Instructor,
This Real Man,
Who,
Being whirled about by maya
In the dream or in the waking state
Views the whole world brokenly,
Through relationships
Of effect and cause,
Of servant and master,
Of pupil and teacher,
Also of father and son,
And others of this nature.

The author of these meditations is evidently sending us back to review this situation in order that we may come to realize that even in the world of $m\bar{a}y\bar{a}$—in the midst of the limitations —the real man, the I, is unchanged, is in no wise bereft of his essential nature. This is so because "I" cannot be put in contrast with all these "yous." The false self, however, is one of the yous, and if the "I" becomes involved in this, and says "I am this" and "This is mine" he is being whirled about by *māyā* in the waking and dreaming states. His actions are then motivated from outside.

Views and actions alternate. According to our view of things we act. If you do not like carrots and obstinately refuse to acquire the taste for them by means of the necessary perseverance, you will not grow carrots in your kitchen garden, or you will not buy them from the market. So the world is changed to some extent by your views, through your acts. That world now reacts upon your body and mind, sets up pleasures and pains, and new likings and dislikings with which you view the world and upon which again you act.

When we regard this process as wide-spread—all of us, including animals and plants and, if I may be so bold, even minerals—we arrive at the conclusion that the whole world exhibits the effects of the outlooks of all the beings who are in it. This is Shankara's view. I have found the same clearly stated in several old Sanskrit philosophical works, which are highly prized in India. Indeed, I read only the other day of an Indian *guru*—one whose teachings are in line with that soberest of all philosophies, the Vedanta—who was asked, in an interview, what is the best thing to do in the case of very serious illness. His reply was that first one should take all the sensible scientific steps to deal with the case practically. Then he went on at some length to say that one must very seriously think about the matter, and see that directly or indirectly, and sooner or later, all such things are an indication of wrong ways of living and thinking, based upon wrong outlooks coming from experience not carefully examined. He said that the tendency of people is to escape from trouble or to dash into immoderate sense-pleasures without taking the trouble to see what they are really doing.

Shankara held to the age-old belief—which is found in all the vast collection of nursery stories and heroic legends with which the mothers of India regale their young, as well as in the old traditional and classic literature—that the human being who does not reach self-realization and thereby release from his present mayavic condition, will be reborn again and again until he succeeds. In these circumstances, it is held, on his return to birth he will meet the results of his actions in the past, obtaining what he has "made for himself." I have met in India sober followers of the yoga methods who say they can remember such past lives, but maintain—as the books also do—that past lives are neither interesting nor useful to know, and that the important thing for us to see and know as clearly and fully as possible is what we are now thinking and doing. In my translation of the yoga Aphorisms of Patanjali, the student will find his statement that the "psychic powers" are an obstacle to the Contemplation.

This belief in a series of births is, however, not a requisite for understanding and living this philosophy. Some believe that the incomplete man after death will find his opportunity in some other way. The important thing for us is the fullest possible present living in the fullest light of our intelligence and of that wide and varied sympathy which is briefly called love. One piece of advice one can give in this connection is this: "Even if you do not believe in your immortality, you had better live and act as if you did"—for it is well known that in later life many people make no fruitful efforts and follow up no fruitful lines of study and thought, because "there is not time for that now."

I beg to be excused for this dissertation, which I felt to be in place because the Vedanta system holds that in every man there is a sufficient present spark of the divine to remind him every now and then of itself, and to leave him never entirely pleased merely with the pleasures of the senses. Indeed, the doctrine goes further and states that in some way all the experiences of life tend to wake each one of us to the reality— or as I have put it, all things when fully contemplated are gateways to infinity. There is something in man which a cow or a hen has not, by which man can wing his way into the empyrean; it is really however only a matter of degree of growth, and that something has been working within, small but not entirely silent, until now the bud is ready to blossom into flower. This is not merely a matter of some mystic inner experience; it is even more an irradiation of the "point of view" which in its turn can make all our life new and bring into it a glow from the pure consciousness and pure joy of our true and essential being. That is enough for now. Let us await the outcome of our meditations.

The statement of outlook through relativity, mentioned in this eighth meditation, is very much in line with modern thought. Each statement is true, within the prescribed conditions. As a little boy I had grand ideas of my father, but it never occurred to me to think of him as a son—the son of my grandfather. Later I learned that the same man can be father and son, brother and husband—and, yes, even in some degree a wife to his life's companion, as she is on occasions something of a husband to him. At the same time master is servant and servant is master, teacher is pupil and pupil is teacher. And what is more, everything is in some degree our servant and our master, our teacher and our pupil, our father and our son.

The height of this relativity is that we do not know whether this body of ours is standing on head or heels, is moving this way or that, is revolving and racing along at what giddy pace and in what direction along with this earth of ours. And the height of wisdom is to accept this situation—like a goldfish in a pond—and see the infinite importance of such relative facts as that I can lift my hand to the plow, my heart to my neighbor, and my will to the impulse of my being. There is freedom and infinitude in these apparently relative and limited powers, for the simple reason that it is quality not quantity that counts in life, and is at last the basis of reality.

The old Vedantists had a nice simile for this truth. They said that we can dream of a snake, and in the dream the snake can bite us—and wake us out of the dream! It is the unreal snake that can sting us out of the dream into the waking state. "Even the Vedanta," says the *Mānasollāsa*, "though in itself false, can be a means for us to awaken to the reality—like a picture." That picture on the wall; showing a rock-bound coast and an angry sea—it is not altogether false, although it is not altogether true. Such is the nature of māyā—it is not unreal, nor is it real. Here again is something which is not one of a pair of opposites, but is a fit companion—or mirror image perhaps—of the incomparable "I."

CHAPTER 27

THE NINTH MEDITATION

The thought with which we begin the ninth meditation is that, after all, even the world, regarded as external, is at last only the one self. In the previous meditation we were thinking that the self is *in* everything; now we have the deeper and more inclusive thought that everything is *in* the self. We have followed a course something like this: the discovery of the all as the basis of the apparent parts, the discovery that the "I" we know is essentially that all, the search for this "I" in any chosen object of thought, and then the attempt to realize the all as enveloping, pervading and in fact being not merely in, but the whole of, everything. We come to the knowledge that the all is to be grasped in terms of "I," not in terms of "it" or "you," so the meditations are intended to lead on *beyond thought* into the new state of consciousness, which will gradually become natural and inconspicuously present, just as the eyes slowly become able to see after we have moved from a lighted room into a dark one. So comes about the dissolution of *māyā* and of the false self.

MEDITATION IX

Devotion to that Glorious Presence,
Infinite Instructor,
Of whom this is an eight-fold form,
Including the animate and the inanimate,
Appearing as what we call earth, water, fire, air,
The sky-matter,
The sun and the moon,
And the life in man,
Beyond whose all-presence

There is naught else
To be found by any searchers.

The infusion of pure self more and more into our lives and the diffusion of illusions need not necessarily produce any sudden illumination, but will more often be like a dawning in the sky; we do not notice it very much when it is there and we have forgotten the darkness that preceded the dawn. In effect it will mean that we have a deeper poise and point of reference within, amidst our experience, and we are not so easily upset by outside occurrences. The false self is becoming more known as but a puppet of ours, less influential in our counsels. And we find the Infinite Instructor with delight, even in things which we may have disliked before. We have now many occasions for the enjoyment of beauty, truth, goodness, harmony, understanding, love and freedom, where we had few before.

This awakening into a life in which first principles and the eternal values are more lived with is not a matter of excitement and novelty, which may easily be titillations of the false self well within the field of *māyā*. We shall not be thinking of the Instructor personally either, or looking mentally for lessons, but we shall be feeling that presence, and finding that we have thousands of occasions of thanksgiving for its divine companionship, in relation to all things. It is not a startlingly new piece of experience or of sensation that is going to sail into our field of vision. We are not looking for a sign. There is no thought of some natural kind of priestcraft in all this, whereby we receive some opening of consciousness through a "you"— some object-person in the external world, who has somehow obtained a "gift of the spirit" and can hand it on. Our unfoldment is like that of a rose—foolish indeed would it be to try to bring the rose to full bloom by pulling out its petals with the hand.

It will now be seen that philosophy—in the Vedanta view— includes feeling along with thought. If philosophy means "love of thought," it is still not without purpose. Science is the exploration of things with thought and the finding of unity there. Religion is the exploration of life with feeling, and the finding of unity there. And philosophy is the exploration of the relations between life and things, and the finding first of harmony and then of unity there. If the facts of our life-impulse are ignored there is no philosophy, but only science. The pinnacle of Aryan thought is reached when no fact of our being or experience is ignored and so the impulses of science, religion and philosophy are blended into one. This pinnacle of thought thus demands the most uncompromising realism.

Just as it contains a rejection of the false self as the basis of our thought about ourselves, so also it rejects false or built-up gods. To build up a god in the imagination and then to pray to that, and to think and think and think about it until it becomes a habit, means that we shall have to work hard and long to break through its influence upon us. But when there is understanding there is devotion, because all things are our teachers—both cabbages and kings—and our natural humility before them (which is due to our intelligent and willing acceptance of our limited position in life, and our recognition that the great quantity of things is the business of a great quantity of life-units, not of only one) renders us pervious to what they have to give. It is related that some Texas cowboys came into a Western town one evening to take pot-luck at the cinema; seeing the playbill outside, one of them shouted: "Hurrah, they are showing Easterns tonight." They were not keen on Westerns!

This ninth meditation was the last of the series, but there is still another stanza in this Song of Praise. This is added to tell about the benefits and results of working at the nine.

STANZA X

Since, in this song of praise,
It has been made very clear that all is self,

Therefore from the hearing of it,
From the thinking on its meaning,
From meditation,
And from reciting it with devotion,
Arises, all by itself,
God-like independence,
And the knowledge of being at one with all,
Combined with great capacity for living.
Also, unimpeded divine power is attained,
Unfolded in eight ways.

There is not much to add in this section of our subject. When I think of God-like independence, I remember
Patanjali's definition of God as unaffected by ignorance, self-
personality, likes, dislikes and possessiveness arising within,
or by action and the results of actions, coming from without.
Certainly we are not to think of God as a ruler, a governor,
one amongst others and against others or with them. To imagine such a being, with such powers, is only to add another
item in the field of mayavic interplay. To think as some do,
that we shall have the pleasure and greatness of being officers
under Him and directors of other men would only be to add
another attribute to the false self.

Divine power is direct power, power not derived. An old
relative of the word "divine" appears in Sanskrit, where it
occurs in a verbal form with the meaning "to shine," [1] in a
noun form to signify heaven or the sky, and in an adjective
form to indicate the divine, the heavenly or supernal. The sun
is the generally accepted symbol for this, as it puts forth its
own powers, while the moon is the symbol for the material
side of things, since it shines only with reflected or derived
light. It is almost synonymous with the word in our text,
which could have been equally well translated "unimpeded
Godness." "Unobstructed living" is a fruitful term for comparison with this, for could we imagine seeing and hearing

[1] *Div.*

and all the rest without the need of obstructions or limitations, consciousness being so powerful as not to be overwhelmed by it all, we should have an idea of life grasping the entirety of things in one thought, without dependence upon particulars. That would indeed be "seeing without eyes" and "hearing without ears."

As to the eight powers which are mentioned in this stanza, I will list them here, though they are not needed in the meditations, since, as one old writer says, if one carries a flower, one enjoys the scent of it without seeking or naming. The powers are regarded as operative at various levels: (1) in the nature of the divine being, (2) in a minor way existing in the devotee's mind, and (3) to some extent cultivable in the yogi's body life in the form of psychic powers. The last condition is not to be sought, but may come unsought, and even then is not to be used for personal gratification—a proceeding which would run counter to the purpose of the meditations. Here is the list:

1. Unlimited smallness
2. Unlimited largeness
3. Unlimited lightness
4. Unlimited heaviness
5. Unlimited vision
6. Unlimited movement
7. Unlimited creativeness
8. Unlimited control

The *Manasollāsa*, commenting on our present text, says that the all-pervading supreme self can enter or reduce itself into the smallest creature as its own self, or expand to include everything. The others logically follow.

In the human mind we do find these powers. It has been stated that external things are characterized by boundaries —circumferences without centers, except in the case of perfect spheres—while the mind operates always from a center and

has no known circumference, no limit to its reach. It can reduce its attention to the smallest thing, or expand it to the larg-
est, can feel as heavy and dull as lead or as buoyant as a zephyr,
can see to the distant stars or "touch the moon with the tip
of its fingers," can think of itself as in distant places and, in the
act, be there, can hold itself aloof or operate in the making
and breaking of forms, and can direct activities in various
channels. In all these respects it differs radically from a merely
material object.

The powers credited to advanced yogis who learn to co-
operate with the life-forces of Nature are classed in the same
way in the puranic or popular traditions. We have accounts of
men who can make themselves heavy at will, so that they cannot be lifted. Not long before my return from India one
floated in a reclining posture in the air, about six feet above the
ground, for quite a long time, in a large assembly. I and my
wife were present, with well-known friends. Traveling in the
"māyāvī body," control of breath, heart-beat and blood-flow,
transmission of thought by mind, and other such things I have
seen. Cases of movement of material objects, and the changing
of one thing into another are related by many. But these are
not cultivated or approved among the serious students, nor
encouraged in the old literature. As Shankara mentioned them,
however, in the text, I have felt that some explanation of them
was due from me in this place. Patanjali's treatment of the
psychic powers has been dealt with at length in my *Practical
Yoga: Ancient and Modern,* published by E. P. Dutton and
Co., Inc., New York. It may be that the "eight ways" referred
to at the end of Stanza X were chiefly thought of by the
author as powers of the unobstructed life, not in any way of
the body or mind. Perhaps we should interpret them only in
the spirit in which Shankara has dealt with the fifteen aids
given in our Chapter 17.

At the end of this series of meditations I must refer again to
the supreme aim of them, which is not to be reached by mere

thinking. There is very great gain in the thinking, and the more of it we do the more we shall realize the distinction between the world of apparent objects—the world of things and minds —and the over-all and underlying One Reality, also the more we shall feel relieved of the pressure of the world. There is immense benefit in this, and if we wish to go on our present course, enjoying life with increasing enjoyment and decreasing pain, the future is rosy before us. We can then live on in the sunny and smiling garden of life as long as we like. But some few are not satisfied with this; there is an open door in this garden wall, and as they wander past it again and again they occasionally peep through and wonder what life beyond the garden would be like. Now and then one of them not only peeps through, but goes through. Call this "nirvana," with Buddha, or "liberation," with Shankara, or "independence," with Patanjali, or "heaven," with Jesus . . . we all know that the meaning can be only one.

PART IV

COMPARISONS

CHAPTER 28

PLATO AND ARISTOTLE

A study of early philosophic thought among the Greeks reveals a variety of outlooks, due to the leanings of different thinkers. There were several distinct types of opinion about the nature of the world even then. The fact is that it is hard for a human being to suspend his own specific character as environment-changer, even when he does sincerely want to see things merely as they are. This positive being cannot refrain from his habit of altering things, so he unknowingly alters the picture to some extent even while he looks at it.

The evolution of philosophy in the West clearly shows this influence. We can distinguish several stages. No doubt early man, like a young child or an animal, unquestioningly accepted Nature as merely things-that-are-there, next as things-to-be-lived-with, and only much further on as a world-to-be-lived-in. In this stage an outlook of duality began to grow—man and the world. From this came things-to-be-modified, featuring man's mature and specifically human type of mind. In the midst of this we now are. Perhaps he will go on to world-to-be-modified; he has already begun to alter the flowers, the trees and the animals, so quite possibly in course of time he will change the earth we tread on and the air we breathe after rearranging the climates and the configuration of the continents and oceans, and other little things like that. It is no wonder that this man, when trying to understand outside things, to some extent mentally remakes them in the process, and that different men have created different philosophies in every human race.

In the history of philosophy in Europe we have generally the spectacle of tyrant kings and priests and tyrant public opinion dictating thought. Certain outlooks were suppressed by whips, and even after that method passed away, certain outlooks were promoted by the prostitution of mental and literary talent for monetary reward. It has always been difficult for unprejudiced thinking to obtain a fair hearing. It is partly because of this that we look back with admiration at the clusters of free thinking philosophers of Greece and of India. The Hindu thinkers are even yet less known in the west than the Greeks, because the exigencies of geography and political history brought their philosophies to Europe later, when the Greek studies had already become well established and fashionable in the centers of learning.

The greatest benefit which Greek thought brought into the modern world was the idea of mind in Nature, conceived as operating somewhat as it does in man. This was clearly a matter of careful thinking, not of what is usually regarded as the mere "projection" which is found in primitive naturism, because it did not pertain to particular objects, but to a perception of the world as coherent and as operating according to certain "laws." Incidentally, to be fair to the primitives, I doubt if we have a right to assume that even they "projected" the idea of life into natural objects on the analogy of the life they found in themselves regarded as objects, when the truth of the matter was much more probably the reverse of this— that they to themselves were not objects, but were first of all only "lives," from which they distinguished and mentally "pushed out" non-life, or things and bodies, only afterwards.

My aim in this chapter is not to present a systematic survey of Greek thought, but only to select certain distinguished philosophers, and show some of their principal opinions along-side the Hindu views.

As to "mind" and "heart" in Nature, we may begin with Anaxagoras and Socrates. Anaxagoras regarded intelligence[1] as the cause of forms and development in Nature, and, later, Socrates found fault with him for leaving out the idea of a final good to which the world is moving, and by which, Socrates maintained, there is an influence in the present determining the future. *Nous* was held by Anaxagoras to be a kind of high intelligence, producing order and regularity in Nature. This involved a distinction between a moving principle in Nature and the mere objects composed of earth, water, fire and air, or the dry, wet, warm and cold "elements." Finding thought operating in himself, producing orderliness in his life, the philosopher went on to attribute orderliness in Nature to a similar cause. He did not ask to *see* this principle with sense-organs, in the manner in which material things are seen, because in himself thought was something unseen, not in the same class with arms and legs, which are objects for sensation.

Although Anaxagoras accepted Nature as one real world, and did not apparently think decisively that it was composed of two totally different things working together as mind and matter (as real dualistic thinkers did later on in Europe), he discerned that it was an intelligent quality of Nature which produced orderliness, or reliable or steadfast forms. One could imagine, with regard to my illustration of the fox and the hens earlier in this book, that sooner or later the animal will not simply accept the tree that he passes as a tree, but will ask himself why the tree remains a tree from day to day, or, if the tree gets bigger, why it grows. He will become aware of a certain degree of regularity and reliability in Nature, not thought of as something else interfering or regulating Nature, but something as much a part of the world as the things them-

[1] *Nous.*

selves. Still, it was thought of as an unseen something in Nature—a "non-material" or mind factor.

This development of thought is similar to that of what I have called the false self gradually appearing in a child—first it knows, but does not know itself; then as it observes more precisely it knows objects as particular things in Nature; next it finds itself to be a particular thing (the false self); then it finds a duality of mind and matter in this thing; producing some voluntary and some involuntary effects; after that it begins to look for both members of this duality also in Nature. Thus philosophy is born. "What?" calls for more particularity; "How?" for special and general past causality; and "Why?" for design, purpose, or what I have called causality from the future. As this philosophy proceeds, in the matter-side duality begins to be regarded as the "what" factor, and the mind-side as the "how" factor; next comes my "outpost" theory, until at last everything has been swallowed up by God or the One Reality. The whole story could be called: "From world to God."

Another thinker of the period, evidently a somewhat different type of man from Anaxagoras—more of the feeling or emotional character—came forward with a theory of feeling in Nature, in the form of love and hate. This was Empedocles. Seeing the attractions and repulsions in Nature, he ascribed them to feeling. In very modern terms we could say he regarded such forces as gravitation and cohesion as "the love-life of the minerals." Development was ascribed to the same cause—a relative triumph of love resulted in the formation of plants, animals and men. Empedocles further held to the idea that Nature is full of transmigrating souls, which would ultimately be released from their wanderings by the perfection of love.

An idea of evolution also came into the philosophy of Anaxagoras, whose "intelligence" was a working principle, not merely moving things about, but being direction within their development.

The course of thought appears to have been somewhat as follows: first mere Nature was noticed, then a principle of intelligence or of love, and then not a mere principle but a set of ideas trying to express themselves. These ideas become working entities in Nature when expressed in living souls or minds, such spiritual souls being then assimilated to the idea of natural souls, brought over as a general belief from more primitive conditions of thought.

This period of Greek thought appears to me to have definitely marked a transit from that primitive introvertness which is the simple unquestioning enjoyment of living to an extrovert outlook. A new subjectivism arose, especially in Socrates, which was essentially extrovert—paradoxical as it may seem.

The rise of Plato and Aristotle appears to me as part of a regular movement in the development of the human mind. In making a philosophic system any philosopher is an artist, in that he is producing a representation of the world in a medium. The musician deals with sounds, the painter with pigments, and both are thereby trying to communicate ideas to other people or to themselves. Art is thus a kind of language, sometimes symbolic in that it suggests wholes by parts, and sometimes conventional, when definite forms are agreed to stand for certain definite things or ideas. The philosopher is not in different case—he is making a system of coherent ideas about life into an idea-picture. His pigments are ideas, and he tries to fit those ideas harmoniously together. As the artist educates us to see what he saw, since we go out from the gallery more observant than before, so the philosopher educates us by his word-pictures to know where he first knew.

Ideas in the mind are of two kinds—percepts and concepts. Percepts are extuitional, that is, they come to us from outside, through the sense organs, as when we see an orange. If oranges had not existed in the world, I am confident in saying that I would never have thought of an orange, I would not have known an object of that shape, size, color, taste and odor. The shape etc. are delivered at the door of the mind, received within as a bundle of sensations, and then recognized as a unit idea. Observing the orange, its attributes or qualities, and its actions (that is, its effect on other things, as for example on us when we eat it), we next think about it, reflect upon it, review it in imagination. This is perceptive thinking. Next we think about it in comparison with other things, that is, we note the points of resemblance and difference, and so we come to a classification, and say that an orange is a fruit. This idea, fruit, is a concept, and is called intuitional because it is an idea rising within the mind, not received from outside. But, it is to be carefully noted, we did not make that idea. It is born within us, yet born from some reality or truth.

This is where we come to Plato. He held that concepts are real; they exist in themselves, apart from our minds; we only become aware of them. There is a world of ideas, class within class, and class within class, ever widening as we ascend, until we reach the supreme idea, which is God, the good. It must be noted that the wider idea includes the narrower idea, but is always present in it. An oak is a tree, and a tree is a plant, but an oak is a plant as well as a tree.

These conceptual ideas, it was held, constitute what we may call a world of ideas, which is not only a real world, but more, it is *the* real world. As compared with them Plato called the percepts "shadows." Plato gave a striking illustration of this when he pictured men as sitting in a cave with their backs to the opening where the light comes in, and seeing their shadows on the wall in front of them. This may be compared with the idea I have expressed in our Chapter 2 in which I described a red cow as an imperfect cow, that is, cowness limited by redness.

Next, there can be a clash among percepts but not among

concepts. So we find Plato asserting that the true is the good, because when there is truth there is harmony, so that knowledge leads to goodness.

It will be noted that this theory of ideas is especially human, that is, beyond the animal. As we have pointed out before, the human mind is combinative and can therefore make things, produce artificial evolutes, with the aid of the hand. The animal adapts itself to the world, but man adapts the world to himself. To that statement we may now add that man can do this because he has concepts. These are at the back of his inventions. "I need," says he, "something to keep the sun off my head." So he makes an umbrella. Something-to-keep-the-sun-off is a concept, without which the umbrella—a percept— would not have been made. The animal, with its more limited mind, would simply shelter under a tree or in a cave, and so would not obtain the greater liberty and power ensured to man by his superior mind, which can respond to ideas.

As to man's own progress; it is a climb to the conception of higher and more inclusive ideas, and so an advance in both truth and goodness, destined to culminate in God. At the same time it is a progressive release from the mere percepts, which dominate him until the conceptual ideas which are born in his mind overcome them. To allow for this progress, which is not expected to go very far in the case of the average man, Plato held the idea of reincarnation, as did the Hindus, the soul being considered by Plato to have normally about a thousand years' interval between two human appearances on the stage of our world.

What, it will be asked, is the practice of progress? It is contemplation. Herein appears the third of the well-known three "eternal values" which Plato contributed to Western civilization—goodness, truth and beauty. If a man has been a slave, obeying orders, and he is suddenly released what will he follow? The answer is goodness, truth or beauty, if he is really a man at heart. The Greek philosophy is thus at the same time a religion, with God as sublime idea pervading the soul, not as master giving orders. Religion is thus man's bond with the eternal, felt in the soul.

In this "religion," the aesthetic sentiment relating us to the world of ideas is beauty; in practice, the yielding of ourselves to the joy of beauty is the means. One way in which this has been expressed relates to the enquiry what an artist is—is he a creator of beauty, or is he a copyist? He is a copyist, because his inspiration is from the divine ideas of which ordinary things are only shadows. He is a man to some degree released from the dominion of mere things, at least when the divine afflatus is upon him, so that in contemplating even the "shadow" of beauty he sees beauty where the common man passes it over.

Next, he has skill to present to others that which he sees, by accentuating its presence, by isolating it to some extent. His statue, let us say, is placed in a museum. It is separated from the mass and clash of sensations that batter us all the time in the market-place and in the street, and often, sad to say, even in the home, and we go to it also in a reverential mood. Thus, we too see the beauty which the artist saw before we did, and afterwards we too will be able in some degree to see it where he first saw it, in the street or in the field. He contemplated the beauty. Perhaps he was lost in rapture and full of intuition. Now we too have seen, we too have contemplated, and we will further contemplate as the result of this good relationship.

If, then, this argument concludes, the artist is only a copyist, and yet he, as also the philosopher, is greatest among humans, and worthy of all our admiration and thanks, what shall we say of the originator of the ideas, God? We cannot say anything, but only bow and rejoice.

If this is Platonism—and I think I have represented it correctly—how does it compare with Shankara's Vedanta?

Well, I have to say that all this extolling of ideas is too objective, from the Vedantic point of view. In it we are too much like an artist painting a picture. Have we perchance taken one of the articles in our world, and elevated it to the rank of leader, and even master, of all the others? After all, when we thus think of ideas, have we not made them into another kind of percepts? In this sort of thinking, are we not perceiving our concepts, so that there is still the "error" of "you" and "I" against which Shankara so emphatically warns us? If we are moderns and occidentals, I fear we have some picture in our minds of those ideas as floating or dancing in space, in a supernatural plane or world. And we may find ourselves looking out for them, or looking up to them. There is an expectancy of some reception of these ideas on our part, and there is some faint thought of ourselves and the ideas as ships which sometimes pass in the night and sometimes meet in the day. Where is that unity which exists, but will never be made by the union of that with this, the union of that idea with this mind? Unity cannot be produced by such a union, or any union. It is to be known by being, whereas the perceiving mind, with its addiction to duality and plurality, destroys the unity in its every act. I fear that every one of that galaxy and hierarchy of ideas or concepts is an "it" or a "you," however high its genus.

The difference is that Vedanta is yoga, not thinking, and although it is yoga by knowledge, its knowledge is not an act of knowing things ("its") or even living conscious beings ("yous"), but of directly knowing the self. And that knowledge is of "I," by the true experience of "I," not overlaid by "its" and "yous." The function of things and beings in our lives is to become gateways to the infinite, through a contemplation which disposes of the distinction between the knower and the known, and, without destroying anything, leaves only pure knowing or pure consciousness. We have glimpses of this occasionally in a kind of waking-sleep which we sometimes spontaneously enjoy in unexpected as well as intentional contemplation.

Having used the term waking-sleep to indicate a condition of ecstasy or enlightenment of consciousness, achieved through contemplation, which is I-ing beyond the yous and its, it is meet that I should say that Vedantists value the sleeping and dreaming states as containing essential values to consciousness as important as those of the waking state. It is a non-Vedantic habit of mind to regard only the waking state as real life, and to say that the dream and sleep can be considered only useful if they subserve something in the waking state. But the Vedanta insists on the essential and independent value of each one of them to consciousness. The dream condition contains qualities both profitable and beneficial, even when our dreams are not remembered in the waking state, as most of them are not. Sleep, too, is psychologically valuable, profitable, and beneficial, even though what happens in it may be, and generally is, totally unknown in the waking state.

If we argue, as between dream and waking, that one state exists to serve the other, we could quite reasonably say, from the standpoint of the dream state, that the waking state exists only as a collection agency to provide materials for dreaming, and again, since waking objects and experiences are remembered with great accuracy in dream, but dreams are difficult to remember on waking, the stream of natural service seems to flow from waking to dreaming. But we must not think of one state as existing for the sake of the other, when in fact there is a mutuality of service. Into the waking state the dream condition brings freedom and clarity and truth, which purify and heal us, and remind us of what our living could be without the cramping, cribbing, confining semi-suffocation of traveling with heavy ballast and pushing against obstacles all the time. My mind searches for an illustration, and I think I have found one—a ship at sea. Let us imagine a ship so well provided with interior mechanism that it could sail through crowded and littered waters without striking any of the innumerable obstructions, and could bring itself perfectly to dock without the aid of tugs or fenders, and with absolutely no concussion. Let us then imagine a man having all the freedom from external limitations which the mind has in dreams, but having also such internal power that he could be as orderly and rational in all that liberty as he now is in the bondage of the waking state. Will that not be so when waking and dreaming have become united in us as power and freedom?

There is some of this attainment in us even now; some freedom in our bondage, and some self-government in our freedom. It is going on; we are slightly aware of it, and can observe it more and more. The three states have even now their own essential unadulterated character, which can be tasted by us, when we very carefully try. Their meaning for consciousness is not entirely unknown to us. But our voluntary evolution will carry the values of the waking state into the others, and will bring the values of the others into the waking state so that in the end the pure consciousness of the sleeping state will not be dimmed by the waking state, and the object-experience of the waking state will not be annulled by the freer consciousness now experienced in the dreaming and sleeping states. In other words, unity and freedom will not deny multiplicity and objectivity. Or, again, an act of consciousness will not involve concentration, meditation and contemplation, but only direct perception.

The fault I have to find with Platonism and other mental philosophies is that they do not leave the door of truth open for us to go through, but only to look through, and so they keep us psychopathically in our old psychological fetters and chains. In the waking state the mind is full of percepts and concepts and we are engaged in working with and among these. In the dream state we stop our working, but still pay attention to the play of ideas within it, but in deep sleep—the kind from which we awake with the knowledge "I slept well," there are no percepts and concepts, but only consciousness— we are never unconscious—knowing itself. It could be called trance, and can become waking trance, whereupon "that which is day to all beings becomes night to the seer, and that which is night to all beings is day to the seer." I have already expounded the utility of the world of objects as aids to concentration whereby consciousness increases its capacity to know, and retains that capacity after the object has gone.

To sum this matter up: the Vedantist lays very great stress upon these three states of waking, dreaming and sleeping[2] as all beneficial. He learns not to overvalue the waking state as compared with the others. And Shankara teaches, as his teachers did before him, that there is a Fourth State,[3] which, however, is not another state but the unity of the three, in which the knowing consciousness achieves that purity of its own being in which it realizes the oneness of being, and thus reaches the end of the long journey of transmigratory life, by stepping off its endless band into the "freedom" [4] of Shankara, the "nirvāna" of Buddha.

This is more filling and deeper than the elevation of even the highest conceptual idea to the divine Throne. If the commonalty have elevated a percept—a glorified man—to that Seat, the philosopher has only gone one further in planting a glorified concept there. The mind will find what it seeks, but the Vedantic yogī gives up all seeking that has the nature of planting, and opens himself in full consciousness to the "being and knowing and joy" beyond any thought of any object, even if that object be the highest concept, the *summum genus*. The seeking is being done, metaphorically speaking, by That, not by this, and so, as I said in my comment on the Song of Praise, it cannot be asked for or sought, imagined or thought, but will find us when the man is ready, when the mind is mature.

And now to Aristotle.

Aristotle has been called the father of modern science. What

----

[2] *Jāgrat, swapna* and *sushupti avasthās.*
[3] *Turīya avasthā.*
[4] *Moksha.*

does this mean? Some have described it as the rise of objectivism. Modern science is based upon a certain belief, the use of which has been confirmed over and over again by experience. It is, rather, a trinity of beliefs, which may be stated as follows: "I believe in the world as a place of truth; I believe in the human mind as a means to knowledge of that truth; I believe that that truth, when known, is beneficial to man." It marks a new mental respect for things known through the senses, apart from any unseen agencies which may be thought to be operating them, and so carries the extrovert tendency of the mind a step further on its downward—and upward—path.

I must explain here my inclusion of "downward and upward path." When the mind goes "downward," that is, immerses itself with conscious intent deeper in matter, or rather pays closer attention to some material thing, it does so in order to rise higher. It retreats, for a longer jump. It submits, for a greater self-assertion. Great concepts are easily born in a mind that honestly and faithfully studies the small things of life.

> One thing at a time
> And that done well,
> Is a very good rule,
> As many can tell—

This is the method of science, which does not despise anything. It is also a good statement of the yoga method, which begins with concentration, then meditates, and finally contemplates, and at the same time has no superiority belief or desire in the background. The method is justified by its leading to greater power as well as greater freedom. What a delight it was to learn that out of half a million kinds of insects in the world only about a hundred are inimical to man; some day if those men who have told us this, or others like them, go on with their small observings we shall know more about that one hundred, and will perhaps learn that in some indirect ways even they are on the whole also beneficial to man. Anyhow, the mind of man is like a giant heart, contracting and expanding in alternate observation and theory, particularity and generality, and so pumping the blood of knowledge through our lives. It will be noted too that this operation gears in with the yogī's experience that every little thing can be a gateway to infinity.

It is a quality very much to be admired in the Greeks that they were by no means one-sided, but were very much on the beam of the balance of interest in inward and outward things. They shone in both work and thought. Their beautiful statues and pottery excite us as much as their philosophic breadth of ideas. If Plato was somewhat biased towards the world of concepts, Aristotle, one of his pupils, soon balanced him by an equal bias towards the world of percepts. But neither of them lost touch with both ends of the beam. And the Greeks never did. But later races moving into a more extrovert cycle have done so, and, following a "downward" phase of human interest, have hailed Aristotle as the father of modern science.

Aristotle's objectivism appeared when he studied not merely things, but changes going on in the world, and saw in them a law of causation at work. As modern scientists are interested as much in forces as in matter, as much in the dynamic as in the static truths of Nature, so was Aristotle, and his formulation of the four kinds of causation well mark his position in this respect.

First he bifurcated the world of objective experience by distinguishing between form and matter. He did not separate them, however, for he declared that we have no experience of matter by itself, but only when molded into form at least to some extent. Forms, in his eyes, were not caused by matter. Matter is one of the four kinds of causes of anything, but is only the material cause, having no say in the production of forms, the cause of which must be sought elsewhere. It can be called a cause because if it was not present no form could be objective. It is therefore of the nature of clay in relation to an earthen pot—and the visitor to the museum in Athens alone knows what a vast variety of pots there actually is!

The other three of the four causes propounded by Aristotle were called (2) the efficient cause, (3) the formal cause and (4) the final cause; the efficient being especially related to reason, the formal to the soul, and the final to God. Forms, therefore, in their origin, belong to what we should call the spiritual side of life; they are brought into objective being by the soul and its operative reason. In this view I think we see something of Plato's influence on Aristotle, for his forms are of the nature of prototypes, like Plato's ideas, of which the forms are ectypes.

Since form is something imposed upon matter by the other three causes, we can proceed to know something of the soul and God by enquiry into the objective forms, as argued earlier in this book, when stating that natural and artificial evolutes are outposts of ourselves. Thus, in Nature, plants were said to have natural propagative impulses from the soul, animals to have moving souls requiring imagination, and man to have reason in service of his soul, this reason being regarded as higher and more positive in its responsiveness to soul, and lower and more passive in its responsiveness to objective impacts from outside. Through the soul there is an *entelechy* or active operation (as distinguished from a mere potency) of form-building in Nature, and therefore a teleological purpose or design showing progress in Nature, not, however, as a continuous process of growth, as thinkers generally regard evolution today, but rather as a series of trials, through soul-impulses, resulting in failure again and again, but constantly getting nearer and nearer to an adequate expression of the original ideas. The highest cause, God, is above or beyond the world, and is the final cause. The first active expression of causality in the world is the soul, which produces the form of the body. Reason is thus the efficient cause, soul the formal, and God the final.

In one of the oldest schools of Hindu thought, named the Analytic,[5] causation is divided into three: (1) the inseparable or material or combinative cause,[6] so called because the cause remains in the effect, like the clay in an earthen pot, or the threads in a cloth, so that, in the trinity of object or substance, attribute, and action or operation, it is only the substance that can be a material cause. (2) The separable or accidental or non-combinative cause,[7] which is so called because it is something incorporated into the effect only as an attribute of the material cause, but is not by any means necessary. Thus the threads used in weaving a cloth may be of a green color, resulting in a green cloth.

(3) The efficient cause,[8] such as the potter or the weaver. There is a fourth cause, not counted as separate, but included in the efficient cause, named

(3a) The assistant cause.[9] This is an auxiliary efficient cause, such as the loom used by the weaver, or the revolving wheel used by the potter.

Aristotle's view differs from that of the adwaita Vedanta, in that he holds God to be the final cause operating in all things, union with whom is the grand event to which all creation moves. God is not the material cause, but the efficient cause of the changes taking place in the world. In the Vedanta, however, God or the One Reality is the material cause of all things, inasmuch as there is no material substance, but the substance of all things is that One. "From what an effect is produced, in that it abides, as a pot in clay, or a cloth in

---

[5] *Vaisheshika;* the principal source-book of this school being the *Aphorisms of Kanāda.*

[6] *Samavāyi-kārana* or *upādāna-kārana.*

[7] *Asamavāyi-kārana.*

[8] *Nimittika-kārana.*

[9] *Sahakārī.*

threads, or a ring in gold"—is a dictum of both the Analytic and Logical schools.[10] This sounds very Aristotelian, and very much like the atomic theory of the scientists of my student days, fifty years ago. But Shankara will not have it so, but maintains that being or existence[11] is the real inseparable or combinative cause of all things. This is something in its own right, and atoms are not. Even dynamism is not. So the real material of the universe must be sought in this reality, and our question becomes: "What is existence?" The answer then is, "It is not any *what*, nor is it something that a what has, but it is the very being that knowing is." The knowing of existence, as I have explained before, is in the I-consciousness, not in the reflection of "its" and "yous" in the mind, not in the manipulations of these things by the mind, but in the pause and poise of mind which allows the I-ness of me to stand for a moment pure and unsullied on the stage of my consciousness. The answer to the question is, "Behold! That thou art," and when the questioner can respond, "That I am," he knows. This implies the ever-presence of the ultimate Divine, and is very different from any sort of climb towards God. In evolution we are only maturing (1) bodies and (2) minds. We are not evolving upwards to God, who is present all the time. As explained before, never at any moment is a "you" the whole of itself, and when we thus discover that we are not something evolving towards God we realize the unimportance of being what we seem. I hope we realize, too, the truth of the statement that every one of us is alone with God. How we struggle to know one another, by thought and love! It is an erroneous kind of knowing that we thus seek, a perpetual looking at rabbits with eagerness to see their horns. The one cause—which is the Whole—is what existence is and what we are, and it is to be known in terms of "I," not of "this."

[10] *Vaisheshika* and *Naiyāyika*.
[11] *Sat.*

CHAPTER 29

THE HINDU SCHOOLS

It is usual to enumerate the old Schools of Hindu Philosophy as six. The word "schools" is not the most appropriate word to describe them; "outlooks" is probably the closest translation of the Sanskrit term.[1]

(1) The Analytical[2] School of Kanāda, sometimes called the Atomistic School. This name arose from its attempt to distinguish the basic things of our experience. Kanāda stated that we are aware of seven factors in Nature, on which all our understanding is based at any time and in any situation. There is something; it has qualities; it has actions; it belongs to some class or group; it has its individual particularity; these things, qualities, actions, classes and particulars are always found in relation to one another; and finally, we are also aware of absences. Thus we take into account, when we are knowing, seven factors:

> Object,
> Quality,
> Action,
> Class (resemblance),
> Particular (difference),
> Relationship, and
> Absence.

This is downright commonsense, and to know these practical factors of our world of experience is of the greatest help in

[1] *Darshana.*
[2] *Vaisheshika.*

the careful observation of anything, so that we may know as well as we possibly can what it is.

Kanāda proceeds to tell us that there are nine kinds of objects or substances or facts: Earth, water, fire, air, ether, time, space, self and mind. In each of these there are various kinds or subdivisions. Under self we have two divisions; God and souls. Some of these things are atomic, and thus constitute the material basis of the world.

The source-book[3] of this school goes into much detail under each of the seven headings. It enumerates, for example, four kinds of absence, namely, previous absence, future absence, mutual or relative absence, and total absence. A study of this very ripe and complete analysis of our experience is very rewarding, and helpful against confusion of thought. In the present book I have made much use of its triplicity of object, qualities, and actions—regarding an object in three ways: what it is, what it has, and what it does.

In its general effects this school presents the beliefs that the material universe is composed of atoms, and that there is a God who is a personal Creator, who moves the atoms, and causes forms. It thus presents the view quite common among non-mystical religions in the Western World, that God governs the universe from outside or above it. Thus God is a self or entity—one of many, but a superior or special one—a thing, in the wide sense of the term; and so is the soul, which has knowledge through union with the mind and the senses.

Like all the Hindu philosophies this outlook has utility in view—the rescue of the soul from its present unsatisfactory condition or predicament, which is to be effected by its complete devotion to God. Its theory of creation can be boiled down to the formula: A makes B, which is not A. This theory is not acceptable to the nondualist Vedantists, as it propounds duality, indeed multiplicity, at the basis of things.

[3] *The Vaisheshika Aphorisms of Kanāda.*

(2) The Logical [4] School of Gautama. If the Analytic School can be described as an enquiry into the nature of our world of experience, this can be called an enquiry into the nature of our knowledge of things. If the first tries to answer the question, "What do we find?" the present one seeks to explain the mental process of our finding. It expounds the logical process, and in so doing exposes its essential weakness—its dependence upon past experience.

Gautama says in effect that we cannot depend upon our sense-perceptions, that they must be submitted at the bar of reason. In the pursuit of truth, reason must come in with its technique of logic to provide a conclusive statement which mere perception cannot give.

Logic is often taken to be a supplement to sense, to be used to gain knowledge where the senses cannot reach. "Mr. Bilkinson has a brain," we say; and we feel quite sure about it —although we have never seen it, and nobody else has seen it —because, "Mr. Bilkinson is a man, and all men have brains." Here we have two pieces of prior knowledge—that Mr. Bilkinson is a man, and that all men have brains. Our inference that Mr. Bilkinson has a brain therefore leads only to a piece of subordinate or inferior knowledge, implied in the premises, so logic can never enlarge the scope of our knowledge, and if it cannot enlarge the scope it is not a means to really new knowledge. So thinking is not a means to knowing, but only to removing errors or inadequacies within a prescribed field of knowledge.

I have criticized this outlook at the outset, because I want to make it perfectly clear that the Vedanta outlook is against dependence upon the thinking mind as the means to truth, and is all for direct perception of the truth. Although it admits inference and the testimony of others as means to knowledge, as described in Chapter 6, these must give way to and depend

[4] *Nyāya.*

upon direct perception before anything is really known. In the Yoga School of Patanjali also direct perception is at bottom the only means to knowledge, for in its process we first give our attention to a thing (concentration), then think fully about it (meditation), then pass on beyond thinking into a pure and powerful gaze at it (contemplation), and in that mind-poise we receive what it has to give.

Gautama says in his *Nyāya* aphorisms that there are sixteen things to take into consideration when making an enquiry. These include the scope and purpose of the enquiry, the doubts or questions we want to clear up, the form of the syllogism and the deduction to which it leads, and the parts often played in human error and deceit by partisanship, prejudice, irrelevance, fallacy, ambiguity, self-contradiction and trickery.

The nondualists appreciate the value of all these things, as they do a large part of the findings of the Analytic School, but they cannot agree with the theory that logic will give men a knowledge of the truth, or the means to bring human life to its fulfillment. In the means to knowledge they place direct perception first, and accept inference, analogy, testimony etc. as of only subordinate value. It is very obvious, is it not, that the best of testimony by eyewitnesses to the fact that grass is green and the sky blue cannot give the knowledge of those colors to a blind man? The Vedantin accepts the great sayings of the Scriptures as divinely inspired, but maintains, as I have amply explained, that they will be understood properly only by the man who has learned to see for himself. Where Gautama and the Logical School follow Kanāda in their belief in God as Master or Ruler of the world, again the Vedantist holds back, and says that ideas like Master and Ruler prescribe a limit to the aspirant's journey to knowledge, and "gum up the works" at the very outset. The Yoga School of Patanjali also maintains that illumination in the mind-poise can come only when there is no prejudice, no prescription of the goal to be reached, no proposition to be proved. Logic has not an open mind, though it is immensely useful and even vital for poking about within a prescribed and limited field.

(3) The Scientific[5] School of Kapila. The original term is better translated as "enumerative." This outlook enumerates what it calls the twenty-five true principles. Its object is to enable the soul to find itself by the knowledge of the true principles, whereby it will be released from bondage to all kinds of things. Its views have a synthetic character differing greatly from the analytic character of the two schools previously mentioned, and very much of its doctrine is acceptable to the Vedantists, who break with it, however, because it posits a fundamental dualism of matter and spirit, which the adwaitī denies. This difference is vitally important, because the liberation aimed at by the Vedantist is not an escape from a real material world, but a self-realization, a release from one's own error, a passage from illusion and delusion into perfect sanity of being.

I have used the word "scientific," and placed this school as the closest to our modern science, because our science is really enumerative. Being so, it compares things by measurement and calculation. In scientific work, when we want to know how hot a bowl of water is, we do not put our hands in and feel its heat, but insert a thermometer, which translates the degree of heat into the motion of mercury or something else on a visible scale. This is measurement, which is really enumeration. Science thus corrects the subjectively-controlled sensory impression with the aid of unprejudiced and almost incorruptible material witnesses, like the thermometer and the yardstick.

I may as well say at this point that this method is not satisfactory to the nondualist, because it, too, is dependent upon a unit which is not true. As logic is defective by dependence on a universal premise ("all men have brains"), which is true

[5] *Sānkhya.*

only by definition and not by completely universal experience, so science is defective by dependence on units and kinds of units which are not infallible and sometimes not properly applicable. Are any two yardsticks *exactly* the same length? Quite probably not. So science is only an approximate truth for practical purposes in dealing with certain things—what we call material things, which have extensity or size, and resistance. It tries to explain the whole by the part. Its arithmetic cannot touch certain other realities. As I remarked earlier on, there is quite a different measure and computation where life is in question. Let two young people get married and they will soon find that $1 + 1$ does not equal 2, but 3 and perhaps more, and in the field of economic production, let us say, ten people work co-operatively with an intelligent plan and they can produce as much as forty or fifty working separately and alone.

Kapila's "enumeration," however, allowed itself a larger field in setting up its twenty-five principles. His first bifurcation of this world of complex experience is into the duality of subject and object[6] or souls and primitive materiality. I do not say "matter" here, because this primitive materiality has three qualities[7] which correspond very closely to our modern material trinity of matter, energy and natural law. These are always found together in Nature, says this school, but in different proportions, so that some things are more sluggish, others more restless, and others more reliable and orderly in their character and actions. Among the many souls there is no one that is special or superior—no God. Such a conception would clash with the idea of the soulness of a soul; if a hand A controls a hand B the latter is no longer a hand, and similarly a soul governed by another soul would cease to be a soul, but would be an object. A corollary of this distinction is that souls are really pure and independent—mere wit-

---

[6] *Purusha* and *prakriti*.
[7] *Tamas, rajas* and *sattwa*.

nesses of the field of Nature, but they feel happy or miserable on account of a "conjunction" with Nature, which is nothing more than the reflection in the soul of the infirmities of the world.

This is not the place to describe all the twenty-five principles, and how they emerge and are related, but I must mention that mind is regarded as belonging to the material side of things, remembering that natural law, or reliability, or harmony, or orderliness, is part of this field, and that it is to that part that the mind with its attendant senses belongs. The conception of the natural world as including body and mind as well as what we commonly call matter is great and grand —an idea of which modern science could be proud, which could solve some of its psychological problems, by a bifurcation between mind and soul rather than between body and mind, as is rather usual. Then indeed could we see the possibility of the potency of mind in all matter, and of all matter in mind. Of course, in this case, knowledge arises by the conjunction of mind and soul. But Shankara's Vedanta will have no bifurcation at all.

The ethical question comes into this system, as it does into the lives of modern atheists and agnostics (who are often notably good people), because it is natural. Nature hangs together, the mind is specially imbued with her harmony, and the feeling-knowledge in the soul will be happiest when connected with a mind that is most perfectly and purely harmonious and least troubled by the conflicts of matter and the restlessness of the energy factor in Nature. There is a natural right and good, as was well expressed in the lines of Alexander Pope in his *Essay on Man:*

> All Nature is but art, unknown to thee;
> All chance, direction which thou can'st not see;
> All discord, harmony not understood;
> A partial evil, universal good.

> And, spite of pride, in erring reason's spite,
> One truth is clear, "Whatever is, is right."

(4) The Yoga School of Patanjali, of which the standard textbook is his Yoga Aphorisms. Quite generally the views of this school are regarded as just the same as those of the preceding—the scientific—but "with God." The emphasis in this outlook is, however, upon what man must do to save himself from his present difficulties. It could be called the school of practical psychology. It contains a carefully planned technique for bringing the mind into a pure condition in which it will at last, through a full discrimination, surrender itself completely to the soul, so that the latter will reach independence, and will reside in its own true nature instead of being colored by the troublesome limitations of Nature. Its theories of the world, the body and the mind, which come in occasionally in the course of the system of mental training which is its chief feature, are quite in accord with those of Kapila's school, but the whole emphasis is upon harmony. There are eight steps of progress which the mind should run through when it wants to attain the poise in which it can reflect the soul. First, the man must be at peace with the world, through an absence of desire to injure, lie, steal, be sensual, or be greedy. Secondly, he must be at peace with himself, through cleanliness, contentment, body-conditioning, self-study and attentiveness to God. Thirdly, he must be at peace physically, by learning to sit quietly in a comfortable, healthy position. Next, his breathing should be regular and peaceful. Fifthly, his senses must be trained out of their ordinary restlessness, so that there will be the peacefulness of noncuriosity about sounds, sights etc. at any desired time. The sixth, seventh and eighth stages are the concentration, meditation and contemplation described earlier in this book and more fully in my translation and explanation of the Yoga Aphorisms in *Practical Yoga: Ancient and Modern.*

Inasmuch as this school accepts the dualism of the preceding one, its teaching is not acceptable to the nondualist Vedantist, but inasmuch as it demands that the yogī shall go into his mind-poise totally without prejudice or specific expectation or theory, its practice is quite Vedantic. But the dualistic theory is implicitly an obstacle to the attainment of the true mind-poise, and all its thoughts about the rejection of coloration by externals, if they mistakenly leave an escapist impulse in the mind, and inasmuch as they do so, will also be obstacles. But Patanjali's analysis of the psychological sources of trouble in human life, containing an equal emphasis against both attraction and repulsion, and a clear statement of the false self or self-personality, are all in line with Vedantic thought and purpose.

The Yoga School does not bring God in as Ruler of the World, but as a picture of the ideal soul, for purposes of meditation—a soul self-governed, and unaffected by the sources of trouble. To this Shankara would raise no objection, for with him there is no objection to idols and images, which have the function of dolls, as assisting the mind to concentrate in its earlier stages. Even the Vedantist can meditate on God, provided he remembers that there is no such external being, and no such being at all unless that is also his own true self.

In some respects the Scientific and Yoga schools resemble another pair that arose in later Greek and Roman times— the Epicurean and the Stoic. Like Kapila, the Epicureans held that the highest good would come from living in harmony with Nature, in the present. Obey the laws of Nature; keep within that moderation which she prescribes in all things; look after your body, your houses, land, horses, cattle in proper measure, and do not worry about past or future. Such was the Epicurean practical philosophy—far from the modern travesty of it which we sometimes encounter in the saying, "Eat, drink and be merry, for tomorrow you die." Like Patanjali, the Stoics seemed to say, "Yes, that is all good. But what of your most precious possession, your mind? Does not this, like your body, need proper treatment and training? Is it not your opinions about things that give you trouble, more than the things themselves?" With such a philosophy, the Stoics were very strong-minded and independent of circumstances, as the Yogīs were and still are today.

(5) The Ceremonial School of Jaimini. I need say very little about this outlook. It holds that the highest good for man will come from a rigid and literal obedience to the ceremonial acts prescribed in the scriptures. These are actions having reference to the unseen forces and beings beyond the range of ordinary human perception and action. The idea is always quite frankly to get something, some favors or assistance from those forces or beings, in the immediate or the remote future. There is considerable preoccupation with the future beyond death, and the means that must be taken to ensure success and a high degree of heavenly attainment and happiness. Sometimes the idea of a *guru* or spiritual Teacher is confused with this method, and he comes to be thought of as one who will give help when appealed to in the "right" way.

The Vedantist also has the highest respect for scripture, but considers that it contains different injunctions for those who want the present kind of a life, though greatly glorified in the future, and for those who have discerned the "true life kept for him who false puts by," and who "want God and turn their backs on heaven." Ceremonies are "the way of prescribed action," but it is the "desire to know Brahman" that leads to the realization of the true self, for that Brahman and self are one.

(6) The Vedanta of Shankara. The principal textbook for this school is Shankara's Commentary on the Vedanta Aphorisms of Badarāyana, and his Commentaries on the Upanishads. I have already described them in various ways throughout this book, introducing one aspect after another by a teaching method rather than a descriptive one.

If the views of the different Schools are thought of in terms of doctrines, one obtains another basis of comparison. These doctrines[8] have been reduced to the simplest terms. If the first School supports the Creation Doctrine[9] (in which A makes B, which is not A), and the third School the Transformation Doctrine[10] (in which A changes into B, which is not A), we may say that the sixth School, the Vedanta, supports the Assumption Doctrine.[11] It means that A does not change into B, or back again, but is only thought to do so, though it must be admitted that the thought is an action producing perceived forms having spatial and temporal characters which can stand their ground. It is all a kind of dance in which the dancer puts himself into different positions, sometimes posing, sometimes moving, in which posing is not the basis because it is a pause in movement, and movement is not the basis because it is a series of poses. The Doctrine denies that there is any material transformation as such, or material causation. Things are assumptive, but are as real as reality is known and felt to be by us. Not one of our categories or conceptions, however, can subsume the rest of them, and so we have to admit that even "reality" is not fundamental. In saying that, we admit the māyā doctrine, which, if illusion, is not a real illusion, but is an assertion that our "reality" itself, though not unreal, is yet not really real. There is something beyond the relativity of things, but the relativity does not deny or exclude it. This is the Indescribability Doctrine[12] which leads us back to the psychological statement that the mind cannot grasp the Self because it is concentrative. Only the self knows the self, but there is self in "I," so the problem will be solved by the I-ing,

[8] *Vādas.*
[9] *Arambha Vāda.*
[10] *Parināma Vada.*
[11] *Vivarta Vāda.*
[12] *Anirvachanīya Vāda.*

when the thou-ing is set aside. The thou-ing is a superstition, a superimposition[13] upon the I.

We resort to analogies. A piece of rope lying on the ground is mistaken for a snake, and the observer steps carefully over it, or jumps out of the way. A post at the corner of the path is in the dusk mistaken for a man, until the observer approaches near enough to correct his superstition (placing over) or superimposition. We say; "Ah, I see now. You are not a snake but a piece of rope." But is it a rope? We have caught ourselves erring in thinking it a snake; are we not still erring? Have we to correct a wrong piece of knowledge, so wrong that go as far as we can it is still a wrong knowledge? Or is it a fancy that there is anything there at all, and even the thereness is a product of the mind? Shall we say that we are "knowing otherwise,"[14] confusing a previously seen object with the object actually present? This cannot be so, because it does not allow for a true seeing of an original or first prior object. Or, shall we say that we are not seeing entirely, because we have not the proper instruments or organs of vision for the purpose?[15] This cannot be so, because then we could never know. Or, shall we say that we are seeing a thing which is absolutely nonexistent?[16] This is impossible, as being contradictory. Or, shall we say that we are projecting our own subjective idea into objective form?[17] No, for this leaves us with no means to account for where we got the idea, or how it arose in the first place. Or, is this world the seeing of an emission[18] or creation by a God or someone else? This could not be without the acceptance of a basic duality, which is absurd. Or, again, is it a reflection of something in something else?[19] Not so, for that

[13] *Adhyāsa.*
[14] *Anyathā-khyāti.*
[15] *A-khyāti.*
[16] *Asat-khyāti.*
[17] *Ātma-khyāti.*
[18] *Srishti-drishti Vāda.*
[19] *Bimba-pratibimba Vāda.*

labors under the same defect. Or, again, is it the seeing of our own emission? [20] In that case we are in the toils of solipsism— there is only one of us, and he is alone!

This last is not impossible, if properly understood, in which case it means that the I in our neighbor, and in you and in me, is absolutely one I. To approach this knowledge correctly we have to remember that there is no I *"in* my neighbor" or *"in* you" or *"in* me." These expressions must be turned inside out. When I and you and he know "I" we shall know our- selves as one. In the meantime we make a collective world, which is one world because we are essentially one, and also is itself very really "I," though very much misunderstood.

So, finally, it comes to this; that the Unproduced Theory[21] is the nearest to Vedantic truth. This states that there is no production, but all is essentially itself, the self. As Gau- dapāda puts it in his Commentary on the *Māndūkya Upan- ishad,* "There is no limitation, no creation, no bondage, no maker, no aspirant, nobody freed—this is the correct knowl- edge." We have only to add to this, "and no 'no,' " and there we are!

Metaphysics must be real metaphysics, not superphysics, a higher materialism, a finer set of goods still on the same old stall. It-knowledge and thou-knowledge must give way to "I." We see now why the author of the *Garuda Purāna* said: "Fallen into the well of the Six Philosophies, the brutes do not understand the chief good; bound in the snare of animal- ism, they are tossed hither and thither in the dreadful ocean of Vedas and Shāstras. Caught in the six waves they remain sophists."

"Sink not the string of thought into the fathomless. Who asks doth err. Who answers errs." Thus said Buddha. Only in contemplation, in which there is no asking, these truths will be known. In the meantime, it remains a fact that the bee goes to

[20] *Drishti-srishti Vāda.*
[21] *Ajāta Vāda.*

the flower, and gets the honey, and that experience is not in vain, as is well taught under this very symbol of honey.

The fifth section of the second chapter of one of the principal Upanishads[22] is called the Honey Section. It is preceded by a dialogue between the ancient sage Yāgnyavalkya and his wife, Maitreyī. He tells her that he would like to retire from the responsibilities of family life, and asks her if she will accept certain property. She demurs, questioning: "Even if all the wealth of the world were mine, would I thereby become immortal?"

Yāgnyavalkya was constrained to reply that she could live the kind of life enjoyed by wealthy people, but that no one could hope to attain immortality by means of wealth. She then replied that the wealth did not interest her but she wanted to know the means to immortality. Her husband then made some statements which have rung down the ages. After asking Maitreyī to listen meditatively, he said:

Not for the sake of the husband, but for the sake of the self, a husband is dear, or—summarizing—wife, sons, property, worlds, gods, scriptures, materials, the universe. So the self is to be seen, to be heard about, thought about and meditated upon. He who regards any of these things as other than the self is thereby shut out from truth. As, on hearing certain sounds, you know that a drum or a lute is being sounded, once you know that that is the sound of a drum or a lute, so, seeing all these things, must one recognize the self.

This is the passage-way from deathlikeness to real immortality, beyond the duality of smelling something, seeing something, hearing something, even knowing something—in all of which there is "another."

Commenting on this, Shankara quotes another Upanishad,[23] which says that all these things are names, forms and actions, and that "All this is only the self," which is "One only,

[22] The Brihad Āranyaka.
[23] Chhāndogya.

without a second"—without duality; as regards which see my remarks on our number-consciousness in Chapter 5. That self, because dwelling in all bodies, is spoken of as the "city-dweller," [24] but the term dweller is inadequate—as all terms must be—and must include coverage and pervasion, the over-all and underlying, as conceptions with which to begin a meditation, which will lead on to contemplation.

"How," then says Yāgnyavalkya, "O Maitreyī, shall one know that by which all this is known? How shall one know the knower?" Immediately following upon this question comes the Honey Section of the Upanishad, which runs as follows:

The earth is honey for all beings; all beings are honey for the earth also—again I summarize—water, fire, air, ether, sun, moon, duty, truth, etc., etc. It is the "city-dweller," composed of light and immortality. It is the self, the immortal, Brahman, all. Just as all the spokes of a cartwheel are fixed in the nave and the circumference, so are all beings fitted in the self, which is without before or after, or inside or outside, the knower of all.[25]

All things nourish one another—this is the meaning of honey. Materially and spiritually, everything is for us a gateway to the infinite, as I have put it earlier in this book. The more we understand the over-all relationship of things, the more fluidity there will be in our ideas of them, in our mental grasp of thingness. In the varied world nothing is basic, but everything has its "floating power." In the mind all our motives are without real purpose, and yet every one of them has its fundamental guidance within. In our thought there are not truths, but only fancies—in our thought, which leads to our makings of things also—and yet those fancies are never without truth. There is no complete error, no complete ignorance—ever. In the world what resists us helps us, as the

---

[24] *Purusha.* Sometimes the human body is called "the nine-gated city," the gates being mouth, nostrils, eyes, ears, etc.
[25] *Brihadāranyaka Upanishad,* II, 5. Much abridged.

ground which obstructs our feet, but is necessary in walking. There is no escape from the self—even māyā belongs to that and is essentially truth.

All this is "from the horse's mouth." It concludes by stating that Dadhich first taught this "honey" to the heavenly twins. Shankara relates this piece of old mythology as follows: When the twins, who were the heavenly physicians, came to Dadhich for instruction, he told them that the king of heaven, Indra, had threatened to cut off his head if he passed the "honey" teaching on to anybody else. The physicians then undertook to escape the difficulty by storing Dadhich's head in a safe place and putting on him in its place a horse's head. He agreed to this plan, and taught the twins the "honey" doctrine through the horse's mouth. Indra fulfilled his threat by cutting off Dadhich's horse-head, and then the twins kept their promise by putting back on his body his own original head.

How shall one know the knower? By knowing anything properly and fully. That is the secret of the Honey Section. If there is no substance in any thing, but only its qualities and actions, its relationships exist and are known and described as objective. Similarly, there is no subjective "substance," no knower but only the knowing. It is the knowing that we call "I," because knowing and being are the same. It would be absurd to think that knowing is an attribute of a substance which is not knowing. What would a knower be when he was not knowing? To understand life we can dispense with substance at both ends of the scale—both objective and subjective.

Every piece of knowing is unitary. Even in the mind an idea is always one thing, not two or more. A utilitarian simplicity envelops the idea of a man riding on horseback— simplicity in the field of intelligent action—but not if one tries to think of a tree riding on horseback, or a giraffe reclining in an overstuffed armchair. Indeed, it is difficult to hold those incongruous pictures in the mind, which keeps skipping from one to the other—tree to horse, and horse to tree—or giraffe to armchair, and armchair to giraffe—but there is no such skipping when the idea is man-on-horseback, for it is one thing. One who knows cities well enough can think a city in one idea. I am sure that a good professor who knows his subject finds it very simple. We may go to it, then, and find the self, or rather self, as many thousands are said to have done. From the unreal to the real is not from one thing to another, but from the complexity of duality and multiplicity to the simplicity of unity. From death to immortality is the same, as error is a matter not merely of thought, but of action and creation, and thus of involvement in a false condition, from which knowledge is the only release.

CHAPTER 30

LOCKE, HUME, BERKELEY,
AND OTHERS

It is not my desire in this and the following chapters to involve the reader in the numerous arguments for and against the various schools of realistic and idealistic thought which have had their vogue in the last few centuries in Europe, but merely to look at the principal teachings of some of the most noted modern philosophers, and examine them alongside the Vedantic traditions. Let us first turn to the English, Irish and Scottish realism, in the persons of Locke, Reid, Hume and some others.

According to realism—belief in the existence and activity of the world, quite independent of any knowledge by any being of any part of it—the odors, tastes, sounds and colors which are delivered at the door of our consciousness tell of things as real as we are and as independent of us as we were of them before they arrived. Living in England as a boy I never saw a mango, and never thought of one of those luscious fruits, and certainly never imagined the distinctive taste of it, but there were at that very time millions of mangoes, in India and other countries and millions of people who had tasted them and knew very well that sensation. If I do not believe in the existence of more "mangoes," and more people, and those people's sensations all independent of my own, I am not a realist. If I do believe in them, I am.

In addition to such direct sensations, we obtain knowledge about the things of the independent world also by reasoning and the testimony of others, who give verbal knowledge.

Sometimes, indeed, we have to correct errors of our senses with the aid of these.

The mind thus reflects in itself objects somewhat as a camera plate receives photographs, but more inclusively, as it also "knows" their qualities and activities. We know directly also that it has operativeness as well as receptiveness. A glance over the seven-fold list of the Analytical School of India mentioned in our last chapter shows that the last four —the noting of resemblances, differences, relationships and absences—belong to the department of operativeness within the mind.

It is to be noted also that this mind has two sets of organs: (1) those for reception from the independent world, namely the sense organs of touch, sight etc., and (2) those for action upon the independent world, namely the action organs, hands, feet, speech, etc. And we may note also here that just as the independent world exists before it is known by this mind, so also the actions done through the body leave their effects in the world after the mind has ceased to be aware of them.

Exactly how the mind receives its images from the world we do not know, nor how it snaps its "plans" into effect. There seems to be a gap between the independent world and the mind. How two such different realities could get together was the big problem that Descartes left for others to face.

Once these sensations are delivered to us through the sense organs, they are retained in memory, and we afterwards play and juggle with them in imagination and thought. It appears that there is thus an inner world of the mind, a world of "ideas" or pieces of knowledge, in which the objects can be moved about with ease, in a manner impossible in the independent world. And we can attend to chosen parts of this inner world of the mind, call up this or that memory, just as we can attend—or very often decline to attend—to chosen parts of the independent world.

Next comes the question: "Is the independent world only apparently outside, but really inside the mind?" It is directly *known* only in the mind, for all knowledge is inside, but, although inside, it is felt to have the character of an invader. Reason tells us that what we know of the independent world is but a small part of it, so even if the part of it that we know is in ourselves there is still the greater part of it outside. In fact the part that seems to be inside is only a copy of a part of that and has imperfections and incompleteness which can be corrected by reference to that world. This is supported by the test of action also, for if we walk in the dark we may knock our nose on a post, or fall over a chair—a post or chair which therefore was not in our mind. Surely the world of the mind is an internal representation of an external reality, plus the internal functions or capacities of imagination, reason, affection and the will. "External reality" includes other minds, as well as things with their qualities and actions, for among those actions we find such as ensue from our own actions upon the world, arising in our thinking, affection and willing.

Many people will think this is laboring the obvious, but statements of "realist" philosophy have to be formulated again and again to counteract waves of "idealist" philosophy which sometimes go to the length of asserting that what we do not know does not exist at all.

It will have been noticed that in the foregoing paragraphs I have mentioned the world and mind as though they were two quite different things—together but different—thus giving an impression of dualism in the field of reality. Our thorough-going realist, however, produces a monism by reasoning that mind also is material and mechanical, as being but a part of the world, just as the out-and-out idealist maintains the reverse, holding that all "material phenomena" are temporary products of mind, or, in some cases, merely orderly fancies in the mind.

This is an appropriate place to examine the relative usefulness of the independent world and the mind-world. That they operate together to sustain each other is obvious. The state of the mind without the ballast provided by the presence of an independent world would be pitiable—something more chaotic than any dream, something analogous to the possession of legs and feet without any hard ground to walk upon, and yet endowed with great restlessness. On the other hand, we cannot picture an independent world of mere substance on which no mind had impressed any forms. The mind and the world quite clearly form a unity, sustaining each other.

The outside world contributes its material to the mind-world, but the mind provides its own "power of reasoning." The ideas in the mind or memories are like furniture in a room; they are "dead thought" just as the pieces of furniture are "dead action"—the action of making a chair is finished in one case, the thinking in the other. The chair and the idea now remain in their respective outside and inside rooms, ready to be used for new action and new thinking. This similarity of the two worlds is very striking.

John Locke will serve as our starting point for a brief study of realism, although he is sometimes classed among the idealists, because, like Kant much later, he considered that our senses do not give us anything like correct pictures of things as they are. He accepted the finding of the famous Rene Descartes, who said, "I think, therefore I am," and argued for the distinction of mind and body, as quite different and separate things. Body was marked by extension, while the mind was characterized by thought.

There was no doubt about the reality of the mind and knowledge, for that, it was held, is directly known, as a little study of it shows.

Locke held that the mind never can rise above or beyond the

ideas arising in sense and mental reflection, though when it is stored with the simple ideas, it can repeat, compare and unite them in a great variety of ways, and thus produce new complex ideas. Our sense-experience of what Locke called the primary qualities of things, including extensity, resistivity and movement, seem reliable, but those of the secondary qualities such as are given in hearing, sight, taste and smell are not found to be accurate. "There is nothing like our ideas existing in the bodies themselves. They are . . . only a power to produce those sensations in us."

Here one must offer a little criticism. The foregoing statement is tantamount to saying that our ideas of things are only equivalents, or "opposite numbers," or symbolic, or codic—more or less accurate translations into a quite different language. But if the mind has no innate ideas of its own, but derives all from Nature through the senses, it cannot be argued that our mental pictures of things are mind-produced, and not to be found in the objects which arouse the sensations. Thus, for example, the color red. On this theory the mind did not invent red. Where then did that color arise? We say that objects have no color in the dark, that is, in themselves. The simple answer must be that the color is carried in the light ray from the sun. If a rose appears red it is because that rose reflects the red-carrying ray, and all we mean when we say that the rose is not really red is that the rose is a reflector or mirror for certain rays and not for certain other rays, so really we are looking at red in the mirror of the rose. We err, no doubt, in attributing the red to the rose, but not in attributing to the rose the character of reflecting the red-carrying rays. The high clouds in the evening sky change color according to the angle of the sun's rays falling upon them; they also are thus mirrors. No one finds fault with a mirror for reflecting and not containing the pictures we see with its aid.

Next, one must not say that the red ray is only a vibration and is not red, unless one admits that the red color exists *some-*

where in Nature and the ray somehow carries it. So there is no error in the sensation as such, but only in the idea that attributes the sensation to a particular form. Locke it was who first pointed out that if you take three bowls of water— one cold, one medium, one hot—put one hand into the cold for a while, and one into the hot, then put both hands into the medium basin, the water will feel hot to the hand which has been in the cold water, and cold to the hand which has been in the hot water. In this case heat does travel from the tepid water into one hand and out of the other hand into the water, so the sensations are reliable but relative. There is heat in Nature, and notwithstanding the imperfections of the senses that is where the sensation came from unless it is pure invention in consciousness.

If we admit that form can exist as such in Nature, we have no justification for an assumption that color or sweetness cannot. Someone asks: "Does the heat in Nature feel hot?" I think we may answer: "As much as the cube feels cubic, or the sphere feels spherical." The heat is there and can be shown by a thermometer. Does the questioner mean: "Is there heat, if no one feels it?" Of course there is. "But heat is a sensation, is it not?" No, it is a fact, as much as a cube is a fact in Nature. Attributes and motions exist in Nature. One recalls the saying of an old Greek mathematician: "Nothing can move in the place where it is, nor in the place where it isn't; so it cannot move at all." The answer is that it can move from one relationship to another. *From* and *to* are realities that come into the mind through the senses.

The fact is that action is the first test of reality. A blind man constructs a three-dimensional mental world after feeling cubes, spheres and other things. The things act among themselves. In the bowling alley, once the ball has left the hand, it travels without the help of our minds, and the ninepins will go tumbling whether we see them or not, and there will be noise and lights.

If anyone now says that colors (*e.g.*) have arisen for utility in evolution, such as that of the flower that calls the bee, and as it appeals to the mind (a blind bee would not see it, and so would not come to the flower) it need not be real color, but only something that will give that sensation to the bee, one must reply that there are thousands of colors, and the flower uses some of them. Human beings are now discovering new colors, by forming new chemical compounds; those colors would never have arisen spontaneously in a human mind.

The Vedantic monist finds no difficulty in this problem of mind and matter. To him they are one. Looking at the world, the mind is concentrating on a part of itself. Since thought ends in action, form is produced, and then inspected. The world is thus the product of a host of minds, all acting, all talking to themselves in form—a host of minds in one world. My mind originates some things; others originate many more. Where I concentrate I see or I create—like a carpenter who could make many things because he knows many things, but is intent on making a table today, because he wants to enjoy the consciousness of that intent. Or perhaps he will look with interest at another's work, thus associating with another mind.

When we feel the solidity of a piece of metal we are communing with the mind of the metal. Our argument was that the forms are outposts of the life in all the kingdoms of Nature, including the mineral. The mind there is experiencing the attributes there, producing the form which is a bundle of attributes by the arrestation of its attention upon them, and, in our sensation, mind contacts mind when form contacts form. In this nonduality there is no contradiction, though there may be plenty of error and false attribution in the realm of ideas. Realism and idealism are thus both incorrect, inasmuch as each tries to make one part the basis of the whole.

Realists think of causation as determinism. They say that the same cause will always produce the same effect. It only means that each thing always acts in the same way, which is an extension of the idea that each thing is what it is. It is from this idea that a mechanistic theory of the world arises, whereby, it is held, the future can be exactly predicted if you have all the data. In connection with this I must first mention Thomas Reid and then David Hume. Reid, the founder of the Scottish School of thought, insisted more decisively than Locke that our knowledge does not produce its objects, but finds them in a real world outside itself. Hume assumed the processes of Nature to be totally nonmental, regarded them as mechanical, and then applied this principle to the mind as a part of Nature.[2] He classified our mental content in two grades: (1) impressions, consisting of sense pictures coming from outside, and such as pleasure, pain and efforts arising from within, and (2) ideas, in which the impressions are reproduced and imagination works.

This is called the theory of sensationalism, because the mind is considered to be a blank sheet on which the sensations write. The inferiority, so to speak, or subordinateness, of the mind is shown by the fact that the least vivid sensation is stronger than the most vivid idea. The flow of ideas, Hume held, is by association. They are held together by (1) resemblance, (2) contiguity and (3) cause and effect. Resemblance is evidently classification, contiguity my man-on-horseback, and cause and effect familiar or constant sequence in Nature.

From this assumption arises the belief that mind is only an extremely delicate and remote reflex system, in which, however, the associations of ideas play a part. Even thinking is regarded as a mechanical reaction. This belief, however, contradicts itself, as we may easily realize by the following example: In a world composed of A to Z, A to Y are all acting

---

[2] It is to be noted, of course, that when it is claimed that man is mechanical, like the mineral, it can equally logically be claimed that the mineral is mental, like the man—further, conscious like the man. Especially is this so as consciousness cannot be explained away.

upon Z, the reaction of which is determined by them. At the same time, however, B to Z are all acting on A, and similarly with all the other letters. So each person is being acted on by all the others, but his action is not totally determined by "others" because he himself is one of the "others." The determinism is gone and there is freedom of everyone to be what he fundamentally is! This confutes any possible mechanistic theory of mind. Similarly in relation to the principle of gravitation I have shown in an earlier chapter that we all have "floating power." We may consider also the feeling of ourselves as making a choice at every moment; if we could have a mind developed in course of time in Nature as a purely adaptive mechanical mechanism, it would not require consciousness at all—there is no reason to assume a difference in this respect between a simple mechanism and a complex one. If we have no freedom, we have no consciousness.

What causes constancy in Nature, and constant sequence? Not material habit. A human form has all its matter changed in a few weeks, but the form remains more or less constant. If there is a mind-habit, however, the form can be constant, although the matter changes. Constancy of form (objects and their qualities and actions) in Nature must therefore be attributed to mind rather than matter—human mind, animal mind, plant mind, mineral mind. In all of them there is unpredictability—very much in man, and least of all in the mineral, on account of its relatively very slow tempo. In this light even the "laws of Nature" slowly change. All this agrees with our theory that all evolutionary forms and artificial forms are "outposts" of ourselves.

What is the matter with the theory of realism? Can we put our mental finger on the spot of its aberration from the truth, and say, "This is where it took the wrong road in thought?" It is, I think, in too much "thinging"—allowing the thing to be too much master in the house of democratic reality. When we consider or look at an object, we must recognize it as a triad of object, quality and action.[3] The world is a complete solid-block interplay of all so-called things, in which the qualities and actions *are* the things. A thing does not *possess* qualities; it *is* the qualities. It does not perform actions, but *is* the actions. Similarly, we do not possess consciousness as a quality; we *are* consciousness.

What I mean by the solid-block interplay is that everything is in intimate touch with other things (take the thingness lightly in your thought) with no empty space between. This is a dance in which the partners are holding each other closely, yet in which there is a frequent change of partners, because it is an elastic world of actions. When I take a drink of water, I am dancing with the water, I am not mastering it. When we catch the high waters of Niagara in a tube and let them in falling turn our dynamos to produce electric power, we are dancing with them, not mastering them. We accept that bundle of thing-quality-action as and for what-it-is, and live with it as-we-are. We do no violence to one another; there can be no violence in this togetherness. There is no internal violence in an organic form when in health. In this way we have a picture of a world of togetherness, in which thingness, though there, is not vital—a picture difficult at first to hold in the imagination, because our wrong habit of thought, making too much of "thing" is hard to overcome.

And now it will be asked: "But where then is the continuity of a being?" The answer is, as already indicated, that there is no continuity in things, but the continuity is in consciousness. The dance is an intimacy of being, which is the knowing of one another. We dance with a stone, an aggregate or community of mineral lives. We build the stone into a wall, and in doing so work in harmony with it, accepting it. We say we know what it is. Our knowing can be more or less superfi-

[3] *Dravya, guna,* and *karma.*

cial.[4] The mineral is life learning stillness by acting stillness, and in so doing manifesting extensity, resistivity, and slow tempo of change. We recognize and accept these qualities when we build our wall. Such a recognition is a very superficial knowing if there is no feeling in it. It is a wooden dance in which we have too much "thingized" our partner. But we feel also something of the life that is there, we too have some enjoyment and experience of that velvety stillness of being —I do not mean that we should *think of feeling* (far, far from it), but we should allow the natural fellow feeling to have its way in us, though we at first may need mental knowledge about feeling in order to overcome a reluctance due to our old habit of too separative thought. Our dance with the stone may be kind or not, but in any case it is part of the great companionship of life. Our knowing of the stone is a community of being. And as all these bundles of qualities and actions are outposts of life, it is natural that our knowing of them in sensation should be a knowing of something that is of the life.

Why have I chosen a stone, of all things, for this illustration? Because if we do not admit life everywhere we establish again the reign of things, and we are back in our original paradox, because—more important, being positive, not negative—it becomes a matter of valuable experience if we do not block our own path of knowledge with the erroneous theory of "thingship." The stone is a phase of life, or a piece of analytic living, in which the analysis never approaches complete separateness from the wholeness of living. Physics and chemistry are only the study of the mineral kingdom, in which for

[4] An animal, in knowing a tree, needs only a very superficial knowledge of its surface. That is enough for its purpose. A man, however, needs to know about its interior substance, and its mode of growth, and its variety, for his constructive and horticultural purposes. A mother or a teacher should know a great deal, especially by sympathy, about a child's mind, which a playmate does not need. A statesman should know more about the interior of people than a tailor, or even a doctor. Never will we be benefited by more knowledge about things than is requisite for their utility.

accuracy, we use mineral "yardsticks." That is enough to serve in the making of our material requirements, but not for knowledge of life or of ourselves.

Incidentally, this distinction enables us to understand what the yoga way of life is. It is following the line of companionship in the three-fold way. If we attend to the rose—make it the center of our attention for the time being, that is concentration. If we observe it and think all about it and thus obtain a greater intimacy with it, that is meditation. Thirdly, if we pass into such communion with it that we forget our *idea* of ourself, this is contemplation.[5] It is something that we do in actual life as well as in the practice of reflection in the mind. It is the height of knowing, in which knowing and being combine. And it is the height of the joy of life.

Let us return to the philosophers. George Berkeley, although an idealist in his conclusions, argued with the realists' weapons. He began with a "new theory of vision," pointing out that we see things as on a flat screen, and then the mind quickly adds depth to the picture by co-ordinating it with its prior experiences of touch and muscular sensation. We then ascribe to the seen things extensity (shape, size), resistivity (solidity), and action (change of position), and rightly so if it is a true fact that one cannot walk through the closed door.

Berkeley, however, judged it to be only a world of idea, a thought-world. He accepted Locke's division of the qualities found in things as primary and secondary. Those qualities already stated, by which things act upon one another, are primary, but those in which they—as I would put it—appeal mainly to mind (sound, scent, sight, taste), are secondary. It seems to me that these can be classed as akin to language, inasmuch as they require interpretation in the mind they appeal to—as, for example, when bees and other insects become aware of the flowers through colors and scents. However,

[5] *Samādhi*, which is "agreement" or harmony.

these colors and scents etc. are qualities of the flower—at least that would be Locke's way of putting it, but Berkeley held that to say that there is a substance there which has these qualities just means nothing at all. The properties are there; they need no support except that of the mind, which they have. Locke held that the primary qualities are real without the support of mind, but this Berkeley denied. If colors are essentially mental so are extensity etc. in which they inhere.

It is an interesting fact, incidentally, that colors, scents, tastes and sounds in plants, animal and human are very largely an appeal to minds, sometimes to attract them, sometimes to repel. The color of the flower is the "dinner bell" for the bee, and the honey is the temptation to closer contact, whereby the pollen is carried abroad. The odor of the skunk, the spines of the cactus and the white coat of the arctic fox have a contrary—a defensive—policy.

Then came Berkeley's great inference, correcting or completing sensory experience, that no object exists except as perceived by mind. Mind is not in the world, but the world is in the mind. When someone asked, "But what of the objects when no one is looking at them?" the answer was that there is always God. This is good Vedantism, if we do not make it dualistic by thinking of God as a being, a creator, but on the contrary, allow for life in *everything*, as in our outpost theory. Then, the extensity of a "thing" is the outpost of a mind dwelling in and working with that limited idea, and thus we have all the reality that any realist can conceive. If extensity means reality, we have it. Reality is a play of real ideas. Such an outlook has come to be called idealism, and usage sanctions the word, though it is properly idea-ism, and the study of ideals is another business.

We come now to another problem which arises when the theories of idealism are carried to "their logical conclusion." [6]

[6] Why does this expression continue to be respected? The term logical really condemns it, for it takes attention away from the practical. "I like

If the world is only in the mind, all must be in *my* mind, because even other minds which I know are within mine. The whole business is like a dream, in which the objects simply do not exist when I am not aware of them. This view, that "I alone exist," is called solipsism. Berkeley's "God," however logically necessary to support the existence of his ideal "world," is still within that world, being only Berkeley's idea! That Berkeley's mind had some passivity and obedience to what he inferred to be others, that his life was not entirely self-willed, was taken as a reason for belief in the existence of other minds—just as the extensity, resistivity and independent actions of other bodies or objects is taken by the realist as reason for belief in a real world outside him. Yet even the apparent passivity and obedience are only "in your dream." There is no escape from solipsism in this view of the world.

I am not sure, however, that there are any sincerely believing solipsists. There is something repugnant about it, from which even philosophers shy away, as a frightened horse does when an old newspaper blows about in its path—there is something that does not fit into its ordered world.

I have two contributions to make to the solipsist idea. First, through the study of dreams. Our dream condition is useful and valuable, because in it our critical faculty is in abeyance. It did not surprise me in a dream to find that lovely grove of cocoanut trees growing on board the steamship on which I fancied I was traveling. There is remarkable detail and clarity in these dreams. This shows me that I have more imaginative faculty in dream than I have when I am awake, when it is jostled and overborne by incoming impressions. Does not the writer who wants to make his perhaps difficult subject as clear

---

pie. Pie is good for the body. Therefore let me eat as much as I can." Well, try it and see. Every fact is hedged round with practical limitations, and act has to be guided by fact, not by logic. Logic is only for finding out what the fact is, and is always based on facts, which provide the general as well as the particular premise.

as possible, require great quietude and freedom from interruption? And why is it that when we wake and try to capture the memory of a dream it very quickly fades, but if we keep our minds very still, scarcely waking, we can to some extent recollect the dream, or parts of it? Because our innate faculty for visualizing is better then than in the waking state. The second thing we learn from dreams is about ourselves. In them we see ourselves more clearly, especially our bare feelings and motives, which we have often rationalized almost out of sight in the waking state. In dream we are honest with ourselves. The soul (if I may use this expression without precise definition just here) sees its own mind for what it is in dreams, without self-deception, and therefore it learns something which it cannot do in the waking state. Dreaming is a valuable condition, and we would be the better, the stronger and the truer for remembering it more, reducing a little the modern habit of dashing at something as soon as we wake. Contemplate, advises the yogī, the knowledge that comes through dreams. I have mentioned this before, but it deserves repetition, lest we forget.

If, then, all our waking life is a sort of dream, as solipsism implies, there is no lack of educative value in that—though we must be practical and say that the waking dream is in the sphere of action, while the dreaming dream is a kind of useful reflection upon its seeings and doings. Vedanta thought gives value to all our three states: waking, dreaming and sleeping, and does not say that dreaming and sleeping are merely a waste of time. I believe that if we go to sleep every night with a feeling of quiet pleasure in the prospect of dreams, we shall get better sleep and better dreams, and come back from them with a lingering trail of purifying knowledge.

As to the state of deep sleep—still further are we then from the hurly-burly of the world's conflict. The soul (I must use that word again) is refreshing itself at the fount of pure consciousness, or nearly pure consciousness, and is there quite selflessly tasting the fruit of experience which ensures its growth. These three correspond to concentration (waking), meditation (dreaming) and contemplation (sleeping). In that last we are enraptured, illumined, and happy, and a mind-action is fulfilled. Therefore do we come out of deep sleep with a feeling that we have been blessed and the sense of being empowered with a new consecration. Surely the Vedanta is right when it says there is no unconsciousness, even in sleep.

In the knowledge of the three states of waking, dreaming and sleeping, we have a most important and useful section of the Vedantic yoga. First we must inspect and think about them and so discover the value of each of them. This will relieve us of the common prejudice which makes us think that experience in the waking state is the only real experience. In comparing waking and dream we can call them both reality—action-reality and dream-reality—or both dream—action-dream and idea-dream. The yoga practice in connection with this knowledge is very simple—go to sleep always in right mood, not carrying your troubles with you. Sleep the sleep not of exhaustion but of anticipation—not rationalized anticipation, which is shot through with limitation, but peaceful undefined expectation. When you relax your body before sleeping (which is also a piece of commonsense in living, though it may require a little practice if we have got it into a bad habit of going to sleep without relaxation), next relax your mind into the absence of desire and ambition, into the enjoyment of mind-being not pushed about by actions and events. In this fuller living you will begin to know peace, which is happiness, excitementless joy. In waking do not try to harness your new peace or power to the old wagon of desires, ambitions and fears; do not shatter it; let it be "with you."

It may be asked, "Why, then, not try to sleep nearly all the time?" There is organic living in the three states. They are not totally different, nor unrelated. They are part of the shuttle-action in the psychological loom. We come to the action-state for honey; we go to the sleep-state for power. Notice these words "come" and "go." Some day we shall say we go to the action-state for honey, and come to the sleep-state for power. That will be the case when knowledge of the false self and the real self is clear. When the three are together there will be fulfillment. Shiva is spoken of as the conqueror of the three cities.[7] Shiva is the patron of yogīs—in the symbolism. The three cities are the three states of waking, dreaming and sleeping. They are all knowledge. The conqueror of the three states enters the fourth,[8] which is not really a fourth but the union of the three.

Now to the second contribution to the theory of solipsism. I have already expounded the practice of "I, you and it"—another most valuable piece of yoga—but let me state it again here. It will come out a little differently, and with a new utility. You are sitting with several friends, or imagine you are. To A you say, "Your arm is muscular, it is strong." To B, "Your complexion and your figure are good; your body is well-kept." And so on, to all the friends. These people have been saying to themselves: "I am strong; I am well-kept," but more careful thought would have led from details such as "My arm is strong," to the whole body, "My body is strong, or well-kept." Looking at your own body you say the same thing, and call it "it." The arm is "it"; the whole body is "it."

Now you turn to A again, beginning a second circle, and think of his conscious mind, and say, "You are clever," and to B "You are good," and so on. This time, when you come round to yourself, you have to be careful not to slip. You must still say "you." There is no difference in attributes, nature and class between the youness of your friends and the youness of yourself. So take a good look at your own you, as well as theirs. You will then become increasingly aware of "I," and of "I" over against and different from "you." You

[7] *Tripurantaka.*
[8] *Turiya.*

will find yourself saying, "My person is my you," just as, "My body is my it." And "I is what I am." You must not start trying to define "I"—lest you make an "it" of "I," like a captive spiritual balloon. By any attempt to define "I" you will plunge yourself in the old error of superimposition.[9]

But now we come to the third circle. In the second round, looking at A, B, and the others, including yourself, you have said, "You, and you and you. . . ." Now, in the third round the formula, beginning the circle with yourself, is "I, and I and I. . . ." This is not merely fanciful. The uneasiness we have in the matter is mental. But if the "saying" is not mental, but "I-al," it will be different. This must be an I-experience, not a thought-fact. It is the wonderful basis of life, not to be grasped by "its" and "yous," but to be allowed fulfillment in us through the devotion of "it" and "you" to "I," which has not outlines, like an it, nor a center, like a you, but is all-pervading, and is freedom and joy. Where is the fear of solipsism now, when the many are one, and man-on-horseback is the undivided truth?

I think everyone will agree that thought and feeling are always found together, but it is not always noticed that there is another partner in each act of consciousness. I am sure that when knowing begins in a child, there is very little "it" or "you" in the picture. There is something very like pure consciousness. The child has no idea of milk, or mother; he or she merely enjoys the consciousness of the taste of milk. Even a grown person drinking milk does not enjoy milk, nor even the taste of milk, but enjoys the consciousness of the taste of milk. This pure consciousness is the knowing of "I," which is there, but unnamed, before the thinking gets to work, entifies milk and mother, and calls the milk "it" and the mother "you." It is only after the babe has entified milk and mother, that he or she entifies himself or herself, and saying "I" mixes that up with an "it" miscalled "I" and a "you" miscalled "I."

[9] *Adhyāsa.*

Let us realize that feeling and I-ing are both forms of knowing. When we look at another person, a you, we first see an it, a face. Perhaps there is grief written on that face, and in a moment the feeling-flow becomes greater than the thinking-flow, so that we become greatly concerned about that "you." There is then a telepathy of feeling—which is a mode of feeling-knowing. The thinking must now stop studying the face with a view to more knowledge about the grief, in order to allow the direct experience.

Beyond that is the still deeper experience of unity in which I meets I, and therein is known "the value of the grief to the soul," or "the impulse of the central urge." This is still another kind of knowing. Quotes were necessary in the last two lines to show that the pure untainted knowing of unentified consciousness is not thus, but only is described thus by the entified thinker.

I want to say that these are real processes in consciousness, without which we are not getting the full content of any experience. When we have them we shall also find the unity of the world, without that division of it into two entities—one "outside" and one "inside" the thinking mind.

The foregoing is Vedantic thought expressed in modern terms. In that philosophy, to know is more than to think. This is not mysticism—closing the eyes to look within. It is opening them more and more. We are not rejecting anything—to look there and not here—but are receiving all.

CHAPTER 31

FROM KANT TO SCHOPENHAUER

Let us now turn to some of the principal points in that wave of German idealistic philosophy which rose with Kant, and took various forms in the thought of his followers or successors, notably Fichte, Hegel and Schopenhauer.

We will first take up the "intuitional" movement inaugurated by Emmanuel Kant, and will see, I think where any tendency to substitute part for whole sets up a philosophic "superstition," and where the absence of that error—as the Vedantists would call it—leaves a basis for reconciliation.

In view of the doubt, raised by the Realists, especially Hume, as to the correctness of our perceptions, Kant addressed himself to the question: "How do we know things?" He answered himself by saying, "In space, time and causation." The senses give us a picture, but it is meaningless (like an artist's picture to a cow) until we have added to it some means of knowing provided from within the mind. These are principally space, time and causation, which are called intuitions (something taught to us from within), which form a sort of network for the interplay of all things. Things would mean nothing to us if we did not think of them in this network, or field of relationships.

This is equal to saying that man has reason, which implies the use of classification, but things in Nature do not classify themselves, or compare themselves with one another as to resemblances and differences. Space, time and causation are very wide categories. Whatever is presented to our consciousness—a percept—is thus something-in-space, something-in-time and something-in-the-field-of-causation.

To apply these categories to things in thought is reasoning. Reason leads to understanding, a piece of understanding being a knowledge of the relations of a group of things in the network. If we come into a large room and see a great many chairs in rows, we reason that there is going to be a lecture or an organized meeting of some kind, whether with talk, or pictures or music we shall judge from other things. The mind "understands" the complex of things that are there then; they form a unit for a purpose. The mind takes them in as a unit; it grasps the whole picture.

Man is greatly concerned with reason, because of purpose. But those chairs and other things have no purpose in themselves. Purpose, however, has put them together and holds them together. It holds the body of a man together, also that of a worm or an amoeba, and even—some say—an atom.

To apply this understanding to everything is to regard the world of forms as fundamentally of the nature of idea, or purpose. This is what Kant seems to have done. He observed that we do not know things-in-themselves, as mere objects, as what in the last chapter we have called "in the outer world," but only in the light of reason and purpose. In these circumstances, the senses are not called upon to present us with pictures of the things-in-themselves, and are not formed and qualified to do so. What things *are* in themselves is unthinkable, because thought is concerned with reason and purpose. Inasmuch as forms (such as chairs and everything else) are shaped with purpose, things-in-themselves have no form, so are not something-in-time, something-in-space, something-in-causation. Even the terrible hardness (to us) of things is on purpose. The world can be understood because it is an idea.

In this very brief summary I hope I have not unfairly represented Kant's philosophy of the world.

Among the things in this world of idea there are not only material things but also living beings. We look into that world and see other minds, other lives. Doing so, we recognize a kinship, and understand that we cannot use those minds for our purposes. They are in themselves incarnations of purpose in their relative spheres of influence. In connection with these therefore arises another intuition, which Kant accepted as that of duty, which makes us say "I ought." There would be no "ought" without choice, he argued, so there is a moral law working in us, relating these persons together. We can do what we like with *things*, because they are only means to our individual ends, anyhow; but not with persons, each of whom is an end in and to himself, not a means to be exploited by others. Kant's treatise against slavery was a practical outcome of his belief in this intuition, and from it also he derived his belief in God.

To substantiate his claim to the intuitional character of our knowledge of space, time and causation, Kant formulated a mnemonic of six letters, ICANMA, to be interpreted as follows:

I stands for *Infinity*. The argument from infinity is that space and time, to put it in my own words, do not occupy space and time. There is no place where space begins or ends —for that would imply a space beyond space, an absurdity. Similarly, there is no time at which time begins to be, or ends. There are no bounds or limits to either. This is called infinity. We do not receive this infinity as a sensation. It is therefore a pre-existent fact in the nature of thought—one of the concepts which distinguish the mind from a camera plate.

C stands for *Continuity*. Just as the artist's picture is only a collection of dots and dashes, so is each picture received in sensation. Similarly, the parts of a chair do not constitute a chair. I think the example of a musical melody is even more effective, because in this case the separate notes, occupying perhaps a half-a-second each, have come and gone—but the mind somehow holds them in a continuity or in a unity, and then there is music, not mere notes.

A stands for *Adhesion*. The notes of music are gone, but

the mind still thinks of the time when they were there. **Or,** an earthen pot is destroyed, but we regard the space which was occupied by the pot as being still there. We do not see that space as space; this conception of space is provided only within the mind.

N stands for *Necessity*. Space and time are necessary because there is no object of sensation that does not occupy space, and there is no happening except in time. The object means nothing to us, except as in space and time.

M stands for *Mathematics*. Sensations and perceptions cannot perform the operations of arithmetic and geometry. These are carried on in the mind. The mind conceives triangularity, for example, and all triangles conform to this.

A stands for *Antecession*. This means that the concepts of space and time antecede the perceptions for which they are necessary. We cannot begin to know what a thing is without their prior presence.

At first sight Kant's statement that we do not know the world is very pleasing to the nondualist Vedantist, as it approaches the theory of māyā; but there the Western philosopher stopped, while Shankara and his teachers went on, and passed on their message: "You shall know the self, and thus what the world is, too." From this standpoint Kant's philosophy, while releasing the mind from the trap of the world, binds the self in the trap of the mind. In his statement of the priority of the intuitions to knowledge he slipped into an assumption. He took for granted what he set out to prove; put certain assumptions into the world, and then discovered them there.

In the ICANMA he gives reasons, derived from experience of the world, for the existence of the network. The network was not known *first*, however, as it should have been if it came first. A mind which had never received any sensation could hardly be presumed to entertain itself with thoughts about mere space and time, with nothing in them. Space and time are not among a babe's first thoughts—I think we can see how it builds them up from percepts, coming through the senses and received as such.

It has to be shown that these intuitions are harmful to the realization of the true nature of things. They are useful in their limited sphere, as enabling the mind to hold a larger grasp, but not as helping him to know either the nature or the utility of things. They form the essential part of Kant's first great work, the *Critique of Pure Reason*, and indeed it must be said that he himself transcended them (except for their limited use, in a purely material sphere) in his second *Critique*, in which his "categorical imperative" (the "ought" and the free moral agent) appears, and again in his third *Critique*, making room for the beautiful and the fit as well. After all, he unfolded the three Greek values—the true, the good and the beautiful, in turn. Vedanta thought—the understanding of life—demands the union of the three, not in a mentalized picture, but in a living experience. I will anticipate just enough of this with the aid of a verse from Emerson:

> The little needle always knows the North,
> The little bird remembereth his note,
> And this wise seer within me never errs,
> I never taught it what it teaches me;
> I only follow, when I act aright.

I will pass on now to some brief criticisms of ICANMA. If it does not help us to know the world as it is we must proceed to something else, must go beyond it for our understanding. If we only want to know the world as we know it, we are only asking for a picture of our own ignorance. That is not real knowledge. Any *a priori* conceptions of reality must be ignorant, for the simple reason that if we knew the fact we would not want to know it. Any idea that we now have of Infinity, Continuity and the rest—yes, even Mathematics—will have to give way to better ideas through the tuition of experience. This network is not an iron frame to last for all eternity, but is a kind of mind-sense, which has its own infirmities comparable to those of bodily sense organs. Using it, the mind interferes with the world it is trying to know, and corrupts the evidence that the senses deliver to its ignorant shrine. I fear they must be classed as inferences, and even then as fallacies.

Infinity. Someone asked, "Who wants infinity? Has it any goodness, truth or beauty about it?" It cannot bark or bite, as James said of concepts in general. Let us look at it. Let me take the point where my pen touches this paper at this moment, and draw imaginary straight lines north, east, south and west, and to the zenith and the nadir—all of them endlessly, to infinity. No one of these lines will be longer or shorter than any other; therefore this point is the center of the universe. So is any other place. This nonsense arose because I brought in the word infinity, and the concept infinity. But it seems to be of no service to reason, because it does not allow the relationships which both reason and experience require. Experience permits me to say I can draw limited lines, and no more.

Continuity. I draw a line with a pencil on a sheet of paper. I say I am making a continuous mark, and that it becomes longer by continuing. This is given to me through the sense of sight. Does my intuition tell me that what I have drawn is not a continuous line, but something else, which, however, intuition is making to appear continuous to me? If there is a quality of extensity connected with objectivity—why should its continuity not arrive to us through sense?

As I extend the line, am I adding to it points, or lumps? If I am adding lumps, each one has extensity or continuity. If I am adding only points, each addition is nothing, as a point has no extensity, and in fact I am not adding at all. Or am I not really lengthening the line, an all-over fact in regard to which continuity is an objective act? The movement of my hand in drawing the line is continuous. Let us go to the babe, which sees the world as one big blur, and gradually analyzes smaller blurs in that continuum, even then giving them more mental discontinuity than they really possess.

Adhesion. If we destroy a pot we do not see that the other things from round about close in to fill up the vacant space. The senses tell us about the gap, but they say, "There is no thing there," not "There is nothing there." However, there is something there—only it is something the senses cannot feel or see. Or if we do not feel even air there, and if in fact there is no resistant material there, the Vedantist will still say that we must take the fifth "element" into consideration, that which constitutes the sky beyond the atmosphere, that is, the ether.[1] Furthermore, he will say that even that ether contains a proportion of the character of the other "elements," and so it too does offer resistance, though too delicate for our senses. That is a bit of the ancient science; which says all things are living together—not in empty space. They are just together, and what looks to us like empty space is not so.

Necessity. No, the concept of space is not necessary. Other things move in ether, not in space. *Mathematics.* A game; if we have presumed its principles or axioms. *Antecession.* An invalid inference, as we have shown.

The fact is that these conceptions are assumptions by the mind, not intuitional truths. They are brought in *to account for* ignorance, to fill up gaps in our world-picture. They are infirmities of the mind, and do not assist the thinker, or the moral agent or the seer. They are small things promoted, parts swallowing wholes. In philosophy they play the kind of role that formerly in religion was filled by an old gentleman with a beard, who at the same time was regarded as omniscient, omnipresent, and omnipotent. They are not universally present, for each one implies a real opposite and establishes a profound duality of thought.

"You talk," someone says, "as if duality were a sin." It is,

[1] *Ākāsha.*

philosophically. It is like calling the universe a tree-on-horse-back, when it is a man-on-horseback. It is calling it two when it is a two, that is, one, as explained in Chapter 5. The practical issue is also involved in this—what I have called the Yoga of the Vedanta, stated in the formula: "The One Reality can be known," by exploring the I, the self—the true, not the false self.

The questions now are, did Kant's successors come nearer to the true monism, and does and can any idealism do so? The especially notable names that come up in connection with the first question are Fichte, Hegel and Schopenhauer.

Every obstacle is a challenge to man, so it was but natural that the immediate followers of Kant should try to find out more about those things-in-themselves which he had de-clared to be beyond the sphere (or the cow-rope, as the Hindu philosopher would put it) of the sensory and intuitional powers of the mind. We have seen that Kant himself discov-ered a purpose in life through his "categorical imperative," shown in the word "ought," which applies only to persons—oneself and others, not to things. I had an example before me just now. My wife said, "I am going out to buy a few things, would you like to come with me?" My reply was, "Yes, I would very much like it, but I ought not to do so, in fact I must not, for I have promised this manuscript to the pub-lisher without delay, so must keep at it." I have a duty to the publisher and the public, not to the pen, to the paper, or to the printing machine. This distinction between things and persons is very important. We have no duty to things. So what are they for, and how do they come to be in this world of persons?

Those who have read this book carefully will have noted that from the beginning this position has been taken up—that things are outposts of mind, creations of mind produced by halts of mind which we call attention, or concentration. If a child wants a toy, why is it? The child wants to enjoy a cer-tain feeling-poise, to linger on a taste of experience, and taste it more. A man is not different. "Life is hunger," says the Upanishad. Without going into all this argument, Kant hit upon the secret in his acceptance of "ought" with reference to persons. If things do not tell moral agents what to do, they could not have created the moral agents in any manner whatsoever; if they had been the creators of the moral agents, they would direct them now. This is all good Vedantism. Perhaps, however, Kant did not allow his study of Pure Reason and his study of Practical Reason to flow sufficiently together to form one river, and so remained in the trap of dualism. But his disciple and successor, Fichte, did essay to relate the two.

Fichte based his philosophic outlook more on "I act" than on "I think," which latter position had been accepted by Kant from the earlier European thinker Descartes. What I do is more important than what I think, because my thinking is only in the service to my doing, which is directed by the "categorical imperative"—one may thereupon argue. So we come round again to the Upanishadic doctrine already quoted: "For the sake of the self all things are dear." So, things exist and present obstruction to man because he needs their resistance in order to be a moral agent, to exercise his will. Instead of a child with its toys, we have an athlete with all his equipment of dumbbells etc. We need the earth in order to walk, although it resists the free movement of our feet. I think, however, that Fichte would have been nearer the mark if he had associated "ought" with desire rather than the will, because it is love that makes the "ought." In announcing love to be the wellspring of duty, Jesus was greatly wiser than Kant or Fichte. We *care* for persons. We "have a heart" towards them. If we like *things*, it is only for the sake of the self that they are "dear." [2] The word can be most accurately translated "beloved."

There is an atmosphere of feeling about Sanskritic philoso-

[2] *Brihadaranyaka Upanishad*, II, 4, 5. The word translated "dear" is *priya*, which is most unequivocally a term implying feeling.

phy which one feels to be somewhat lacking in the European, and which is necessary to the understanding of life. There is a knowledge which emerges into our consciousness as a result of the spontaneous impulses of affection which we lack if we merely place love in a mental category or system. Here again Jesus was marvelously right, and the mental philosophers fall short of monism by making love an attribute of the soul instead of its being.

It is interesting that Fichte's dumbbell theory—as I am calling it—was worked out in the karma-theory of India long, long ago, in the days of Krishna and even in those of his remote predecessor, Rāma. I have discussed it in Chapter 12. Well understood, it asserts that we get what we have worked for, and then that educates us. We work because we desire. We desire because we need.

When speaking thus of reason, love and will, I must allude to Fichte's regard for the unity of the mind, whereby he considered these three to be functions, not faculties. They are not separate departments or portions of the mind, but are the mind working in certain ways, and they are synthetic in their effects. Through this mind there is growth and purpose in life in the world, to which end the "not-self" (the dumbbell) is set up and comes into being. This making of a "not-self" implies that Nature is at basis a world of ideas, even if objectified. Further, it is a world of self, even if exteriorated. So Fichte's philosophy is a form of idealism—the world as idea or expression of idea. The exterioration can never be total, so the resistance can never be total, so the things have not a total thingness, and that is why you cannot find the thing-in-itself —that is the way I work it out, and that is perhaps what Fichte meant when he regarded things as mere shadows of the function of reason. These things are still only means to ends, having no intrinsic value; they exist for the self. But even then, inasmuch as the self in each of us acknowledges other persons who also express the will in their actions, there must be an absolute or over-all will, accounting for the whole of Nature and persons, and moving them from within with a divine intent. This thought flowed naturally from the unquestioning acceptance of many selves.

Hegel comes next—born twelve years later than Fichte and surviving him by seventeen years. Hegel shook the Western philosophic world with his wonderful discovery that what we are witnessing in life is "Becoming," and that this primary fact is so inclusive that it disposes of the mystery of nothing. In the process of removing "nothing" from being we arrive at "becoming!" This is the grand inference that set the world agog and left many of the philosophers gasping like fishes thrown out of water. Some even said that this was carrying reason too far.

The proposition is simplicity itself, however, if we begin it in the right place, where Hegel must have begun it. He must first have "seen" it for a fact, for it bears the mark of a piece of complete direct experience, not inference, and certainly not testimony.

To understand Hegel's discovery, you must look *first* at the world as Becoming. Do not say, "I can see things and persons that are. I thus see what exists, that is, being. Next, if you ask me, I am aware of empty spaces, and I think of what might be there and then say there is nothing there, and that is non-being." It will not do; you have obstructed your mental vision with that old bugbear of space. Look at Becoming first; then you will see that within that idea there is something that now exists, and something that doesn't but will do so. Then you look at being and non-being; the facts being and nothing are equal and necessary components, or rather residues of this analysis. It is not that being and nothing combine to make becoming, but that becoming is the reality which has a head and a tail, just like the elephant which the little boy was too small to see all at once. While removing the nothing you have the becoming. So please do not start all over again and ask: "But do you mean to say that 'nothing' exists?" I mean to say that "nothing" is; we experience it, but if you want me to say that it is a kind of being, meaning by being those things which you experience which are not nothing—well, I just won't.

Now, when you have found the meaning of Becoming, do not throw it away again, as Hegel did, at least when he said: "Reason governs the World and has consequently governed its history. In relation to this independently universal and substantial existence—all else is subordinate, subservient to it, and the means for its development." [3] If such statements are to be made and accepted only as mind-pictures, as idols, all is well (like the worship of Krishna with four arms), but to objectify the Becoming is to obscure it and lose the vision.

We can look at past and future in the Becoming. What is going on here, said Hegel, is a progressive realization of the idea of spirit, finding itself, or rather coming to itself and "contemplating itself in concrete actuality." This is somewhat like the old theory of archetypes—divine and perfect ideas which are to express themselves ultimately in form. There are two ways, however, of looking at such archetypes. One is to regard them as models or patterns of something to be made; the student or artist tries over and over again, constantly getting nearer to the "ideal." The other is to regard them not as outside models, but as inward impulses which give direction to all the life-functions, and will thus at last bring the student or artist to a realization of himself, he being the end (as Kant would have put it), and the forms or makings being only means, to which no honor or duty is due, and which may be broken without compunction. In the latter case, that of the inward archetype, one must of course reach one's realization through the "I," as before explained.

Hegel did not, I think, mean to *explain* Becoming by assuming the reality of non-being. It is only in a secondary way that we can invest non-being with the garment of reality—

[3] Trans. by Sibree, in his *Philosophy of History*.

not at all if by reality we mean being. Becoming is more than being. It is the reality of the world—of what is known. If I am right in this view of Hegel's meaning, we may say he came very near to the Vedantic theory of *māyā*, which says the world is the "indescribable" because it cannot be put in the category of being nor in that of nothing. "Pure being"— it is a question of agreeing upon the meanings of words—is not mere being, but is the Becoming which includes the nothing.

Hegel marks out three stages of the Becoming, working itself out in the history of life, realizing itself in mind in Nature. First there is the "feeling" stage, feeling here being a very obscure kind of knowledge. Then comes the stage of the subjective mind, with its reasoning kind of knowledge. The third is a stage of freedom, in which will and idea are one. I interpret these in terms of religion as (1) the stage of personal desire, very groping, (2) the stage of "Thy will, not mine, O Lord," which every orderly person and every scientist is carrying out, and (3) the stage of the illuminated soul, in which "Thy will and mine are one, O Lord," in which the purpose of everything is known, the Lord vanishes and "the Universe grows I."

These views may be criticized as somewhat speculative in view of the modern findings of morphological growth in plants and other such things, which do not follow such a regular and progressive pattern as was formerly thought. But this is not the ground on which the vision (as I have called it) of Becoming is to be judged. A tree throws out millions of wasted seeds—is it in the mere hope that some of them will find a place to grow, or is there in it an artistry aiming at better seeds, like an artist throwing off his many pictures? Without such an artist-impulse would seeds have become what they now are? We can trace the Becoming in any one line of forms, but life breaks into form this way and that way, it gropes, and gives up or backs off, and tries again, with little purity of Becoming until the illumination or third stage is reached. As seen through its forms, it seems to go "underground" when some of its forms are destroyed, but in the morning, when we come and look again at the garden, lo, new forms are there.[4]

I cannot think that Hegel's method was merely dialectical. His teleology was implied in the vision of the Becoming, and there is as much monistic outlook in his discovery that forms are agencies for self-realization, as there was in Fichte's dumbbells. Hegel indicated that nothing really goes astray from the one purpose, when he wrote: "Those manifestations of vitality on the part of individuals and peoples, in which they seek and satisfy their own purposes, are at the same time the means and instruments of a higher power, of a higher and broader purpose of which they know nothing."

For purposes of this study we may put aside Hegel's excursions along various bypaths, but I feel it necessary to counteract his—very ignorant—criticisms of Hinduism. In this mood, he could write: "The element of worship in Hinduism corresponds to its conception of God. God is here substance, the undetermined, abstract, contentless emptiness and vacancy. Now, worship means essentially the annulling of the separation between God and Man, the Reconciliation, the restoring of the unity and identity of God and Man. Hence, in Hinduism what man has to do in order to become identical with God is to empty himself of all content, to become that very vacancy which God is. Thus the state *aimed* at is an emotionless, will-

---

[4] I was much impressed in this matter when I read, years ago, Sir Arthur Keith's statement about the embryo: "There is a recapitulation of ancestral history as the human embryo passes through its ripening stages, but this recapitulation is masked by the display of characters which are wholly of recent origin. Nor need this surprise us. What should we think of a builder who in the erection of a palace insisted on 'recapitulating' all the evolutionary stages which lie between a hut and a palace? In the development of the human body, as of that of every other living thing, we find a strict observance of the principle of economy. If an ancient feature is reproduced, it is because it is a necessary part of the scaffolding for the new." From *Concerning Man's Origin*, by Professor Sir Arthur Keith.

less, deedless, pure abstraction of mind, in which all positive content of consciousness is superseded. God is here a pure abstraction, and man, in becoming the same abstraction, becomes identical with God, attains 'union with Brahma.' Thus worship aims at the complete submergence of consciousness."

This is unfair. It should be laid down as a rule—it is a moral rule—that in the comparison of religions one should compare the best of one's own with the best of another's, and if one alludes to the worst of another's one should compare it with the worst of one's own. There is too much of the comparing of the best of one's own with the worst of another's, and that worst of another's is easy to find, for there are thousands of writers in every religion who cannot avoid reading their own imperfections of character and knowledge into even the best of their national or family traditions.

These statements about Hinduism are not true. When the Scripture, trying to speak of God, says, "Not this, Not this," it obviously means *all* this, including the "not-this," so we must say—even as Herbert Spencer could not avoid doing with his "unknowable"—it implies *more than this, not less.* The substance Hegel talks about is described by him as "this," and God as a void, which is also a "this." And the Hindu goes into contemplation, not as an unconsciousness, but as an illumination of mind, which is a realization of something more than this, though indescribable in terms of this, in which "our consciousness" looks like blindness in comparison with the new. In fact, Hegel's own opinion about the fundamentality of Idea partakes of his tendency to this error of mistaking parts for wholes. He said: "The purpose of the Universe is the complete realization of the mind of God in actuality. Philosophy is the knowledge of the Idea by itself. Then the Idea becomes the Absolute Idea or Self-consciousness." This is by no means fundamental, and besides Self-consciousness is here presumed in the very seeking of it, however dimly and darkly, and leaves us with only a process mistaken for an end.

We come now to the last name I have selected for this brief study—Schopenhauer. He did not find Hegel's theory that the foundation of things is in Idea at all satisfactory. If we think of creation by idea, we see it to be true enough, but only in our environment. "Walking the plank," as explained in Chapter 8, could teach us that. In ourselves, thought precedes creative action, and we see that dimly and deviously the same order prevails even in the lower reaches of evolution. It is not that the world is merely passive, however, for thought also receives instruction and new ideas from the world. "But you cannot have it both ways," cries out the consistent thinker. This, however, is only apparently so; a closer inspection shows us that the mind is instructing or rather awakening itself (not being awakened) to the realization of its own latent possibilities by and through the creation. The created thing is thus really only a *pause of thought*, and not a thing in itself. Forms are then puppets in the mental stream, and to regard them as something purely external, standing up in their own right and on their own feet as the mind does, is to be under an illusion. Schopenhauer said that there is no thing-in-itself behind these forms, but the reality is behind the mind, and is the Will.

The German philosophers who preceded Schopenhauer were too intent on a mental picture of life and reality. But we have to experience what life is and know it whole, not merely have an idea of it. It seems as if the European philosophers had not this comprehensiveness, but that they were trying to interpret the whole drama of life in terms of mind —a case of making a part the cause or basis of the whole. Truly, however, if we can say that in some way the self is educating itself or awakening itself (all these similies being only poor and temporary substitutes for the truth of the matter) with the aid of mind and things, we must also say that the world is not real in the full sense of the term, and yet it contains and presents the reality, for it is never entirely bereft of it in the limiting processes of idea and creation.

Schopenhauer propounded Will as greater than Idea, and declared the world an illusion. May we say that he came nearer to the truth than those who have held the *Idea* to be basic? I think so. Because, while ideas rule the world, something else rules the ideas.

Let us look again at the relation between will and idea in the mind. If you sit quietly and watch the flow of ideas, cat—milk—cow—shed—roof—shingles—wood—trees and so on, you can suddenly pounce, and say, "Hey, stop, I want to look at those trees." You can govern that flow of ideas. What pounces? The will.

There is a will working in and through us, and it is our own will, and is indeed a better self than the ideas and concepts in which we commonly bathe. It gives order, while the drift moves towards decay. Everywhere in Nature we find a central urge, a will to live, the instinct of self-preservation, and more than that, of self-enhancement. I have claimed it even for the mineral and the atom. If we are advocates of the will, we cannot ask with what idea in view the will does its pouncing and thus controls the series of events. The will is a wiser seer than the reason is. We must not allow ourselves to fall back from the heights of will into the slough of ideas. If this will has a purpose, we must not think of that as an idea being brought to fulfillment. It can be only the purpose of life known in the will by experience of life. It appears that just as an animal needs to know only the outside of the tree for its purposes, and the man needs to know also the inside material of the tree for his purposes, we need to know still more of it for our "ought" purposes, and still more for our "reality" purpose. For the "ought" we must live affectionately. For the real we must live in the essential purpose or motive of life known in the will. This is the deepest intuition, but not a retreat within. It is our deepest need and hunger, and is reached only after and through love.

The essential will-to-live should not be confused with desire-to-enjoy. The latter is feeling for things, and, later, feeling for persons. This desire, which is essentially love, is behind thought, but behind the desire for company of things and persons is the fount. Schopenhauer saw this so deeply that he could write: "The individual character of each is to be regarded as his free act. He himself is such because he once for all wills to be such. For the Will exists in itself even in so far as it appears in an individual; it constitutes, i.e. the original and fundamental Will of the same, independent of all knowledge. . . . From this it follows that the Individuality . . . is not through and through mere phenomenon, but has its root in the thing-in-itself, in the will of the individual. . . . All genuine merits have their root not in the mere phenomenon, but in the thing-in-itself." [5] He added that the structure of the will is innate, and that it is incapable of any improvement through culture.

In this, Schopenhauer as philosopher was far from being the pessimist that he was with regard to life in the world. He placed man, that is every man, on such a pinnacle of being that the contrast of that with his condition in the world was indeed painful. But there was an inconsistency in this—at its greatest when he wrote of the world as a place of struggle for suffering and dying souls. He should have seen—and felt—what we may call the joy of being in the will to be, present behind all the suffering. This being is joy. It is the obstructions to life that give us pain, and that we abhor. Life is, otherwise, "wonderful, dear and pleasant unto each." We must hand it to Fichte that he saw the obstructions as "dumbbells." To Buddha, however, we owe the most unexpected and enlightening thought in this field. When he gained his illumination, he sang:

"I, Buddh, who wept with all my brothers' tears,
  Whose heart was broken by a whole world's woe,
  Laugh and am glad, for there is liberty.
  Ho, ye who suffer, know
  Ye suffer from yourselves . . . ." [6]

Then he described the world as a place of sorrow! With this paradox he showed "the way to bliss." It is indeed a great joy when we stop placing our happiness in this or that material gain, and find it in the living itself—even on a "low plane"—in the *manner* in which we meet the stream of events. There was no pessimism in Buddha. Quite the reverse. He found the secret of life, and its joy.

Although Schopenhauer was not able to see man's freedom in the midst of apparent bondage, as Buddha did, he was able to see his essential freedom, when he wrote of man beyond the mire of mind. I like to think how in his own corner he must have enjoyed his work—his philosophy—and the pleasure which must have been his in his literary artistry, which stands out far above that of all other thinkers of his time.

There is really no natural, nor philosophical, pessimism. We cannot deny the joys of natural living, in which every play of limb and function—walking and running and the luxury of sitting, breathing and eating etc.—are all sheer delight, as the animals well know. Even games, which are fighting in moderation, are the height of pleasure. When we tire of them it will be time to let them go. But in the meantime, what folly to preach or practice a doctrine of repugnance, which can leave us only in an enlarged mire of dislike, and bring us not one whit nearer to freedom from dependence upon the things of the world.

Some may say that to nominate will instead of idea as the basis of reality precludes ultimate knowledge as such and negates all philosophy. "Go act, and do not talk, or even

[6] *The Light of Asia*, by Sir Edwin Arnold.

think, except for small and temporary ends!" This would be true, were it not that will is also a kind of knowledge, so that we can say to thought, "I do not want your mental pictures, your flat and unprofitable substitutes for living." When we analyze this mind, with its thought, liking and will, we really find that all these three functions are modes of knowing. Thought knows about things, and when we try to know persons and purposes by thought we kill them and dissect them in the process. Liking gives us more intimate contact with things, and affection with persons, the latter setting in motion, I believe, a telepathy different from the sense-contacts which serve to connect the thinking-mind with its world of objects. We invest even things with personality when we like them, and then we do not really desire them, but rather their companionship. And the will? We see it governing likes and dislikes, because it is the key to the true pattern of living. Likes and dislikes are not random where it has its sway, because it, too, is a mode of knowing—but it is knowing of that which is beyond thing and beyond companion, which keeps all this dance of things and companions in order and in unity. Where it comes in, beyond the false self, stands "I," and inasmuch as "I" knows and trusts itself my life will follow its true orbit, and be true without the need of means and ends.

CHAPTER 32

EMERSON, AND OTHER AMERICANS

We turn to America, and I pick out for my first example Ralph Waldo Emerson. My first discovery here is that we have something I did not find among the German or the English-Scottish group of famous and typical philosophers whom I selected for comparison with Shankara and his teachers, the nondualists of Vedantic thought. The point of difference is that Emerson cannot be classed as either Idealist or Realist, because he is both of these things at the same time.

Though Emerson read the philosophies of the whole world, he was not selective, nor eclectic. He did not pick out any one as suiting him best, nor did he seek to make a new combination by putting together chosen pieces from different sources, with that patchwork coat effect that the eclectic method must always show, because it does not grow but is made. But Emerson started with an advantage over all those others, that he stood at the beginning of a new race and a new world and did not need to carry his head over his shoulder to appease a tradition. His companions in the new world were nearly all people who had left the past, and were prepared to go forward with hand and with brain, as the case might be, in their work of establishing the new.

Even among those forward-facing people not all could be as free as Emerson, for he was a man without bitterness. He did not allow one idea to capture him and obscure the rest, nor permit any ancient wrongs to blind him to the virtue and truth which were a part of their perpetration, and even of their perpetrators. He met and welcomed each new experience with his whole soul, and spoke and acted from the same vantage point. He leaves us therefore with a curious feeling that it was hardly a man who spoke, but Nature and the pulse of Nature that spoke through him, and apprised less articulate observers of their own vision and thought newly coming to birth for the new human age.

I came as a visitor and then a resident to this country, after long maturity in Europe and the East, and so could and can see in the movements and thoughts of the throngs and the schools and the homes the sprouting and budding of a new time spirit, which, if I may say so, is still a little youthful and clumsy, but is somehow natively even if only half articulately very sure of itself, and I can see also that it belongs to the future and the skies as well as to the earth and the present, and is really onward and upward. Perhaps even Emerson did not go far enough when advising the coming generation to hitch their wagons to the stars; they begin to show signs of hitching the stars to their wagons, which is something more.

There will perhaps be an end to this growth when it has gone a certain length, as each man's body grows, and even each thought of his, as the trees and animals stop at some point, as far as form and type are concerned. We may expect a period to this race-forming, which will then be followed—as was the case in older races and nations—by a ripening and the production of a fruit that can feed the world, soften the declining days of the old, and shelter the birth and growth of new children, consanguinous and adopted, in all parts of the earth. If I were to try to name the new era, I would say it is characterized, whether consciously or not, by an inward-rising feeling of sympathy and companionship with other men and all things, which in the Teutons who preceded us was kept somewhat in abeyance by their intentness on the power of thought and the narrowness that its clear and potent issues so often required. The new spirit seems to say: "There may be enemies, but we regret it, and we take no joy in the conflicts that may arise, nor in the victories that must ensue." There has been a release from the old mental pride, with its odious comparisons; the new ark of the covenant is being carried in all the sacredness that ever was, but with joy and cherishing, not with pride.

And now, perhaps, I shall be called upon to make good my estimate of this new philosophy of life by quotations. Well, there is not room here for much of that, but luckily each can do it for himself, for the Essays are to be found in most libraries and many of the homes, and I need only say, "Open the book at any page at random, and you will find such an ever-present central mood of the kind of which I have spoken, that whatever may be the topic with which it deals you will see that the treatment of it shines with this new outlook, and is indeed sustained by it." I open the Poems, and cull some verses from those that spring to the eye. Here is a bit from *Each and All:*

> Little thinks, in the field, yon red-cloaked clown
> Of thee from the hill-top looking down;
> The heifer that lows in the upland farm,
> Far-heard, lows not thine ear to charm;
> The sexton, tolling his bell at noon,
> Deems not that great Napoleon
> Stops his horse, and lists with delight,
> Whilst his files sweep round yon Alpine height;
> Nor knowest thou what argument
> Thy life to thy neighbour's creed has lent.
> All are needed by each one;
> Nothing is fair or good alone.
> I thought the sparrow's note from heaven,
> Singing at dawn on the alder bough;
> I brought him home, in his nest, at even;
> He sings the song, but it cheers not now,
> For I did not bring home the river and sky. . . .
>
>   . . . .
>
> I inhaled the violet's breath
> Around me stood the oaks and firs;
> Pine-cones and acorns lay on the ground;
> Over me soared the eternal sky,
> Full of light and of deity;
> Again I saw, again I heard,

The rolling river, the morning bird;—
Beauty through my senses stole;
I yielded myself to the perfect whole.[1]

I turn the pages, and choose the secret of all intuition and idealism from "Destiny":

That you are fair or wise is vain,
Or strong, or rich, or generous;
You must add the untaught strain
That sheds beauty on the rose.
There's a melody born of melody,
Which melts the world into a sea.
Toil could never compass it;
Art its height could never hit;
It came never out of wit;
But a music music-born
Well may Jove and Juno scorn.[2]

And the Realist. Here he is in "Woodnotes":

When the pine tosses its cones
To the song of its waterfall tones,
Who speeds to the woodland walks?
To birds and trees who talks?
Cæsar of his leafy Rome,
There the poet is at home.

. . . .

Knowledge this man prizes best
Seems fantastic to the rest:
Pondering shadows, colors, clouds,
Grass-buds and caterpillar-shrouds,
Boughs on which the wild bees settle,
Tints that spot the violet's petal,
Why Nature loves the number five,
And why the star-form she repeats:
Lover of all things alive,

[1] From *Poems*, by R. W. Emerson. Riverside (1883-1904) Edition. Houghton Mifflin Co., Boston and New York, pp. 4-6.
[2] *Ibid.*, p. 31.

Wonderer at all he meets,
Wonderer chiefly at himself. . . .[3]

Therein is shown the attitude of this sort of philosophy—
a nasty word in these glades, if it implies intentional outlook,
and not the spirit in a man, as it here does. Let us look at the
picture of Nature's action, or the environment that we meet.
We shall find it to be purely scientific, for it admits no chance
where reason is employed; the out and the in come from the
same stock. Here is a portion of the little poem entitled "Compensation":

> The wings of Time are black and white,
> Pied with morning and with night,
> Mountain tall and ocean deep
> Trembling balance duly keep.
> In changing moon and tidal wave
> Glows the feud of Want and Have.
>
> . . . .
>
> Man's the elm, and Wealth the vine;
> Stanch and strong the tendrils twine:
> Though the frail ringlets thee deceive,
> None from its stock that vine can reave.
> Fear not, then, thou child infirm,
> There's no god dare wrong a worm;
> Laurel crowns cleave to deserts,
> And power to him who power exerts.
> Hast not thy share? On winged feet
> Lo! it rushes thee to meet;
> And all that Nature made thy own,
> Floating in air or pent in stone,
> Will rive the hills and swim the sea,
> And, like thy shadow, follow thee.[4]

Emerson was thus very conscious not only that all things
in Nature speak, as it were, of some perfection, but that the

[3] *Ibid.*, pp. 33-34.
[4] *Ibid.*, pp. 270-271.

relations between them—or the occurrences of life—also are
not fortuitous. This comes out very clearly in his poem "The
Rhodora." After describing how he found the little flower in
the woods, he concludes:

> Rhodora! if the sages ask thee why
> This charm is wasted on the earth and sky,
> Tell them, dear, that if eyes were made for seeing,
> Then Beauty is its own excuse for being:
> Why thou wert there, O rival of the rose!
> I never thought to ask, I never knew;
> But in my simple ignorance, suppose
> The self-same Power that brought me there brought you.

It was not only in fate and Nature that Emerson perceived
a divine unity. It is true that in youth there was something
of a flight from men, as seen in the poem "Good-Bye," but the
vision soon righted itself. As early as 1841, in a letter to
a friend, Emerson could write of himself as "an admirer of
persons. I cannot get used to them; they daunt and dazzle me
still. . . . Blessed be the Eternal Power for those whom fancy
even cannot strip of beauty, and who never for a moment seem
to me profane." [5]

The little poems on "Heroism" and "Friendship" show how
the One and the many meet in mutual help like the clasp of
two hands:

> Ruby wine is drunk by knaves,
> Sugar spends to fatten slaves,
> Rose and vine-leaf deck buffoons;
> Thunder-clouds are Jove's festoons,
> Drooping oft in wreaths of dread,
> Lightning-knotted round his head;
> The hero is not fed on sweets,
> Daily his own heart he eats;
> Chambers of the great are jails,
> And head-winds right for royal sails.

[5] *Ibid.,* p. 496.

O Friend, my bosom said,
Through thee alone the sky is arched,
Through thee the rose is red;
All things through thee take nobler form,
And look beyond the earth,
The mill-round of our fate appears
A sun-path in thy worth.[6]

And all is summed up in the "Spiritual Laws," which tells of the "living Heaven," our actual world which our prayers should respect:

The living Heaven thy prayers respect,
House at once and architect,
Quarrying man's rejected hours,
Builds therewith eternal towers;
Sole and self-commanded works,
Fears not undermining days,
Grows by decays,
And, by the famous might that lurks
In reaction and recoil,
Makes flame to freeze and ice to boil . . .[7]

And who shall say that there is no solidity in all these contemplations, when Emerson could write, so long ago:

Atom from atom yawns as far
As moon from earth, or star from star.[8]

I must remember that I am not writing biography, but a note on the new philosophy, which is as old as the hills, but has been obscured for a while. It is a philosophy of self-awakening, not of acquisition. "Shakspeare is the only biographer of Shakspeare; and even he can tell nothing, except to the Shakspeare in us." It is a philosophy of being. And that is what the

[6] *Ibid.*, pp. 272 and 274.
[7] *Ibid.*, p. 275.
[8] *Ibid.*, p. 339.

Vedanta also was and is, with its four Great Sayings, taken one from each of the four Vedas: (1) That, Thou art; (2) This is the Self, the One Reality; (3) I am I, the One Reality; and (4) Knowing is the One Reality.[9] Central is its statement that being, knowing and joy are one, the same.

This new philosophy is not at variance with these Great Sayings, this finding of the One Reality everywhere, by acceptance and innocent penetration, not by the rejection of what is disliked—that pit into which Schopenhauer fell, but which, too, indicated a vision, a partial vision, the vision of the idealist which must breed pessimism when it mislays the present Real, because man himself is not immersed in the bad, but is the standing refutation of his own philosophy. I know that Hindu literature is spattered here and there with the same misogyny, and that the *vairāgya* which should be translated "uncoloredness" is often turned into "repugnance" or at least "surfeit." But an early surfeit is born of shallow heart; it is like a small stomach which cannot take a meal, and leaves its owner meager and sallow. And the false surfeits rationalized from fear of discomfort and pain are a great trap for the unwary on this path.

Quite different is the new Naturism, which is healthy, not a wind that blows one about, or along, or away. In it there is a new realism, which finds Nature to be the teacher, inspiring a friendly, not servile, reverence; and there is also a new idealism, which does not set the mind up as a mentor, proposing rules to make Nature intelligible, but rather evolves man as prospective liaison between her earthly kingdoms, looking to the day when he shall have become the living index of her warring hopes and powers, and the balance-wheel of their harmony. As Emerson put this process: "As a man's life comes into union with Nature, his thoughts run parallel with the highest law. . . . Intellect agrees with Nature. Thought is a

[9] *Tat twam asi; Ayam ātmā Brahma; Aham Brahmāsmi; Prajnānām Brahma.*

finer chemistry, a fairer vegetation, a finer chemical action. It agrees also with the moral code of the universe." [10]

I have taken Emerson as a type and plenteous fountain of the new philosophy, with no thought of setting aside others. As in Greece, as in Germany, and as elsewhere, the philosophers come in groups, and it matters little who is who. Among the Concord group the emphasis was on modes of intelligent living rather than physics and metaphysics—on deeds more than words, as befitted the new times. A glance at the titles of Emerson's Essays, First Series, shows this. They are "History," "Self-Reliance," "Compensation," "Spiritual Laws," "Love," "Friendship," "Prudence," "Heroism," "Self-Reliance," "The Over-Soul," "Circles," "Intellect" and "Art." Turn to the essays themselves, and you find them all opalescent to unity. At the very outset, in the verses introducing "History," we have:

> There is no great and no small
> To the Soul that maketh all,
> And where it cometh, all things are
> And it cometh everywhere.

Or, from the poem "Musketaquid:"

> The cordial quality of pear or plum
> Ascends as gladly in a single tree
> As in broad acres resonant with bees;
> And every atom poises for itself,
> And for the whole.

These two verses alone are enough to found a whole volume of idealism—Kant's first book in a nutshell. And another:

> I am owner of the sphere
> Of the seven stars and the solar year,

[10] *Natural History of the Intellect.* Notes: Riverside Centenary Edition, p. 430.

> Of Caesar's hand and Plato's brain,
> Of Lord Christ's heart, and Shakspeare's strain.

Here is solipsism, with a difference. The essay on "History" offers a condensed critique of the whole subject, with illustrations. After this we may turn to "Prudence," with its:

> Scorn not thou the love of parts,
> And the articles of arts.
> Grandeur of the perfect sphere
> Thanks the atoms that cohere.

This is realism. The four verses, read together, harmonize perfectly—and all the rest fit in. Life is living, thought is thinking, and "God offers to every mind its choice between truth and repose; take which you please—you can never have both."

Thoreau and Alcott and others all participated in the new movement, but it was Emerson who lived widely, without rules, more able to be with the spirit everywhere, and thus proved safe from the substitution in thought of part for whole.

This movement is one, like that of old Vedantic times, which rested upon the acceptance of Nature as simply observed. Thoreau and Channing appear to have been more interested in observing detail than Emerson was, and so when they walked with him they could show him many things. His mind leaped to the contemplation, theirs more to the concentration. He therefore more set the spirit of the age, while they caught its movements. He saw the same thing everywhere, even in the new particulars his friends showed him. This in no way reduced his delight in the new perceptions, for every time it was the same Being whom the forms adorned but did not disable. He was like the lover whose pulse quickens every time he sees his mistress in a new dress. If he had been a Hindu he would, no doubt, like Rāmakrishna, have reverenced Kālī the mother and understood her moods, without any cloud before the vision of the One Reality.

The spirit of science, however, was on the move. In its most modern form it means the supplementing of the senses for closer observation—of the small in our microscopes, of the large and the distant in our telescopes. All its lessons have shown us that the world is of one piece, that the same spirit which is in the saddle in the globe is also in the atom. The mystery of being that water is, is the same mystery that hydrogen and oxygen are, and combination or disintegration present no change to this Vedantic eye. Knowledge is power, giving new pattern to all this dancing. The shuttle action proceeds—one minute we are immersed in the dance, a minute later we are looking on. When this yogī that each of us is comes fully into his own he will find himself dancing and looking on at the same time.

Bergson came on the scene, observed, and found *change* everywhere, so fully that he could say that the static appearance of things is only an illusion of the intellect—like the apparent circle of fire seen when a torch is whirled in the darkness. Change is the substance of reality. But every assertion breeds its opposite, and even Bergson could not deny himself expression in language, which, even if it is the music of knowledge, depends upon the unchangingness of the meanings of words. If the word "change" changes, the constant principle is gone. If it does not change, change is not there. The Vedantist author of *The Nectar of the Glorious Precepts*,[11] avers at the very beginning that stillness of the eye is necessary for accurate vision, stillness of the mind for accurate perception of what is in the eye, and stillness of the self for understanding what the mind has seen. And where is music without notes, walking without steps, thinking without poise on ideas? Ever-present change arm in arm with ever-present

[11] *Shrīvākya-sudhā.*

poise is nearer the fact, and their union announces a deeper reality embracing both, but ungraspable in thought because thought proceeds by comparison and classification, and there is no second with whom to compare or classify that one.

This is not to say that we cannot know. It is on this point that the Vedanta differs from modern thought, because its "knowledge" is a form of yoga, and yoga is beyond mind. There is a weakness in this statement, too, for when we say "beyond mind" that beyond also is a concept of the mind. So Vedanta, at last, cannot state the truth and does not pretend to do so, but rather warns us where our darkness lies. I suppose that even Herbert Spencer, in announcing the existence of the "unknowable," and Thomas Huxley, whose "agnosticism" meant, he said, not merely that we do not know, but that we cannot know, the ultimate truth, were not without their mental reservation, that there may some day be for us a resurrection and ascension into a truth, a new consciousness, which the māyās of mind and form shut out. The fatal error of the Church has been to accept the truth of the ascension, make it a "fact," and then put its foot down hard upon those who are finding it.

The old Vedantists said that we are not totally without this experience, which we call "sleep." I have, in an earlier chapter, discussed their views on the dreaming state, and the implications of our partial education by dreams. I remarked, I think, on the short-sightedness of science—for a long time —in its assumption that our dream state could be without utility, in an evolutionary pattern of life. "In sleep," Shankara said, "consciousness is pure." [12] We come from the trance saying there was nothing there! Then the sages shake their heads over us mournfully, as who would say, "What did you expect? Some more of this? But 'not-this, not-this' is the key." When we read of the blind man who had his sight restored

[12] *Commentary on the Vedanta Aphorisms*, I, 3, 15; II, 1, 6; II, 3, 18; III, 2, 7; III, 2, 35.

and said he saw men "like trees walking," we can well understand his psychology, but had we been present we would have counseled him: "Not trees, not trees; try to look without that."

There is a common belief among the old Hindu thinkers, which is something more than an animistic belief, that the mind has a material reality of its own, compounded of substance finer than air, by which it retains even a material integrity apart from the body. It is there that inhere in the mind itself the colors and sounds etc. which it relates to incoming sensory impressions in the brain, and thereby—across the gulf of thingness—communicates, in the sympathetic language of sensations, with other minds who are working and jostling and dancing in our joint world of extensity and resistance. I have already mentioned, perhaps, that it is an interesting fact that colors in Nature seem very constantly to be a signal to affect other minds—at least minds first and bodies afterwards. Even the background of greens in leaves is very intelligent, as being an excellent foil for the variety of reds and yellows on one side and blues and violets on the other, in the flowers. This language of color will perhaps be studied some day by a patient scientist who will watch and catalogue the responses called out by the several heraldic signs, from whom and to whom.

In a prophetic mood I could be tempted to say, with an allowance for errors in translation, that the freed minds sing to one another, and so convey the color directly that in our world is frozen into resistant form. Is that where the colors come from, and is that why music seems to us so peculiarly divine or free? I recollect a brief conversation with a Hindu friend one day, in an interval between listening to some compositions played on the *vīnā* by an expert. My companion said, in effect, that while listening and enjoying the music, the greatest delight of it was that it cleared the mind of all thoughts.

Reverting to that statement about mind beyond body, I

would like to give my testimony, for what it is worth, not only
to the general belief in India that minds can and do sometimes
communicate at great distances, but can travel also. Samples
of these experiences were mine in such circumstances as to
convince me beyond the shadow of a doubt. It is a matter of
the greatest interest that Dr. J. B. Rhine, of Duke University,
and his helpers, have recorded thousands of test cases of
thought-transference, and that he has observed that the operation takes place free of the usual condition of diminution by
distance which occurs when impulses of sound and light fan
forth into our atmosphere and ether. In dreams, too, there are
often communications from other minds—more readily accepted than in the waking state—not only direct, but from
thoughts and feelings which appear to have been left by others
on the very walls of the rooms in which we may sleep and
have the dream. There is no great personal use in disentangling
the mixture of psychological excitations, idea and dream pictures, but there is great value in letting their light into our
lives, for they carry much instruction when remembered un-
critically, and in general tend to a ripening of experience which
filters at favorable moments into our waking state.

It is generally assumed that the mind is all known, but it is
reasonable to expect that we shall make discoveries in it which
will be as startling as those which we have uncovered in the
natural world. Even in the quiet process of ordinary living
something in the mind grows like grass in the night. At an
early stage of growth that greenery is like a mist, and we look
at it from an angle to make sure we have not been deceived by
some optical illusion, but a few days later the presence of the
green is commanding and solid to the vision. I remember one
Hindu monk, who used occasionally to come and live near to
my dwelling for weeks together, and with whom I was on
very cordial terms, who once, deciding that his body was getting too stout, obtained a pair of dumbbells with which to exercise. They were exceedingly heavy—the Hindu rarely does

anything by halves. One day he inadvertently dropped one of those things on his bare foot. It was a bad smash, which put him on crutches for a long time, but the point of the story is that when I happened to go to his room shortly after the accident he was wincing with pain and roaring with laughter as nearly as possible at the same time. It was the picture of himself, who had been so complacently philosophical a short time before, suddenly disillusioned by so very undramatic an event, that caused his laughter. But it showed to me that his philosophy was not words, not even ideas, but behind these a growth of the soul or an emergence of spiritual reality into the mind.

I knew another, a very young man, of similar type, with whom I spent months checking over some Sanskrit translations. We lived door by door at that time, and were constantly meeting. He, too, had adopted the monkish life—much to the disappointment of his parents, who wanted a grandson—a resigned disappointment, however, in a land where it often occurs, and in special cases is not frowned upon by tradition or scripture—but it had not impaired an incorrigibly jovial mood with which he was naturally endowed. He was fond of quoting Richard III's soliloquy on winter's blight, and used to laugh most heartily at misfortunes. I never knew anyone else so constantly getting into scrapes and troubles as he, and it was usually no one else's fault. I am trying to say that the emergence or reflection of the spirit into the mind, is not a matter of highly colored heroics, as some expect—but a gradually dawning freedom which is not noticed to be an attribute of personality, but is, rather, an alteration in the stance of personality.

After saying that knowledge of the One Reality is to be had only through yoga, and not through mere thought, a question naturally arises as to what ordinary thought is for. In a fox, it is to find the way to the hens and to avoid pitfalls by the way. In a man it is to serve the conscience (or categorical imperative, as Kant called it). In man, the central urge has provided a new motive to suit the new human adventure, the new phase in the conflict between self-preservation and self-enhancement. Motive is feeling or emotion, which gives interest, and in this degree it is called love. Love is a kind of knowledge, an awareness of "other lives." With it we begin to live in others, and cannot ignore the wounded bird or the lost child, or, to be more positive, we feel the need of companionship in living. Our new hunger is for friendship, and we find that when it is satisfied it enhances experience.

The sea of troubles on which this new impulse launches us is worth while. The proof of the pudding is in the eating. Life in the world of action goes on under this impulse, with thought as its instrument, concerned in finding or making that pudding. If the pudding is all right, we say to thought, "Good boy! Your ideas were correct." In the world of action, the waking state, correctness in this service is truth. It is goodness, in the sense in which we say, "This pie is good," or, "This is real pie."

The theory that thought is instrumental to action, and success in action is the test of its truth, is called pragmatism. The scientist thinks of a new idea to solve a problem. He calls it an hypothesis. He tries it out. It works. It is added to his collection of true ideas. I have brought the subject in here because it is a very important school of philosophy, developed in America, and well in line with the new naturalism. William James played a most important part in demanding for this kind of thought a more prominent place than it had before. If I am a bee, and I see a red flower moving in the breeze, I say, "There is the dinner-flag," and that is truth. If the bush could be asked what it is doing when it makes the flowers, and could reply, it would say, "I am putting up the bee-calls." Colors, shapes etc. are techniques which have established themselves pragmatically. Experimentalism, though often called by the same name, is liable to fall into mere empiricism. When we dissect a dead body and describe all its parts, we do not discover what a body really is. In this view we come near to the Hindu theory of the counter-correlative, according to which a chair in a world of no men would not be a chair, but simply some pieces of wood of various shapes fastened together in a certain way. This principle carries back to the finest components of anything, even to the atom, the electron and whatever may be beyond.

The adoption of the social test in pragmatism puts us well on the way to the theory of the whole propounded in our first chapter. The thing must "fit in" with other things and beings; they are the test of its truth. Error is just a misfit. We cannot say, "This is what truth is," but "This is what I mean by truth." Substance is not truth. If I show you a pot and tell you that this is a piece of clay, that is not the truth. If it were, clay would be a dance of electrons, and I do not know what electrons would be. Or, if I bring water, and say, "Here is some oxygen and hydrogen for you," it would not be the truth.

Thus, it seems, pragmatism is not concerned with the One Reality. Well, opinions differ, but William James definitely wrote that monism is superstition, that both concepts and percepts are realities, but the perceptual flux has more life in it than concepts, which are static or dead. Similarly, one could put it, the cloth is more important than the yardstick that measures it, though the yardstick has its use. The concept of a dog, said James, cannot bark and bite. If concepts were innate truths, he argued, we would have a concept to explain Being itself, but we have not. The fundamental fact in life is Life, and everything is relative to that. Intellect is its servant, not its curator. The universal truth cannot be explained—that is, it cannot be subject to the paradox of knowing a thing by comparison with something else—but James could not quite leave it out of his philosophy, so he became much interested in the study of religious experiences, believed in the power of faith, and concluded that some kind of theism is essential to the happiness of human beings.

This pragmatism is well on the way to Vedanta. It, too, recognizes the pragmatic value of the intellect in its limited sphere, but is essentially concerned with the yoga which extends knowing beyond the net of thought and even of love. Where James objects to absolute idealism, saying that it does not account for the existence of our finite consciousness, Vedanta calmly replies that it is not finite—that is a mistake. And when he says in effect "My pluralism accounts for evil, but your monism does not," he meets the answer that there is no evil—that too is a mistake. And when he says, "The world seems very real," he is countered by "What? With all its relativity and paradoxes? Wait till you have seen the Real!" The fact is that if, when we speak of monism, we mean a one, we are still in the mental net, but if, meaning *the one*, we are prepared to go as "I" through the will, the imposer of unity even in diversity, into the freedom of the self, we reach the one without a second.

Running my eye along the line of later thinkers, I find Professor Whitehead standing up like an Everest in these Himālayas, and am led to stop and ask myself if this is an illusion or the real thing. Will this, too, wash away in the winds and rains of inspection and judgment? Let me work upon it and compare it point by point with Vedantic and Emersonian realism.

Professor Whitehead has some condensed expressions which will help us to be brief. First let us take up his "Presentational Immediacy," along with "Symbolic Reference." We see a colored shape, compare it with memories of previous experience, and decide that it is a chair. The colored shapes are symbols, or indicators; we do not see the whole thing. It requires inference and judgment to know that the whole thing is there. There can be mistakes in such inference and judgment. We can attach our colored shape to the wrong memory, and conclude wrongly. Right or wrong, the world of objects is not directly affected by this knowledge—"Nature is closed to mind." I am in the world; the world is not in me; the world extends beyond my ken; the world existed before my time; my activity intends to find and affect an actual world, beyond myself. The foregoing statements are summarized.

It is necessary to admit experience of "world," not merely "thing," and this involves interplay of things in an actuality called solidarity—"In Presentational Immediacy, or sense-perception, the world is disclosed as a community of actual things like ourselves. The relatedness of spatial extension is a complete scheme, impartial between the observer and the perceived thing. The way in which each actual physical organism enters into the make-up of its contemporaries has to conform to this scheme."

Here we have unity in the form of relatedness; these things cannot leave one another alone; they bump. To quote again: "Thus the disclosure of a contemporary world by Presentational Immediacy is bound up with the disclosure of the solidarity of actual things by reason of their participation in an impartial system of spatial extension." This bumping brings in "Causal Efficacy." Causal Efficacy means that functioning is conditioned by environment. Our bodies can be bumped—and are bumped, in fact, quite often—and when moved into a new environment, even without our consent, carry with them our sense-organs, so that our sensations now arise in the new environment, and with them our minds have to deal, unless they retire within their own castles of illusion, the world of dreams.

One could not ask for a better statement of the actuality, or reality, of the world, with its variety of things, existing whether we know them or not. Not only existing, but acting without apparent contact (gravitation, magnetism, etc.) and, in what we class as organisms, even signaling to other organisms (flower and bee). "Thing" evidently does not mean mere object, but qualities or attributes and actions as well. Sensation touches our three means of correct knowledge also here; for there is no objection to inference as a means to knowledge of what the actual is, or rather, of more about it than is given in sensation, as shown in the interpretation of symbolic reference.

Why has this situation arisen, that the senses have developed only to the point of giving us symbols or parts instead of the whole thing? My answer is that the fox does not need to know the whole tree, and we do not need to know about the dinner bell—the sound is enough for our purposes. Why should one say to oneself—"Ah, that is the brass bell, colored somewhat golden, standing about five inches high, with a model of a little bull on top, which I brought from Trichinopoly—or was it Chittoor?—which is being rung by the blonde maid in a black dress and a white apron, who is the daughter of Mrs. Timkins, living in the little street near the canal, which, and so on, and so on"? The fox does not want to know more about the tree than the sensation that a tree gives him. What is the matter then, with this being called man? He is on the make, and the fox is not. As I said before: the animal adapts itself to its environment, but the man adapts his environment to himself. But even the man goes only so far in wanting to make. He, too, has no use for the thing in itself; his making is circumscribed by a limited desire. At first his desire is for pie, a little further on, for sweetheart and wife—not a picture, nor an animated doll, but, as Sir Walter Scott put it, woman, in our hours of ease so coy and hard to please and at other times a veritable angel. He wants to live with life—he needs its challenge, some salt and pepper to make him know that he is alive. The philosopher needs other philosophers—why else would I spend months in writing this book, and going to publication, and receiving for it hardly enough to keep me in pie, when I could get much more working as a gardener or teaching chess to innocent young men? Now we are getting warmer in our question why mind and consciousness came in at all. The cat has its head out of the bag. Here it comes.

Nature is only a conversation—minds in communication—and a book. Rather, conversations and books. All minds in their actions upon others are ringing dinner bells, calling us to feasts of reason and flows of soul. The odor of the new-turned earth speaks peace—does the mind know any peace except in such communion? Can it invent peace? Can it retire into peace? Can it find peace anywhere but here? Everything recites its own lesson, and we call it an attribute. It is more than an attribute; it is the source of sensation—which is much more than a symbol; it is a throb of consciousness, enjoyed in communion. All things are outposts of consciousness, forever talking—someone said that thinking is only talking. Not talking across space. There is no room in this plenitude for space—only for real things. There is extensity and resistivity, as solid and hard and lasting as you please. These are the books. There is earth, water, fire, air, ether.[13] Because of extensity there are directions[14]—North, South, East, West, Zenith, Nadir, and between—but no space, only fulness of being, and when the time comes it will all fold up like a scroll and fade like a dream, leaving no empty space behind.

This is Realism, not that which says all is mind, or all is matter, or all is this or that. Yoga is that mind-operation in which no projection of the part mars the perfect communion of the whole, and that is the knowledge to which Vedanta calls.

[13] *Akāsha.*
[14] *Dish.*

INDEX

Absence, principle of, 236
Abstracts, 39
Accomplishments, the six, 81, 119
Action, as thought, 47; and reality, 257; dead, 255; rules of, 59
Action-meditation, 159, 173
Actor, simile of, 44
Advertising, aggressive, 97
Affirmations, undesirable, 88
Agreement, principle of, 117
All, and each, 20, 176, 204, 293
America, 291, 292
Analytic, school, 233, 235
Anaxagoras, 220
Animal, mind in, 37
Apples, don't fall, 189
Archetypes, theory of, 282
Aristotle, 229, 231
Artist, evolution of, 36; function of, 225
Atom theory, 17, 236
Attention, paying, 47
Austerity, undesirable, 93, 140
Awareness, of thoughts, 70

Balance, bodily, 93; emotional, 73; mental, 65
Becoming, theory of, 281, 282, 283
Bee, "dinner bell" of, 264, 306
Being, the infinite, 45; true, 178; true and false, 168
Belief, and disbelief, 70, 114
Bergson, 301
Berkeley, 263, 264
Blake, quoted, 66
Bodies, complete, 51, 56; series of, 44

Body, training the, 92
Bose, Prof. J. C., 23
Brahmā, 138
Brahman, 56, 62, 133, 141, 144
Breath, regulation of, 144
Buddha, 140, 186, 247, 288
Burns, Robert, 9

Calmness, 144
Camera, simile of, 253
Carpenter, example of, 48
Cat, and king, 188; example of, 19, 149, 180
Casuality, 21, 187, 190, 201; not material, 35, varieties of, 232, 233
Centers, and circumferences, 216
Ceremonial school, 244
Ceremonies, 96
Cessation, of dependence, 94
Change, doctrine of, 301; tempo of, 113; two kinds of, 55
Changing, and thinging, 54, 260
Character, building of, 97, 160
Child, 221, 269, 278
Clerk-Maxwell, Prof, 41
Coiled One, the, 139
Columbus, example of, 163
Combinativeness, 55
Companionship, 65
Concentration, and will, 164; bodily aids to, 92; imprisonment by, 168; in action, 48, 159; in teaching, 51; is grip, 49; mood of, 119, 140; power of, 43, 142; technique of, 146, 148, 180; the highest, 144; universal, 46

313